DICTIONARY OF LAST WORDS

MID-CENTURY REFERENCE LIBRARY

DAGOBERT D. RUNES, Ph.D., General Editor

AVAILABLE

Dictionary of Ancient History
Dictionary of the Arts
Dictionary of European History
Dictionary of Foreign Words
  and Phrases
Dictionary of Linguistics
Dictionary of Mysticism
Dictionary of Mythology
Dictionary of Philosophy
Dictionary of Psychoanalysis
Dictionary of Science and Technology
Dictionary of Sociology
Dictionary of Word Origins
Dictionary of World Literature
Encyclopedia of Aberrations
Encyclopedia of the Arts
Encyclopedia of Atomic Energy

Encyclopedia of Criminology
Encyclopedia of Literature
Encyclopedia of Psychology
Encyclopedia of Religion
Encyclopedia of Substitutes and
  Synthetics
Encyclopedia of Vocational Guidance
Illustrated Technical Dictionary
Labor Dictionary
Liberal Arts Dictionary
Military and Naval Dictionary
New Dictionary of American History
New Dictionary of Psychology
Protestant Dictionary
Slavonic Encyclopedia
Theatre Dictionary
Tobacco Dictionary

FORTHCOMING

Beethoven Encyclopedia
Dictionary of American Folklore
Dictionary of American Grammar
  and Usage
Dictionary of American Literature
Dictionary of American Maxims
Dictionary of American Proverbs
Dictionary of American Superstitions
Dictionary of American Synonyms
Dictionary of Anthropology
Dictionary of Arts and Crafts
Dictionary of Asiatic History
Dictionary of Astronomy
Dictionary of Child Guidance
Dictionary of Christian Antiquity
Dictionary of Discoveries and Inventions
Dictionary of Etiquette
Dictionary of Forgotten Words
Dictionary of French Literature
Dictionary of Geography
Dictionary of Geriatrics

Dictionary of German Literature
Dictionary of Hebrew Literature
Dictionary of Judaism
Dictionary of Last Words
Dictionary of Latin Literature
Dictionary of Mathematics
Dictionary of Mechanics
Dictionary of Mental Hygiene
Dictionary of New Words
Dictionary of Physical Education
Dictionary of Russian Literature
Dictionary of Science
Dictionary of Social Science
Dictionary of Spanish Literature
Dictionary of the American Language
Encyclopedia of American Philosophy
Encyclopedia of Morals
Encyclopedia of Pastoral Psychology
Personnel Dictionary
Teachers' Dictionary
Writers' Dictionary

DICTIONARY

OF

LAST WORDS

Compiled by
EDWARD S. LE COMTE
Columbia University

PHILOSOPHICAL LIBRARY
New York

TABLE OF CONTENTS

PREFACE

Dying words have a better than usual chance to survive. There are reasons, reasons rooted very deep in human nature, why men pay particular attention to them and preserve them. They answer an expectation. The interest, because so natural, is older than anyone can say. It is and has been for uncounted centuries the daily stuff of legends and biographies and histories and ballads, has pointed many a moral and adorned many a tale. Peoples far distant in time, place and customs have joined in the feeling that the utterance which is never to be followed by any other is by that very fact significant. Sometimes we remember nothing else, nothing of Nathan Hale or Captain Lawrence except their last words. Those who have never read Goethe in prose or verse can still tell you that he said on his deathbed, "More light!" Indeed it is debatable whether any words of Jesus Christ (except for the Lord's prayer) have been more often repeated than "Into thy hands I commend my spirit"—repeated by legions of Christians on their own deathbeds. Death is the great heightener. When the thing that is said would have been under any circumstances wise or fine, it is especially so under *this* circumstance. Death can make even triviality momentous, and delirium oracular. Last words have an aura about them, if not a halo.

Men's expectations in regard to dying words have been influenced by whether they themselves were preoccupied with this world, or the next. In the latter case there was a hope for some intuition, some confirmation of faith, some interpretable vision, from the hoverer between time and eternity. In the other case, what last flash of character or

final summary comment might not be forthcoming? **Listen**
ing at a deathbed is not necessarily morbid. It is a visit
at the cave of possible wisdom, or at any rate the turning
on of an additional psychological light.

Sir Thomas Browne and Walt Whitman approach the
subject from these different angles. The seventeenth-
century philosopher and physician declared, "Men sometimes, upon the hour of their departure, do speak and
reason above themselves; for then the soul, beginning
to be freed from the ligaments of the body, begins to
reason like herself, and to discourse in a strain above
mortality." Whitman it behoves to sound more modern.
"Last words are not samples of the best, which involve
vitality at its full, and balance, and perfect control and
scope. But they are valuable beyond measure to confirm
and endorse the varied train, facts, theories and faith
of the whole preceding life." Who is looking at what
quotations?—it will always come down to that.

The earliest names are great names (great partly because they have been preserved)—kings and patriarchs and
philosophers—Cyrus the Great and Jacob and Buddha,
Joseph and Confucius. The people gather reverently
around their leader, the sons around their father, for his
last instructions and advice. And the words are handed
down. And when they do not exist, it is sometimes necessary to invent them, as Xenophon perhaps invented the
interminable speech he assigned Cyrus in the *Cyropaedia*.
The question becomes one of appropriateness rather than
of truth.

It must be admitted this is no area of study for the
scientific historian who likes his facts well authenticated.
Except in the case of public executions, and apart from
statements in the handwriting of the deceased, it is all
tradition, all hearsay, depending often on a single inter-

ested witness (by which is partly meant, not *dis*interested). Fable is always possible: even at executions there are strange disagreements among the few who were close and should have heard. And yet the condemned are alone in being fully aware of what is coming and in being given explicitly the chance to speak before assembled witnesses. If they are misheard, what chance, the scientific historian will ask, has he whose auditor must bend low to catch the faintest of whispers? William Pitt the Younger is represented by an English anthologist as having said, "How I love my country!" The usual version is, "How I leave my country!" But maybe he did murmur "love" and was misunderstood. The doubt is typical. What great men have shared the advantage of "Dutch" Schultz, the gangster, who, as he lay raving in Newark City Hospital, with a slug in him and a fever of 106, was assigned a police stenographer to take down in shorthand his every word? Rarer still—although the domestication of tape recorders may yet change that—is the case of Kalakaua, king of the Hawaiian Islands, who, in his supreme moment, in San Francisco in 1891, called for the new Edison "machine that talks," and faltered a fragmentary message to his people, the wax recording of which is now in the Honolulu Museum.

But cautionary remarks and peculiar or typical cases can be taken up later. First comes definition. The present dictionary, easily the largest of its kind, alone in being documented, and the first to be published in this country since 1901, gathers together 1664 quotations that are in each case the last recorded words, according to a source which is always specified. In the majority of the cases the words were spoken, but in other cases written words are used: either because this was the last mode of communication, as with suicides or those dying in solitude, or because the last spoken words are not on record and there was something written reasonably near the time of demise that could be taken as a substitute.

The rhythm of such a book is naturally short. There are no quotations over 220 words, but wherever a quotation is started it is continued through to the end without cutting: the last words are faithfully given (apart from an inconsistency, reflected here from the sources, in regard to the formal closes and signatures of letters).

The persons included are famous, by standards illustrated by such works as *Webster's Biographical Dictionary,* the *New Century Cyclopedia of Names,* or the *Dictionary of National Biography* and the *Dictionary of American Biography.* Some have a claim to entry only by noble birth, or by connection with the famous—blood-relationship, marriage, friendship, service—and a very few are borderline cases that might not get into a standard reference work, but that broaden interestingly, and in some historical context, the representation here.

The result is so varied and wide-ranging as to defy rigid classification, and the order may as well be alphabetical, even for browsing purposes. The fortune of the alphabet brings together, as would any other accident, some notable contrasts and potential comparisons, as, for instance, between two well-born Alberts, one with his "gutes Frauchen" on his mind, the other with "Herr Jesu" (compare, for the two worlds again, Bannister and Barbusse). Leopold II said, "I am hot;" Lepelletier, "I am cold." Charles XII seems to be answering Charles IX. Prince Peter and Hugh Peters dare their enemies to do their worst. Danks grieved over being alone; Danton was fiercely proud before an audience.

The great and world-renowned are here, some of them never greater than in their deaths. And of course there is a host of lesser figures, requiring for most readers a word or phrase of identification. Here also are the infamous—assassins, celebrated criminals of all kinds, including war criminals.

Many die describing their symptoms and sensations. Others are bent rather on saying some sort of farewell to life. Some die with the gift of prophecy that Socrates (in Plato's *Apology*) and Hotspur allude to as belonging to the dying; others are surprised in the midst of their plans. There are ironies and whimsies and wonderful ambiguities, not arranged by any dramatic poet. We see the brave and the angry and the frightened, the repentant, the unrepentant, and the puzzled. There are all degrees of irreverence, from the jest (despite the legal maxim that "no one is presumed to trifle at the point of death") to the curse. There are martyrs bearing witness to their faith in the midst of tortures. There are suicides writing their lonely notes, lovers with the name of their beloved on their lips, warriors proving themselves so to the last. Some, not necessarily poets, write verse, while three poets make their final comments in foreign tongues, Byron in Greek, Schiller in Latin, Albert Pike of Arkansas in Hebrew. A few spoke rounded paragraphs. Most are brief, unless they are writing, and some never finished what they had to say. The unifying fact is that here is human nature from a single vantage point: make of it what you will. Whatever is expected, there is a good chance of finding it.

All this is not to say that there are not patterns. Customs and religions and repeating circumstances supply them. Some deliver themselves of last words from a sense of duty, and one can see the regularization of this in China, where it was customary to ask the dying person formally for them. It was in response to such a bidding that the empress Tzu-hsi spoke her unfeminist warning. Worthy words would be engraved on wood and inscribed in the family records. In Japan—and in China also—it has not been unusual to compose a poem: Tojo's is a recent example. If one does not volunteer, one may be asked. In the Western world the dying have often had to reckon with some very importunate attendants, who were determined at practically any cost to force out a message or response. To mention one secular example, there is an experimentalism almost—and perhaps quite—cruel in calling back the great mathematician Lagny from the depths to see if he could still give the correct answer to the square of twelve. Religions furnish their pattern, as with the Christians who, instinctively or by explicit instruction, breathe the name of Jesus at the last. An Egyptian would say, "I am Osiris, and rest in Him. Let me pass through the gate." Or he would utter the well-known death-formula: "I am, I am, I live, I live, and when I awake in peace I shall not be in corruption." The plain secular opposite is the cry of the Roman gladiators to the emperor: "Morituri te salutamus." So, too, repeating circumstances bring forth similar responses, as in the considerable number of cases where executioners are asked either (a) to hurry, or (b) to wait.

Even the great and famous remarks are again and again discovered not to be unique. The British had Rear-Admiral Carter, although they did not make so much of him, one hundred and twenty-one years before we had Captain Lawrence. Goethe was imitated by Laurence Oliphant. Nathan Hale was anticipated by Mark Barkworth, a Catholic hanged in England in 1601, who, told "to remember that Christ Jesus died for him," replied: "And so do I for him, and I would I had a thousand, thousand lives to bestow upon him in this cause." But these were not his very last words.

It may be, as Virginia Moore argued a few years ago (and Francis Birrell before her), that there are fashions in dying. Certainly the eighteenth century in England, and in France up to the French Revolution, yielded a remarkable number of self-conscious deathbeds, where calm, if not absolute piety, reigned. But later times do not produce such regular fruit, and the seeker of Zeitgeist must beware of finding only what he is looking for.

There is always what might be called the seamy side of an interest: evidence abounds that eighteenth-century Englishmen fed not only on the words of good men, but on the last sayings, if only as falsely reported in pamphlets, of those who were getting their just deserts at the foot of Tyburn tree—Jack Sheppard, Jonathan Wild, and all their tribe. So, too, the gist of what the Earl of Essex said on the scaffold in 1601 was put into rhyme in more than one broadside ballad still extant, while a couple of others were freely invented, as Defoe and Fielding did with Wild, feeling (like so many reporters of last words) that the spirit, not the letter, was what counted.

What, too, of the parodies, which have a range that includes cartoons (sometimes very didactic—"Let's try to beat the train"), indecorous jokes (one revolves around a last-minute revelation of maternity—see Ezra Pound's Canto XII), and a song made popular by Miss Ethel Merman, the song about Miss Otis, the lady who "regrets she will be unable to lunch today" (because she has to go to her own hanging). (Goethe's mother declined an invitation on the grounds that she was busy dying). Does anyone believe that it happened, or is it merely a macabre joke, that a window-cleaner who lost his footing on the top floor of an office building was heard to say as he plunged past the third floor: "I'm all right, so far!" That Western predecessor of Mark Twain, "John Phoenix," gives "A Very Mournful Chapter" to the "Death and Spirit Resurrection of Squibob." Squibob dies, but a little later sits up in bed, exclaiming, "Look here, old fellow. By George! I quite forgot my last words." His are—he first borrows from three American statesmen—"Here's luck!" Mark Twain himself pokes fun at the practice in *A Tramp Abroad,* in the chapter on the French duel. M. Gambetta carefully determines in advance of the duel what his last words shall be. (So the ranting Captain Hook in *Peter Pan* makes his dying speech prematurely, "lest when dying there may be no time for it.") Of course a French duel never hurts anyone unless the combatants catch cold, but M. Gambetta does drop from fright, faintly murmuring, "I die for . . . for . . . perdition take it, what *is* it I die for? . . . oh, yes,— FRANCE! I die that France may live!" All such parodies indicate the deep interest in, the enormous importance of, the thing parodied, even as burlesques of Homer are testimonials to the greatness of Homer.

To return from literature to life, there are exceedingly indecorous last words on record for real persons. What Rousseau's *Confessions* reports of the Comtesse de Vercellis is an odd case in point. Another involves Robert Henryson, the Scottish Chaucerian poet, who is supposed to have addressed to a witch some very plain Chaucerian words, in rhyme at that, but his modern biographer, Marshall W. Stearns, calls the "anecdote . . . open to doubt, for there is evidence of confusion in chronology"— an objection that is charming for its refusal to go into, or even mention, the question of witches! The deathbed of Horace Greeley has been the subject of persistent rumors that make it impossible to include with confidence the pious remark attributed to him in some biographies. L. D. Ingersoll, writing close to the event, declared, "What he really said in his waning moments was quite as different as 'La Garde meurt, et ne se rend pas,' was from what Cambronne really said at Waterloo. It need not be repeated." It has been repeated, but, since there is such a gulf between authorities, the only reasonable thing to do is to leave Greeley out.

In fact the whole collection divides between formal and informal last words, and there will be those who feel that all the latter kind are indecorous or pointless and should not have been included. That is to say, the broad difference is between remarks that are meant as messages, to a small or large circle (with prayers and religious formulae in a special niche as not addressed to human beings at all), and those exclamations, descriptions of symptoms, casual requests and comments, family intimacies, irrelevances, and incoherences that frequently even the thickest biographies suppress as adding nothing to the stature of the speaker. This compiler, having gone to school with the son of a very prominent American who died in his prime, wrote the son asking for his father's last words; the inquiry was passed on to the attending physician, who replied, "I am deeply conscious of my obligation to history to divulge any last words he may have spoken, but am unable to do so for the reason that your Father was unaware of his approaching death and therefore uttered no last pronouncement." There is the difference again: there are always last words but often they are not noticed or passed on unless they constitute a "pronouncement." The apology for the other kind, the casual monologue or dialogue, must lie in its human or intimate biographical interest, and although some of the remarks are almost unbearably pathetic, the impulse to drop or censor was conquered by the feeling that what was made public once may be made public again. But there can be no doubt that some formal statements which now pass as last were in fact followed by words of a different character that have gone unrecorded. So far as some books are concerned—for example, Stevenson's *Home Book of Quotations* and *Chambers's Encyclopaedia* — Diderot's last words were, "The first step toward philosophy is incredulity." This, said to his daughter, comprises his last formal words. But what he retorted to his wife's remonstrance when he took an apricot are his actual last words.

Most of the casual remarks slip easily into a transcendental meaning. Consider the number of persons who said they would—or wanted to—go to "sleep," or who referred to light or darkness, or who expressed fondness for "home." One has to go no further than Abbott and Adam for delusions parallel in their poignancy. Or there is Page: "Here Alfred, take this spade." That was not meant to be grim, but death is a master ironist. Leichhardt describing how he "came right on Mount Abundance, and passed over a gap in it with my whole train" sounds like Bunyan's Pilgrim and his party. And that once well-known book lies behind Will Bill Hickok's pledge: "with wishes even for my enemies I will make the plunge and try to swim to the other shore."

If there is not ambiguity, intended or unintended, there may be characterization. In view of his stress, in *The Way of All Flesh,* on the importance of money, it is right for Samuel Butler to have inquired, "Have you brought the check-book, Alfred?" Personages as different as Nijinsky and Anatole France and Charles W. Eliot ended with some version of the word "Mother." Who can say that this basic return is uninteresting or unrevealing? One would not ordinarily associate George Washington and André Gide, yet they came to the same conclusion—"'Tis well"; "C'est bien." And what made those twain meet, Chuang-Tzu and Demonax—was it thought, or character?

The most outrageous attempts at humor have been made, in modern times, by criminals. There was George Appel, from Chicago, who, as the guards were strapping him to the electric chair, told the official witnesses, "Well, folks, you'll soon see a baked Appel!" Jack Rybakoff, gambler and small-time racketeer, adhered, like Rothstein, to the underworld code in refusing to tell the police who shot him: "Me mudder did the job." If this is crude, there are the sly English: see Palmer and Peace. Deacon Brodie is the most gentlemanly in Charles Whibley's *Book of Scoundrels,* and he gives us real-life parody. A saying widely attributed to Hobbes—it is probably a confusion with something in Motteux's Life of Rabelais—is, "Now I am about to take my last voyage—a great leap in the dark." So Brodie asked and answered a question. "What is hanging? A leap in the dark." Brodie "faced the last music with a bravery and a cynicism which bore the stamp of true greatness." It has been said that it is better to live well than to die well, but it has also been affirmed that it is better to die well than to do neither.

The literature of death is wide, books on executions being one important and helpful branch. Another drawn on here is collections of last letters, of which there are two in German. On the periphery of the subject are books that deal with death-scenes, such as Feodor Wehl's *Der Ruhm im Sterben* (Hamburg, 1886), Thomas H. Lewin's *Life and Death, being an Authentic Account of the Deaths of One Hundred Celebrated Men and Women* (London, 1910), Luis A. Rodriguez's *Las Grandes Muertes de la Historia* (Mexico, 1938).

The history of collections of last words can be briefly told. The Greeks and Romans are well covered in W. Schmidt's *De Ultimis Morientium Verbis* (Marburg, 1914). A very few dying words are occasionally to be found in books that carried on the *ars moriendi* tradition of the late middle ages and Renaissance, such as Thomas Lupset's *A Compendious Treatyse, Teachynge the Waye of Dyenge Well* (1534). Montaigne and Bacon both displayed an interest in the subject, the latter in his essay "Of Death." Subsequent centuries saw various evangelical publications, for example W. C. Brownlee's *Dying Testimony of Believers and Unbelievers,* a work designed to show the deathbed strength and happiness of believers in contrast to the torment and terror that beset infidels. Brownlee, in the nineteenth century, draws profusely on the tract by the Puritan divine Thomas Brooks, whose *Apples of Gold for Young Men & Women: & a Crown of Glory for Old Men & Women. Or the Happiness of Being Good Betimes,* first published in 1657, reached a 22nd edition in 1814. Such pious synopses, gathering crucial evidence from the dying, still appear. For instance, a Canadian publication of 1913, M. C. Pritchard's *Pebbles from the Brink,* mingles the unidentifiable, such as "Happy John, A Policeman," "An African Convert," and "Mr.—" (who told his wife she was sealing his damnation), with the misspelled—"Venble Bede," "Bellyarmine," "Hobbs," "Ignatus," "Nender," and "Voltair" (who, as several others of these books know, departed "Alternately praying and blaspheming, this wretched man"). (Indeed, the stories about the deathbed recantation of Robert G. Ingersoll were such as to force his friends and relatives who had been present to issue an affidavit of denial in 1906.) The freethinkers, not to be outdone, produced at least one answer, G. W. Foote's *Infidel Death-Beds.*

In a more neutral category are Joseph Kaines' *Last Words of Eminent Persons* (London, 1866) and Walter R. Egbert's *Last Words of Famous Men and Women* (Norristown, Pa., 1898), which pave the way for Frederic Rowland Marvin's extensive compilation, *The Last Words (Real and Traditional) of Distinguished Men and Women, Collected from Various Sources* (New York, 1901). Marvin's book contains a little over six hundred names, arranged alphabetically. A discouraging number of these quotations the present compiler has been unable to pin down, and therefore unable to include, but Marvin did an impressive piece of work, for all his exasperating reticence about his "various sources." There have been only two separate (secular) publications since, both issued in London in 1930: *Last Words of Famous Men* by "Bega" (A. B. Codd), which lists some five hundred names (none of them belonging to the twentieth century), and *The Art of Dying, An Anthology* by Francis Birrell and F. L. Lucas, which goes chronologically through two hundred and seventy-two. Virginia Moore gives in her interesting history of dying, *Ho for Heaven!* (New York, 1946) some two hundred potentially relevant quotations, but they are mostly duplications of those in Birrell-Lucas.

Among the dictionaries of quotations, H. L. Mencken's and Burton E. Stevenson's are notable, the latter putting over a hundred under "Death: Last Words." Walter Fogg, *One Thousand Sayings of History* (New York, 1929), has seventy-four.

All these twentieth-century books have been valuable to this compiler, at the least as a stimulus to research, but he has not been able to borrow from them so much as he would have liked, for three reasons. First, they present as last words what often turn out not to be last words at all, though they may deal with death, be excerpts from wills, or sound in other ways appropriate. Take Stevenson's quotation for Alexander Wilson, the ornithologist: "Bury me where the birds will sing over my grave." It is a shame to lose this (and many others) by investigating it, but, alas, Wilson's friend and biographer, A. B. Grosart, distinctly says, "While in good health he had, in a conversation on death, expressed a wish to be laid in some rural spot where the birds might sing over his grave." James Madison's remark (also put by Stevenson in the ultimate category), "I always talk better lying down," was uttered some years before death. "Bega" is often quite frank in this practice, quoting from Lincoln's Second Inaugural Address, saying after a quotation from John Abernethy, "He lingered another year and died tranquilly," giving for Sir William Herschel ("*d.* 1822") a note written in 1819, and for Thomas, Lord Erskine ("*d.* 1823") lines "From the *Farmer's Vision* (printed privately in 1818), showing his love of animals."

Admittedly one can define "last words," if one likes, as any utterance made at a time when the speaker or writer is contemplating his own death, although he may be a youth in perfect health with fifty years of life and work ahead of him. (Such a definition, by the way, would exclude many truly last words—of those without any intimation of the coming event.) The DICTIONARY, however, has aimed—for the sake of consistency and of a survey of human history from a uniform vantage point—at being literal about last words. There have been difficulties, as when authorities differed, or when some few subsequent words were reported only indirectly or summarily. Sometimes an arbitrary choice had to be made after all. Frequently the variants do belong to the last days, even to the last hour, and the problem is one of learning their sequence. In the case of such lingering illnesses as that of Louis XIV or Charles II (who apologised for being "a most unconscionable time a-dying"), where many words were noted down, but not dated—let alone time-clocked, it seems impossible to tell now what were actually the last. In other cases, the actual last words are by no means the best-known. For instance, there are three familiar variants for Thoreau: 1. A visitor asked him what his hopes were for a future life. "One world at a time!" he said. 2. He was asked if he had made his peace with God. "I have never quarreled with him." (This bears a family resemblance to Heine's "God will forgive me—that is his *métier*,"—which was not *his* last word either.) 3. "I leave this world without a regret." It is fair to call all these dying words ("dying" being a less limited adjective than "last"), and very char-

acteristic they are. But the two words that later came
from Thoreau in his delirium, although they are not epi-
grammatic or even syntactic, will strike many readers as
not less appropriate. Of course there is no denying that,
often, keeping to the known facts brings a loss, qualitative
or complete. Sir Philip Sidney's reply to the dying soldier,
"Thy need is greater than mine," gets replaced; more un-
fortunately still, Oscar Wilde's "I am dying beyond my
means" does not, for though it is known that these were
not his last words, it is not known what his last words
were: so, too, with Richard I's forgiveness of his assassin:
"Let him go, but not empty-handed. Give him a hundred
pieces when you free him from those chains." The close
student of last words is constantly being reminded of the
wisdom of James Gordon Bennett's advice to a cub re-
porter, "Remember, son, many a good story has been ruined
by oververification." Indeed, the lastness of (to say nothing
of the meaning of) Goethe's "Mehr Licht" has been questioned by some biographers, who add to it, but this is
carrying heresy too far. Where good authorities, who are
apparently being thorough, differ, one has a right to the
aesthetic choice.

Stevenson's quotation for Alexander Wilson brings out
a second liberty of collectors to be looked at askance—com-
posing direct quotations out of indirect. Biographers inform us that Lord Macaulay "had told his butler that he
should go to bed early, as he was very tired." Only the
Home Book of Quotations professes to know his exact
words: "I shall retire early; I am very tired." While this
sort of conversion may be no greater than the liberty one
necessarily takes in translating from a foreign language, it
probably should be avoided for those who spoke English,
whose exact phrasing and perhaps crucial overtones of
expression are our proper concern. It is true that in certain older English boogs—e.g., Clarendon's *History*—it was

a matter of style to employ the third person (as it is employed today, from policy, in transcripts of Presidential press conferences), and one feels—and sometimes there is corroborative evidence—that the *ipsissima verba* are arrived at by merely shifting tense and person. Still more justifiably may this be done with foreign sources—to arrive at Bruno, for example, or to translate Tacitus or Plutarch.

Of course a general study of dying could have a section devoted to the content of last words in those cases where we do not have them direct, and it would be, like the rest of the book, full of both fine and curious things. James Bryce said he would go out and look at the stars. Charles Lamb murmured the names of his dearest friends. Swinburne in his delirium rolled out fragments of Greek choruses. Hundreds are on record as having prayed a prayer that was not overheard. Pierre Bayle asked if his fire was kindled. Hamilton Fish wrote his own temperature, and Alexander Woollcott, stricken at a broadcast, set down on a card the telephone number of his heart specialist. Francis I warned his son not to be dominated by a woman. Susan B. Anthony went through a roll-call of great feminists. P. T. Barnum wanted to know what the circus receipts had been during the day at Madison Square Garden. All these and numerous others are lost to a DICTIONARY OF LAST WORDS, although such a book undoubtedly is preserving, without having any means for knowing it, other contents in a phrasing that was made up later.

But—and this is the third and last caution to be insisted on—one should give a source and shift the responsibility that way. Fogg and Moore never name their authorities, Marvin, Birrell-Lucas, and Stevenson seldom. (Bega gives only the surname of an author, which is sometimes not enough to be grateful for.) Consider the remark assigned to Queen Elizabeth, "All my possessions for a moment of time!" This does not sound like her, and after considerable research one is still left wondering how much further back than the nineteenth century it goes. And who was it that first imagined that Beethoven said, "I shall hear in heaven"? Miss Moore is particularly confusing, as when she attributes to "Lord Elgin" what was said by Lord Eldon, and to "Sir William Lawrence" what was said by Sir Henry Lawrence. Marvin has Stafford entered twice—first under "Howard, William" and then—with different last words!—under "Stafford." Indeed any collection of size will be lucky if it escapes the even readily traceable errors that dog this whole field. Miss Moore quotes Maurice, Comte de Saxe, as having said, "I have made a beautiful song," a rather prima donna statement that gets cleared up when one learns that the French was, "La vie n'est qu'un *songe*"! Without explanation the same writer gives for Joan of Arc, "Water! Water! Jesus!'" as if the saint were asking for the fire to be put out, whereas she was really asking for holy water. As Bega relates it, the last wish of Louis Eugene Cavaignac was "to hear Chopin play, and the latter, who had a great aversion to illness, was induced to come. As he played, the dying man rose from his bed and appeared in the room. His mother rushed in to get him back, but he said—'Don't fear, mother. I heard the music of the spheres sung by angels; it did me good.'" Cavaignac might well suppose that this was angelic music, since he died in 1857, and Chopin had died eight years before! Both dates are supplied on different pages of Bega, who also names the same authority for the dying words of both men—Engel.

Marvin and Bega occasionally enter names only to admit that there are no last words on record. This may be a waste of space, or it may be a useful reminder that for many of the great we possess no quotations, genuine or false. Or at least the false are not well-known. There is a human tendency for someone to step in and try to fill the breach. Recently, in a syndicated column, words for General Custer were supplied, in all historical seriousness, apparently. "Where did all those damned Indians come from?" No doubt this is the right thing for him to have said, but it was not explained how, if he was slain with all his men, it got reported. To be sure, more than fifty persons have come forward at one time or another and claimed to be the sole survivor at Little Big Horn, but, amid such an embarrassment of potential riches, we shall stubbornly suppose that history heard the last from Custer in the words that Lt. W. W. Cooke (q.v.) wrote at Custer's direction, the famous message for Benteen.

A list of the completely missing would have to include England's four greatest poets before the nineteenth century—Shakespeare, Chaucer, Spenser, and Milton, the greatest poets and historians of Greece and Rome, and Plato and Aristotle, most of the leading creative figures of the Renaissance, and Lincoln and Alexander Hamilton, the latter of whom lay "surrounded by a wife and friends so distracted they forgot to treasure for posterity the few broken words he could still utter." Add Lenin and Stalin: it might seem odd that, as the Current Digest of Soviet Press confirms, the propaganda value of assigning last words to Stalin has not been taken advantage of, but of course there is other evidence of the desire of Stalin's successors to play him down, rather than up. His last public utterance was at the 19th Party Congress in October, 1952 (five months before he died), a speech that ended: "Down with the War-mongers!" Certainly last words have been a rallying-point. The Reverend Dudley A. Tyng's dying words—among his last—gave rise to the hymn, "Stand up for Jesus." At the time of the Centralia, Illinois mine blast, notes scrawled by the trapped miners on cigarette wrappers and other scraps of paper made up the entire front page of the New York daily, *PM,* of April 1, 1947, as the best persuasion for increasing safety measures in mines. The same newspaper carried, seventeen days later, an advertisement by the Palestine Resistance Committee quoting Dov Bela Gruner, who had just been hanged by the British: his last words were compared to Nathan Hale's.

Dr. Johnson said, "A man will turn over half a library to make one book." This compiler, who wishes he had been a staff, and who was, indeed, provided with one quotation and sometimes two or three by each of certain friends and correspondents named on the next page, has ransacked several libraries, turning over thousands upon thousands of books (and newspapers and periodicals), in seven languages. None will envy the unrivalled opportunity for error and for regrettable omission. Corrections and worthy additions will be welcomed, for their own sake and against a possible second edition. There are those who could, if they would, furnish authentic quotations that have never been made public before, but the attitude of Marshall Field's widow is understandable, wherever it prevails. "Mr. Field's last words," she told reporters, "were for me and not for the world."

E.S.L.

ACKNOWLEDGMENTS

For providing him with, or calling his attention to, material used in this book, the compiler wishes to thank the following: Caroline Bancroft; Walter Hart Blumenthal; Richard Chase; Istvan Csicsery-Ronay; P. G. Downes; F. W. Dupee; Nancy Hale; James D. Hart; Henry B. Herman; Karl F. Heumann; Michael J. Laffan; Samuel Loveman; Donald Maher; Addison M. Metcalf; William Nelson; Nuala; John Burnett Payne; E. L. du Plessis; Rella Ritchell; Mark Schorer; George R. Stewart; S. D. Wakefield; Philip Wintner; Anthony E. Zipprich.

Note

Except where used initially, suspension periods (. . .)
indicate, not omission of any words, but a break in time
or an interruption (such as another person's speaking).

DICTIONARY OF LAST WORDS

A

ABBOT, Robert (Bishop of Salisbury):
*Come Lord Jesu, come quickly, finish in me the work
that Thou hast begun; into Thy hands, O Lord, I
commend my spirit, for Thou hast redeemed me.
O God of truth, save me Thy servant, who hopes and
confides in Thee alone: let Thy mercy, O Lord, be
shewn unto me: in Thee have I trusted, O Lord, let
me not be confounded for ever.*

ABBOTT, Charles, Baron Tenterden (lord chief justice):
Gentlemen, you are all dismissed.

ABD-ALLAH BEN-ZOBAIR (to his followers):
*No one need ask where Abd-allah is; whoever wants
him will meet him in the first ranks . . . O my Lord,
the troops of Syria are assailing me in great numbers,
and have already torn aside a part of the veils that
cover thy sanctuary. O my Lord, I am weak and oppressed on all sides. Send thy phalanxes to my aid.*

ABDALRAHMAN III (written):
*I have now reigned above fifty years in victory or
peace; beloved by my subjects, dreaded by my enemies, and respected by my allies. Riches and honours,
power and pleasure, have waited on my call, nor does
any earthly blessing appear to have been wanting to
my felicity. In this situation I have diligently num-
bered the days of pure and genuine happiness which
have fallen to my lot: they amount to FOURTEEN:
—O man! place not thy confidence in this present
world!*

ABERDEEN, Lord Haddo, 5th Earl of:
Perfectly comfortable.

ABERNETHY, John (surgeon):
Is there anybody in the room?

ABIMELECH (who killed all his 70 brothers except one):
Draw thy sword, and slay me, that men say not of me, "A woman slew him."

ACCORAMBONI, Vittoria (as she fell, stabbed):
Jesus! . . . I pardon you.

ACHARD, Saint:
'Tis enough, my brothers: till now I have struggled against my illness; I have forced myself to conceal from you the pain tearing at my bowels; now that the malady has reached my vital parts I can no longer dissimulate. What I enjoin above all, the one thing needful, is to take care lest the author of evil sow hatred among you and break the peace of the brethren. You are not unaware that hatred cleaves man from God and closes heaven to him. No suffering can expiate hate; it is not redeemed by martyrdom; it is a stain that all the blood in us would fail to wash. So I go to join my fathers. Place my body in the midst of the sepulchres of our brethren.

ADAM, Dr. Alexander (Sir Walter Scott's schoolmaster; spoke as if in the classroom):
That Horace was very well said; you did not do it so well . . . But it grows dark, very dark, the boys may dismiss.

ADAMS, Abigail (to John):
Do not grieve, my friend—my dearest friend. I am ready to go, and—John, it will not be long.

ADAMS, Alice or Alicia (long surviving sweetheart of Nathan Hale, twice married but not to him):
Where is Nathan?

ADAMS, Henry (to his secretary-companion):
Dear child, keep me alive.

ADAMS, John (mistaken):
Thomas Jefferson still survives.

ADAMS, Dr. John (principal of Phillips Academy in Andover; last entry in journal, Sept. 28, 1862):
This day I enter my ninety-first year. The year just closed has been one of trial and deep solicitude. My country! oh my country! I do not expect to see peace restored during the short remainder of my stay, but I am earnestly looking forward to that everlasting rest which remaineth to the people of God. God reigns. He will accomplish His purposes. Amen and Amen.

ADAMS, John Quincy:
This is the last of earth! I am content.

ADDAMS, Jane (asked by the doctor if she would like a little water):
Always. Always water for me.

ADDISON, Joseph:
See in what peace a Christian can die!

ADELAIDE, Marie (mother of Louis XV; told by the Marquise de Maintenon, "Madame, you are going to God"):
Yes, my aunt.

ADLER, Alfred (psychoanalyst):
Kurt [his son's name].

AGASSIZ, Louis R. (naturalist):
The play is finished.

AGATHA, Saint:

Lord Jesus, Who hast created me and preserved me from my infancy, Who hast shielded my body from stain and my soul from the love of the world, Who hast enabled me to triumph over all my sufferings, receive my soul now, in Thy mercy!

AGATHON the Abbot, Saint (asked, "Art thou not confident that thy works have been according to God's will?") :

I presume it not, until I have come before Him; for otherwise are the judgments of God, and otherwise the judgments of men . . . Show me your charity, and speak not to me, for I am wholly occupied.

AGESISTRATA (mother of Agis, king of Sparta; offering herself to the noose) :

I pray that it may redound to the good of Sparta.

AGIS (king of Sparta, sentenced to death) :

Weep not, friend, for me, who dies innocent, by the lawless act of wicked men. My condition is much better than theirs.

AGNEW, Sir Andrew (Sabbatarian promoter) :

Did the doctors really say I was NOT to get up? . . . If they said so, then I won't get up; but I feel well. . . No, I will keep them [the pillows] as the doctors left them.

AGRESTIS, Julius (centurion, whose word was doubted by the emperor Vitellius; suicide) :

Since you require some decisive proof, and I can no longer serve you in any other way either by my life or death, I will give you a proof which you can believe.

AGRIPPINA (to the assassins sent by her son Nero) :

Smite my womb.

AINSWORTH, William Harrison (historical novelist; last sentence of last letter) :
> *Dr. Holman thought me much wasted since I last saw him, and so I am no doubt. Your affectionate cousin, W. Harrison Ainsworth.*

AKIBA Ben Joseph (Palestinian rabbi; martyred under Hadrian; referring to Jehovah) :
> *One.*

ALBERT, King of Belgium:
> *Follow the path for another fifty yards. I am going back to the foot of the rocks to make another climb. If I feel in good form I shall take the difficult way up; if I do not I shall take the easy one. I shall join you in an hour.*

ALBERT, Prince (of Victoria) :
> *Good little woman.*

ALBERT, called Alcibiades (Margrave of Brandenburg) :
> *Lord Jesu!*

ALCOTT, Louisa May (author of *Little Women*) :
> *Is it not meningitis?*

ALDERSON, Sir Edward Hall (judge; asked how he felt) :
> *The worse, the better for me*

ALDRICH, Thomas Bailey (author) :
> *In spite of all, I am going to sleep; put out the lights.*

ALEXANDER the Great (asked to whom he wished to leave the throne) :
> *To the strongest.*

ALEXANDER (King of Judea; to his wife) :
> *Do thou therefore, when thou art come to Jerusalem, send for the leading men among them [the Pharisees], and show them my body, and with great appearance of sincerity, give them leave to use it as they them-*

selves please, whether they will dishonour the dead body by refusing it burial, as having severely suffered by my means, or whether in their anger they will offer any other injury to that body. Promise them also, that thou wilt do nothing without them in the affairs of the kingdom. If thou dost but say this to them, I shall have the honour of a more glorious funeral from them than thou couldst have made for me: and when it is in their power to abuse my dead body, they will do it no injury at all, and thou wilt rule in safety.

ALEXANDER VI, Pope:
I come. It is right. Wait a moment.

ALEXANDER I (Emperor of Russia; when they raised the window blinds) :
What a beautiful day!

ALEXANDER II (hit by bomb in St. Petersburg) :
More quickly...inside ... carry me to the palace ... there . . . to die.

ALFONSO XIII (King of Spain; kissing the crucifix):
Spain: my God.

ALFORD, Henry (dean of Canterbury; wanted the Archdeacon thanked for the funeral service) :
Yes; will you move a vote of thanks for his kindness in performing the ceremony?

ALI PASHA, called The Lion of Janina (assassinated) :
Go, my friend, despatch poor Vasiliky, that these dogs may not profane her beauteous form.

ALLEN, Ethan (told by the parson, "General Allen, the angels are waiting for you!"):
Waiting, are they? Waiting, are they? Well, God damn 'em, let 'em wait!

ALLINGHAM, William (poet):
I am seeing things that you know nothing of.

ALTGELD, John Peter (governor of Illinois):
How do you do, Cushing? I am glad to see you.

AMBOISE, Georges, Cardinal d':
I believe . . .

AMBROSE, Saint (when the name of Simplicianus was mentioned as a possible successor to him as bishop):
Old though he be, he is the best of all.

ANAXAGORAS (philosopher):
Give the boys a holiday.

ANAXARCHUS (philosopher; pounded to death with pestles):
Pound, pound the pouch containing Anaxarchus; ye pound not Anaxarchus.

ANAXIBIUS (Lacedaemonian general; ambushed):
Men, it is good for me to die on this spot, where honour bids me; but you hurry and save yourselves before the enemy can close with us.

ANDRÉ, Major John (hanged as British spy):
It will be but a momentary pang.

ANDREW the Apostle (crucified):
O cross, most welcome and long looked for; with a willing mind joyfully and desirously I come to thee, being the scholar of Him which did hang on thee; because I have been always thy lover, and have coveted to embrace thee.

ANDREW, James Osgood (Methodist Episcopal bishop):
God bless you all!

ANDREWS, Eusebius (royalist; before being beheaded):
Lord Jesus, receive me!

ANDRONICUS I (Eastern Roman emperor; mobbed):
Oh, Lord, have mercy! Wherefore wilt thou break a bruised reed?

ANGOULÊME, Duchess of (daughter of Louis XVI):
My God, I am going to beg pardon for my sins; help Thy humble servant in this moment which is to be decisive for me for all eternity.

ANNE, Queen (of England; handing the white staff of the Lord Treasurer to the Duke of Shrewsbury):
Use it for the good of my people.

ANNE of Austria (wife of Louis XIII):
My hand is swollen. It is time to depart . . . [to Milord de Montaigu, weeping at the foot of her bed] Monsieur de Montaigu, consider what I owe to God, the favor He has shown me, and the great indulgence for which I am beholden to Him.

ANSELM, Saint:
Yes, if it be His will, I shall obey it willingly. But were He to let me stay with you a little longer till I had resolved a problem about the origin of the soul, I would gladly accept the boon; for I do not know whether anyone will work it out when I am gone. If I could but eat, I think I should pick up a little strength. I feel no pain in any part of my body; only I cannot retain nourishment, and that exhausts me.

ANTOINETTE, Marie (having stepped by accident on the executioner's foot):
Monsieur, I beg your pardon.

ANTONINUS PIUS (Roman emperor; asked the password):
Tranquillity.

ANTONY, Saint:

I indeed go the way of the fathers, as it is written, for I perceive that I am called by the Lord. Promise to bury me secretly, so that no one shall know the place, save you alone, for I shall receive my body incorruptible from my Saviour at the resurrection of of the dead. And distribute my garments thus. To Athanasius, the bishop, give one of my sheepskins, and the cloak under me, which was new when he gave it me, and has grown old by me; and to Serapion, the bishop, give the other sheepskin; and do you have the hair-cloth garment. And for the rest, children, farewell, for Antony is going, and is with you no more.

ANTONY, Mark (to Cleopatra):

You must not pity me in this last turn of fate. You should rather be happy in the remembrance of our love, and in the recollection that of all men I was once the most famous and the most powerful, and, now, at the end, have fallen not dishonourably, a Roman by a Roman vanquished.

AQUINAS, Saint Thomas (on receiving the Eucharist):

I receive Thee, redeeming price of my soul. Out of love for Thee have I studied, watched through many nights, and exerted myself; Thee did I preach and teach. I have never said aught against Thee. Nor do I persist stubbornly in my views. If I have ever expressed myself erroneously on this Sacrament, I submit to the judgment of the holy Roman Church, in the obedience of which I now part from this world.

ARAM, Eugene (English schoolmaster and murderer; asked on the scaffold if he had anything to say):

No.

ARATUS (Greek general; slowly poisoned; on a friend's seeing him spit blood):
These, O Cephalon, are the wages of a king's love.

ARCHIMEDES (to the Roman Soldier):
Stand away, fellow, from my diagram.

ARETINO, Pietro (satirist; doubtful last words after unction):
Keep rats away, now that I'm all greased up.

ARGYLL, Marquess of (executed on charges of collaboration with the Roundheads) :
I desire you, gentlemen, and all that hear me, again to take notice, and remember, that now when I am entering on eternity, and am to appear before my Judge, and as I desire salvation and expect eternal happiness from Him, I am free from any accession, by knowledge, contriving, counsel or any other way to his late Majesty's death; and I pray God to preserve the present King His Majesty, and to pour His best blessings on his person and government, and the Lord give him good and faithful counsellors.

ARGYLL, Archibald, 9th Earl of (on the block, repeated three times):
Lord Jesus, receive me into Thy glory.

ARMISTEAD, Lewis Addison (brigadier general in the Confederate army at Gettysburg; put his hand on the cannon, waved his sword):
Give them the cold steel, boys.

ARMSTRONG, Major Herbert Rowse (executed for the poisoning of his wife Katie):
I am coming, Katie!

ARNAULD, Angelique (abbess of Port Royal):
Jesus, oh Jesus, you are my God, my justice, my strength, my all.

ARNOLD, Benedict (calling for his old Continental uniform of a major general):
Let me die in my old uniform. God forgive me for ever putting on any other.

ARNOLD, Thomas (headmaster of Rugby):
Ah, very well.

ARRIA (Roman matron; when her husband Caecina Paetus was ordered by the Emperor Claudius to put an end to his life and he hesitated to do so, she stabbed herself and handed him the dagger):
Paetus, it doesn't hurt.

ARTAGERSES (adherent of Artaxerxes II; to Cyrus the Younger):
O most unjust and senseless of men, who are the disgrace of the honoured name of Cyrus, are you come here leading the wicked Greeks on a wicked journey, to plunder the good things of the Persians, and this with the intent of slaying your lord and brother, the master of ten thousand times ten thousand servants that are better men than you? as you shall see this instant; for you shall lose your head here, before you look upon the face of the king.

ARUNDEL, Philip Howard, Earl of (charged with saying mass for the success of the Spanish Armada):
Jesus, Mary.

ARVERS, Félix (French poet; calling back his confessor):
Ah! Coquereau, I forgot to mention one of the greatest faults of my life. . . . I have spoken badly of Charles X!

ASCHAM, Roger (English humanist):
I desire to die and be with Christ.

ASTE, Marcello, Cardinal d' (assuming a sitting position):
I wish to die sitting, in tribute to the most worshipful will of my good and precious Jesus.

ASTROS, Paul, Cardinal d':
Neither life nor death nor any being can separate us from Him.

ATCHESON, George C., Jr. (diplomatic aide to General MacArthur, as the plane with him and twelve others crashed near Hawaii):
Well, it can't be helped.

ATTICUS, Titus Pomponius (Epicurean):
How much care and diligence I have employed to restore my health on this occasion, there is no necessity for me to state at length, since I have yourselves as witnesses; and since I have, as I hope, satisfied you, that I have left nothing undone that seemed likely to cure me, it remains that I consult for myself. Of this feeling on my part I had no wish that you should be ignorant; for I have determined on ceasing to feed the disease; as, by the food and drink that I have taken during the last few days, I have prolonged life only so as to increase my pains, without hope of recovery. I therefore entreat you, in the first place, to give your approbation of my resolution, and in the next, not to labor in vain by endeavoring to dissuade me from executing it.

AUBIGNE, Agrippa d' (Huguenot commander and poet):
It comes at last, the happy day:
  Let thanks be given
  To God in heaven,
While we learn pleasure in His Way.

AURELIUS, Marcus (asked by the tribune for the watch-word):
Go to the rising sun, for I am setting.

AURELIUS, Quintus (a rich man who found himself on on Sylla's proscribed list):
Woe is me, my Alban farm has informed against me!

AURUNGZEBE (emperor of Hindustan; letter to his favorite son):
Soul of my soul . . . Now I am going alone. I grieve for your helplessness. But what is the use? Every torment I have inflicted, every sin I have committed, every wrong I have done, I carry the consequences with me. Strange that I came with nothing in the world, and now go away with this stupendous caravan of sin! . . Wherever I look I see only God . . . I have greatly sinned, and I know not what torment awaits me . . . Let not Muslims be slain and the reproach fall upon my useless head. I commit you and your sons to God's care, and bid you farewell. I am sorely troubled. Your sick mother, Udaipúrî, would fain die with me . . . Peace!

AUSTEN, Jane (asked if she wanted anything):
Nothing but death.

AUSTIN, Stephen F.:
Texas recognized. Archer told me so. Did you see it in the papers?

B

BABAR (nickname of Zahir ud-Din Muhammad, founder of Mogul dynasty of India; making at the sick-bed of his son Humayan a prayer that was answered):
O God! If a life may be exchanged for a life, I who am Babar gice my life and my being for Humayan.

BABINGTON, Anthony (conspirator; still alive when taken down from the gallows):
Spare me, Lord Jesus.

BACHAUMONT, Louis Petit de (memoirist, copied down a scandalous song referring to the adulterous and pregnant Marie, duchesse de Durford, ending):
> *Lovely Mary,*
> *Were I the archangel for you,*
> *Destined that work to do,*
> *How I would worship you,*
> *Lovely Mary!*

BACHMAN, John (American Lutheran clergyman and naturalist; of a relative):
I love her—I love you all.

BACON, Francis (letter to the Earl of Arundel and Surrey):
My very good Lord,—I was likely to have had the fortune of Caius Plinius the elder, who lost his life by trying an experiment about the burning of the mountain Vesuvius. For I was also desirous to try an experiment or two, touching the conservation and induration of bodies. As for the experiment itself,

it succeeded excellently well; but in the journey (between London and Highgate) I was taken with such a fit of casting, as I know not whether it were the stone, or some surfeit, or cold, or indeed a touch of them all three. But when I came to your Lordship's house, I was not able to go back, and therefore was forced to take up my lodging here, where your housekeeper is very careful and diligent about me; which I assure myself your Lordship will not only pardon towards him, but think the better of him for it. For indeed your Lordship's house was happy to me, and I kiss your noble hands for the welcome which I am sure you give me to it, etc.

I know how unfit it is for me to write to your Lordship with any other hand than mine own; but in troth my fingers are so disjointed with this fit of sickness, that I cannot steadily hold a pen.

BAEDEKER, Dr. F. W. (missionary):
I am going in to see the King in His beauty!

BAGEHOT, Walter (economist; refusing his sister's help in adjusting his pillows):
Let me have my own fidgets.

BAILLY, Jean Sylvain (guillotined in the French Revolution; a voice said, "You are trembling, Bailly"):
My friend, I am cold.

BAINHAM, James (Protestant martyr):
O ye papists! behold, ye look for miracles, and here now you may see a miracle; for in this fire I feel no more pain, than if I were in a bed of down: but it is to me as a bed of roses.

BALBOA, Nuñez de (while being led to execution he was preceded by a herald crying "Such is the punishment imposed on this traitor, this usurper of the rights of the crown"):

That is false. I always have served my king loyally and sought to add to his domains.

BALDWIN, Elias Jackson (gambler):
By gad, I'm not licked yet.

BALZAC, Honoré de (written):
I can no longer read or write.

BANCROFT, George (historian):
I cannot remember your first name. ["It is the same as yours, Mr. Bancroft—George."] *What is your last name?*

BANNISTER, John (comedian):
My hope is in Christ.

BARBUSSE, Henri (author; wanted a delegation sent to strengthen action in the war in Ethiopia):
Telephone and say that they must still enlarge it. . . Always larger, broader, more universal. . . It's the only means of saving the world.

BARHAM, Richard Harris (author of THE INGOLDSBY LEGENDS):
As I laye a-thynkynge, the golden sun was sinking,
O merrie sang that Birde as it glitter'd on her breast
   With a thousand gorgeous dyes,
   While soaring to the skies,
'Mid the stars she seem'd to rise,
     As to her nest;
As I laye a-thynkynge, her meaning was exprest:—
   'Follow, follow me away,
   It boots not to delay,'
   'Twas so she seem'd to saye,
   'HERE IS REST!'

BARING, Maurice (author; asked, "What would you like for lunch, dear Major?"):
Whatever you would like me to have.

BARNATO, Barney (English speculator; before jumping overboard):
What's the time?

BARNAVE, Joseph (apostate from Jacobinism; stamped with his foot on the scaffold):
This then is my reward?

BARNEVELD, John of (champion of Dutch independence; to the executioner):
Be quick about it. Be quick.

BARRE, Jean François le Fevre, Chevalier De La (condemned to death for having mutilated a crucifix):
I did not think they would put a young gentleman to death for such a trifle.

BARRIE, James M.:
I can't sleep.

BARRON, Clarence Walker (financial editor):
What's the news?

BARROW, Isaac (divine):
I have seen the glories of the world.

BARRYMORE, John (to Lionel) :
You heard me, Mike.

BARTON, Clara (founder of American Red Cross):
Let me go! Let me go!

BASEDOW, Johann Bernhard (educational reformer):
I want an autopsy made for the benefit of my fellow men.

BASHKIRTSEFF, Marie (diarist; seeing the candle by her bed burnt almost to its socket):
We shall go out together.

BASS, Sam (desperado):
The world is bobbing around.

BASTIAT, Frédéric (economist):
I am not able to explain myself.

BAXTER, Richard (Puritan writer):
Death, death. O I thank Him, I thank Him. The Lord teach you to die.

BAYARD, General George Dashiell (fallen at Fredericksburg; dictated):
My black mare and sorrel horse I give to you, father. There are about sixty dollars in my pocket-book. There are papers in my trunk to be turned over to the Department (Quartermaster's), to settle. Once more, good bye, beloved father, mother, sisters, all. Ever yours, George D. Bayard.

BAYARD, Pierre Terrail, seigneur de (called "le chevalier sans peur et sans reproche"; at the defeat of Romaguans mortally wounded, asked to be placed at the foot of a tree to "die facing the enemy"; a certain constable who had just fought against France spoke words of pity to him):
It is not I who am to be commiserated, but you, far more, who fight against your king and your country.

BEARD, George Miller (physician):
Tell the doctors it is impossible for me to record the thoughts of a dying man. It would be interesting to do so, but I cannot. My time has come. I hope others will carry on my work.

BEATON, David, Cardinal (protesting to the conspirators):
I am a priest; I am a priest! Fie! fie! all is gone.

BEATRIX (Bavarian grand duchess; letter) :
To the Duke of Bavaria:
Neumarket, March 11, 1447
Our warm devotion and all love and goodness in our power. Noble prince, dear brother, it is proper that you should know that we fell ill last Monday, and though we had hope of getting the better of our infirmity, we notice that the weakness and sickness is going from bad to worse. Therefore we beg you in all friendliness to send promptly one or two of your councillors here to Neumarket, so that if God the Almighty calls us, your brotherly affection may know what sort of departure we made.

BEAUMONT, Rev. Joseph (Wesleyan minister; conducting service, announced the hymn):
Thee, while the first Archangel sings,
He hides his face behind his wings.

BECKET, Thomas à (murdered in Canterbury Cathedral):
I am prepared to die for Christ and for His Church.

BECKFORD, William (author; writing to his daughter):
Come quick! quick!

BEDDOES, Thomas L. (poet; end of suicide note) :
I ought to have been among other things a good poet; Life was too great a bore on one peg & that a bad one.—Buy for Dr. Ecklin above mentioned Reade's best stomach pump.

BEDE, the Venerable (ecclesiastical historian; anxious to finish his translation of the Gospel of St. John, to the scribe):
Write quickly. . . Well, thou hast spoken truly 'It is

finished.' . . . Glory to the Father, and to the Son, and to the Holy Ghost.

BEDELL, William (Bishop of Kilmore in Ireland):
I have kept the Faith once given to the Saints; for the which cause I have also suffered these things; but I am not ashamed, for I know Whom I have believed, and I am persuaded that He is able to keep that which I have committed to Him against that day.

BEECHER, Catharine (daughter of Lyman; propagandist for female higher education; written):
I hope to be in Phil. in about ten days. I am stronger than for yrs. but take no new responsibilities.

BEECHER, Henry Ward (American clergyman; asked by the doctor how high he could raise his arm):
Well, high enough to hit you, doctor.

BEECHER, Lyman (Presbyterian clergyman; quoting the words of St. Paul):
I have fought a good fight, I have finished my course, I have kept the faith; henceforth there is laid up for me a crown, which God, the righteous Judge, will give me at that day. . . That is my testimony—write it down—that is my testimony.

BEETHOVEN, Ludwig van (when the wine he had asked for came) :
Too bad! too bad! it's too late!

BEHAINE, Monseigneur Pierre Pigneau de (bishop of Adran):
Here I am finally—here I am at the end of the tumultuous career that, whatever my repugnance, I have kept to for so long. My troubles will soon be over and my true happiness is coming, since I have all confidence in the mercy of my God. I willingly leave this world where I have been thought happy in that

I have had public admiration, been respected by the great, esteemed by kings. I can't say that I regret all these honors—it's just that they add up to vanity and trouble.

BELL, Alexander Graham (dictating, though his wife said "Please don't hurry"):
But I have to. So little done. So much to do.

BELL, Sir Charles (Scottish anatomist; to his wife):
Hold me in your arms.

BELLARMINE, Robert Francis, Cardinal (ended with the Creed):
. . . and in life everlasting, Amen.

BENEDEK, Ludwig August von (general; lines to his wife):
Relieved to hear that you feel better. I had a very bad night—am now stronger. Your poor Louis.

BENEDICT, Brevet Brigadier-General Lewis (who fell in battle at Pleasant Hill, Louisiana) :
Colonel, rally your men and advance as soon as possible.

BENEZET, Anthony (educator; to his wife):
We have lived long, in love and peace.

BENJAMIN, Judah P. (lawyer; letter):
What I require is warmth—will it never come?

BENNETT, Arnold (to Dorothy C. Bennett):
Everything has gone WRONG, my girl.

BENSON, Robert Hugh, Monsignor (brother of A. C.):
Arthur, don't look at me! Nurse, stand between my brother and me! . . Jesus, Mary, and Joseph, I give you my heart and my soul.

BENTHAM, Jeremy (utilitarian):
I now feel that I am dying; our care must be to mini-mise pain. Do not let the servants come into the room, and keep away the youths; it will be distress-ing to them, and they can be of no service.

BENTON, Thomas H. (congressman) :
I am comfortable and content.

BERANGER, Pierre (lyric poet):
My God, my God! enlighten us. Inspire in a united mankind the love of the good, the love of well being . . . To do good, to live for others—that's happiness. Charity, charity, for all the world to be happy. . . Widows, small boys—help them.

BERENGER de Tours (heretical ecclesiastic):
Today, on the day of His Epiphany, my Lord Jesus Christ will appear to me, either for Glory, as I in my repentance should like, and as I hope, or for Con-demnation, as others would like, and as I fear.

BERLIOZ, Hector (composer; note):
A thousand greetings to Balakirev.

BERNADETTE Soubirous (of Lourdes):
All this is good for heaven! . . Blessed Mary, Mother of God, pray for me!—a poor sinner, a poor sinner.

BERNADOTTE, Count Folke (U.N. Mediator in Pales-tine; assassinated; after inspecting a bullet in his wheel and when a newspaperman shouted "Good Luck!" as he drove on):
I'll need it.

BERNARD of Clairvaux, Saint (to his monks) :
I know not to which I ought to yield—to the love of my children, which urges me to stay here; or to the love of God, which draws me to Him.

[22]

BERNARD, Claude (physiologist; when he began to feel cold and a traveling rug was placed over his feet):
This time it will serve me for the voyage from which there is no return, the voyage of eternity.

BERRY, Charles Ferdinand, Duc de:
Blessed Virgin, have mercy.

BERULLE, Pierre, Cardinal de (blessing his congregation):
I do bless. . . May Jesus and Mary bless, rule and govern.

BESSARION, Johannes or Basilius (Roman Catholic prelate and Greek scholar) :
Thou art just, O Lord, and just are Thy decrees; but Thou art good and merciful, and Thou wilt not recall our failings.

BESTOUJEFF (Russian revolutionary hanged with Pestel; when the rope broke):
Nothing succeeds with me. Even here I meet with disappointment.

BEZA, Theodore (Protestant theologian; of his beloved Geneva):
Is the city in full safety and quiet?

BICKERSTETH, Edward (evangelical clergyman) :
The Lord bless thee, my child, with overflowing grace, now and for ever.

BILLINGS, Josh (pseudonym of H. W. Shaw, American humorist):
My doctors East ordered rest of brain, but you can see I do not have to work my brain for a simple lecture—it comes spontaneously.

BILLY THE KID (real name William H. Bonney; outlaw):
> *Who is there?*

BIRON, Armand Louis de Gontaut, Duc de (was eating oysters and drinking wine when the executioner came):
> *Take this wine. You must need some in your profession . . . [to his fellow prisoners] It's finished, gentlemen. I leave for the great voyage.*

BISMARCK, Prince Otto Eduard Leopold von:
> *I do not want a lying official epitaph. Write on my tomb that I was the faithful servant of my master, the Emperor William, King of Prussia.*

BLACKIE, John Stuart (translator):
> *The Psalms of David and the songs of Burns, but the Psalmist first . . . Psalms, poetry.*

BLAKE, William (to his wife, of the songs he was singing):
> *My beloved, they are not mine—no—they are not mine.*

BLANDY, Mary (whose lover induced her to poison her father, in 1751):
> *Gentlemen, don't hang me high for the sake of decency. . . I am afraid I shall fall.*

BLAURER, Ambrosius (Swabian reformer):
> *O my Lord Jesus Christ, this made you in your great thirst desire nothing, but you were given gall and vinegar.*

BLOMFIELD, Charles James (bishop of London):
> *I am dying.*

BLÜCHER, Field Marshal Gebhard Leberecht von:
> *Nostitz, you've learned many a thing from me. Now you are to learn how peacefully a man can die.*

BLUM, Robert (German political agitator; tried to decline the blindfold):
I want to look death in the eye. . . . I die for freedom. May my country remember me!

BLUNTSCHLI, Johann Kaspar (Swiss statesman):
Glory be to God in the highest, peace on earth, good will towards men.

BOAS, Franz (anthropologist):
It isn't necessary to wear oneself out repeating that racism is either a monstrous error or a shameless lie. The Nazis themselves have recently had to appreciate the accuracy of the facts that I have brought together on the European emigrants of America.

BODWELL, Joseph R. (governor of Maine; wanted to be returned to his chair):
Get me there quickly.

BOEHME, Jacob (mystic):
Now I go hence into paradise.

BOGUE, David (divine; delighted to hear that a certain doctor was come):
Is he?

BOILEAU, Nicholas:
It is a great consolation to a poet at the point of death that he has never written a line injurious to good morals.

BOLEYN, Queen Anne:
Friends and good Christian people, I am here in your presence to suffer death, whereto I acknowledge myself adjudged by the law, how justly I will not say: I intend not an accusation of any one. I beseech the Almighty to preserve His Majesty long to reign over you: a more gentle or mild Prince never swayed

[25]

*sceptre. His bounty towards me hath been special.
If any one intend an inquisitive survey of my actions,
I entreat them to judge favorably of me, and not
rashly to admit any censorious conceit; and so I bid
the world farewell, beseeching you to commend me
in your prayers to God. . . . To Jesus Christ I commend my soul!*

BOLINGBROKE, Viscount (statesman and philosopher;
to Lord Chesterfield):
*God who placed me here will do what He pleases
with me hereafter, and He knows best what to do.*

BOLIVAR, Simon:
*Let us go. They have no use for us here! José! Bring
the luggage. They do not want us here!*

BONAPARTE, Madame Elisabeth (Jerome) (sister-in-law
of Napoleon; when someone mentioned nothing was so
certain as death):
Except taxes.

BONAPARTE, Pauline (Borghese) (sister of Napoleon,
princess of Guastalla; looking at herself in a mirror) :
I always was beautiful!

BONIFACE, Saint (as boiling lead was poured into his
mouth):
I thank Thee, Lord Jesus, Son of the living God!

BONNET, Charles (Swiss naturalist and philosopher;
had a delusion that a servant had stolen important papers—his wife, humoring him, promised to bring in the
"culprit", who would admit his guilt):
So he repents? Let him come and all will be overlooked.

BOOTH, Edwin (actor; asked by his little grandson,
"How are you, dear Grandpa?"):
How are you yourself, old fellow?

[26]

BOOTH, John Wilkes:
Tell my mother—I died—for my country. . . . I thought I did for the best. . . . Useless! Useless!

BOOTH, Junius Brutus (actor and manager):
Pray, pray, pray.

BOOTH, General William (of the Salvation Army; to his son):
I'm leaving you a bonnie handful. Railton will be with you.

BORGIA, Lucretia (letter to pope Leo X):
Most Holy Father and Honored Master: With all respect I kiss your Holiness's feet and commend myself in all humility to your holy mercy. Having suffered for more than two months, early in the morning of the 14th of the present, as it pleased God, I gave birth to a daughter, and hoped then to find relief from my sufferings, but I did not, and shall be compelled to pay my debt to nature. So great is the favor which our merciful Creator has shown me, that I approach the end of my life with pleasure, knowing that in a few hours, after receiving for the last time all the holy sacraments of the Church, I shall be released. Having arrived at this moment, I desire as a Christian, although I am a sinner, to ask your Holiness, in your mercy, to give me all possible spiritual consolation and your Holiness's blessing for my soul. Therefore I offer myself to you in all humility and commend my husband and my children, all of whom are your servants, to your Holiness's mercy. In Ferrara, June 22, 1519, at the fourteenth hour. Your Holiness's humble servant, Lucretia d'Este.

BÖRNE, Ludwig (political writer and satirist):
Pull back the drapes! I'd gladly see the sun. . . . Flowers . . . Music.

BORODIN, Alexander (composer; letter to his wife about the dance "tomorrow" at which he died):

I shall say no more about it and leave the description of the festivity to the more expert pen of your other correspondents.

BORROMEO, Saint Carlo (asked if he wished the Viaticum):

At once.

BOSCO, John (founder of the order of the Salesian Fathers):

Thy will be done.

BOSSUET, Jacques (pulpit orator) :

Lord, I suffer grievously, but I am not confounded. For I know in Whom to trust. Thy will be done.

BOUFFLERS, Chevalier Stanislas Jean de (poet and courtier):

My friends, believe that I sleep.

BOUHOURS, Dominique (grammarian):

I am about to—or I am going to—die: either expression is used.

BOURBON, Louis de (bishop and prince of Liège; to his assailant):

Mercy, mercy, my lord of Aremberg, I am your prisoner.

BOURG, Anne Du (falsely accused of the assassination of Minard; executed):

My friends, I am not here as a thief or murderer, but on account of the Gospel . . . My God, forsake me not, that I forsake Thee not.

BOUVIER, Auguste (Protestant theologian):

My God! . . . My God!

BOWDITCH, Henry Ingersoll (physician; asked if he suffered):
No, dear,—wish that the end would come.

BOWDITCH, Nathaniel (American mathematician and astronomer; as he sipped some water) :
How delicious. I have swallowed a drop from 'Siloa's brook that flow'd fast by the oracle of God.'

BOWLES, Samuel (newspaper editor; to his nurse):
You may be sure that in another world there will be always one soul praying for you.

BRACE, Charles Loring (social-service worker; reading in the paper of the success of the sanitarium on Long Island):
I wish you would send this to Mr. Potter.

BRADFORD, John (Protestant martyr; to his fellow at the stake):
Be of good comfort, brother; for we shall have a merry supper with the Lord this night. . . . Strait is the way, and narrow is the gate, that leadeth to eternal salvation, and few there be that find it.

BRAHE, Tycho (Danish astronomer):
Let me not seem to have lived in vain!

BRAHMS, Johannes (after drinking a glass of hock):
Ah, that tastes nice, thank you!

BRAINERD, David (missionary to the Indians):
It is another thing to die than people have imagined.

BRANDT, S.S. General Karl (Hitler's personal surgeon; as they put the hood over his face):
It is no shame to stand on this scaffold. I served my fatherland as others before me. . . .

BRASIDAS (Spartan general in Peloponnesian War):
These men do not mean to face us; see how their spears and their heads are shaking; such behaviour always shows that an army is going to run away. Open me the gates as I ordered, and let us boldly attack them at once.

BREITINGER, Johann J. (Swiss critic):
Living or dying, we are the Lord's.

BREMER, Fredrika (novelist):
Ah! my child, let us speak of Christ's love,—the best, the highest love!

BRERETON, William (executed with Anne Boleyn):
I have deserved to die, if it were a thousand deaths. But the cause wherefore I die, judge ye not. But if ye judge, judge the best!

BRIGGS, George N. (governor of Massachusetts; to his son) :
You won't leave me again, will you?

BRINDLEY, James (engineer; was visited by some canal builders who could not make their canal hold water):
Then puddle it. . . . Then puddle it again—and again.

BRISBANE, Albert (American advocate of Fourierism; to his wife):
My love, turn me over . . . towards you.

BRISBANE, Arthur (journalist):
This is the best of all possible worlds.

BRODERICK, David C. (California senator):
I die; protect my honor.

BRONTE, Anne:
Take courage, Charlotte; take courage.

BRONTË, Branwell (brother of the Brontë sisters; to the last prayer):
Amen.

BRONTË, Charlotte (to her new husband):
Oh, I am not going to die, am I? He will not separate us, we have been so happy.

BRONTË, Emily (to Charlotte):
If you will send for a doctor, I will see him now.

BROOKE, Gustavus Vaughan (actor; shipwrecked; asked if he would go in the lifeboat):
No! no! Good-bye. Should you survive, give my last farewell to the people of Melbourne.

BROOKE, Sir James (rajah of Sarawak; starting a letter):
My dear Arthur—

BROOKE, Rupert (poet; as a friend helped to lift him into the pinnace that was to take him to the hospital ship):
Hallo!

BROOKE, Stopford (man of letters; as the news was read him):
It will be a pity to leave all that.

BROOKINGS, Robert (philanthropist) :
I have done everything I wanted to do. This is the end.

BROOKS, Elbridge Gerry (Universalist minister; asked how he felt):
My head is pillowed upon the bosom of the dear God.

BROOKS, Phillips (Episcopal bishop):
Take me home. I must go home.

BROWN, Rev. Abel (anti-slavery agitator; fancying he was being mobbed):
Must I be sacrificed? Let me alone, every one of you!

BROWN, John (biblical commentator):
My Christ!

BROWN, John (asked if he was tired, standing on the scaffold as the soldiers deployed):
No, but don't keep me waiting longer than necessary.

BROWNING, Elizabeth Barrett (asked, "How do you feel?") :
Beautiful!

BROWNING, Robert (a telegram being read that *Asolando* was nearly all sold out):
How gratifying.

BRUCE, Robert the (who had vowed to go on a crusade):
I will that as soon as I shall be dead, you take my heart from my body, and have it well embalmed; you will also take as much money from my treasury as shall appear to you sufficient to perform your journey, as well as for all those whom you may choose to take with you in your train; you will then deposit your charge at the Holy Sepulchre where our Lord was buried. You will not be sparing of expense, but will provide yourself with such company and such things as may be suitable to your rank; and wherever you pass, you will let it be known that you bear the heart of King Robert of Scotland, which you are carrying beyond seas by his command, since his body cannot go thither. . . . Gallant Knight, I thank you— you promise it me, then? . . . Thanks be to God! for I shall now die in peace, since I know that the most valiant and accomplished knight of my kingdom will perform that for me which I am unable to do for myself.

BRUNO, Giordano (philosopher; burned at stake for heresy) :

*I die a martyr and willingly. My soul shall mount
up with the smoke to paradise.*

BRUTUS, Marcus Junius (at Philippi, before calling on
one of the bystanders to kill him, quoted):
*O wretched Valour, thou wert but a name,
And yet I worshipped thee as real indeed;
But now, it seems, thou wert but Fortune's slave.*

BRYAN, William Jennings (written):
With hearts full of gratitude to God.

BRYANT, W. C. (up after having struck his head on
the pavement):
*Whose house is this? What street is this? . . . Would
you like to see Miss Fairchild? [his niece]*

BUCER, Martin (reformer; three fingers pointing up-
ward):
He governs and disposes all.

BUCHANAN, George (Scottish humanist; summoned to
answer for something objectionable in his writings):
*Tell the people who sent you that I am summoned
to a higher Tribunal.*

BUCHANAN, James:
O Lord God Almighty, as Thou wilt!

BUCHANAN, Robert (poet and novelist):
I should like to have a good spin down Regent Street.

BUCHER, Johann Peter (jurist):
*Now farewell. Permit me to close my tired eyes in
sleep.*

BÜCHNER, Georg (poet):
*We do not suffer too much, we suffer too little, for it
is through suffering that we attain God. We are
death, dust, ashes—how should we dare to complain?*

BUCKINGHAM, George Villiers, 1st Duke of (to his assassin Felton):

Villain!

BUCKINGHAM, George Villiers, 2nd Duke of (letter):

To what situation am I now reduced! Is this odious little hut a suitable lodging for a prince? Is this anxiety of mind becoming the character of a Christian? From my rank I might have expected affluence to wait upon my life: from religion and understanding peace to smile upon my end; instead of which I am afflicted with poverty and haunted by remorse; despised by my country and I fear forsaken by my God. I am forsaken by all my acquaintance, neglected by the friends of my bosom and dependents on my bounty; but no matter! I am not fit to converse with the former and have no abilities to serve the latter. Let me not however be forsaken by the good. Favour me with a visit as soon as possible. I am of opinion this is the last visit I shall ever solicit from you.

My distemper is powerful; come and pray for the departing spirit of the poor unhappy Buckingham.

BUCKLAND, Frank (inspector of fisheries):

God is so good, so good to the little fishes, I do not believe He would let their inspector suffer shipwreck at last.

BUCKLE, Henry Thomas (historian; of the traveling companions in his care):

Poor little boys!

BUDDHA, Gautama:

Beloved, that which causes life, causes also decay and death. Never forget this; let your minds be filled with this truth. I called you to make it known to you.

BUDGELL, Eustace (Grub Street author; suspected of theft; suicide note):
What Cato did and Addison approved
Cannot be wrong.

BUDGETT, Samuel (Bristol merchant):
O dear!

BUGEAUD de la Piconnerie, Marshal Thomas Robert:
It is all over with me.

BULL, George (theologian):
Amen.

BULL, William (Congregationalist minister) :
Bless the Lord.

BULLER, Sir Redvers (general):
Well, I think it is about time to go to bed now.

BÜLOW, Hans von (pianist and conductor; asked how it was with him):
Ba—d.

BUMBY, Rev. John Hewgill (clinging in the cold river to a canoe):
O dear, dear, dear me! We are dead.

BUNSEN, Christian Karl, Baron (Prussian diplomat; as he took a visitor's hand):
Very kind, very glad!

BUNSEN, Baroness:
Amen.

BUNYAN, John (author of *Pilgrim's Progress*):
Weep not for me but yourselves: I go to the Father of our Lord Jesus Christ, who will, no doubt, through the mediation of his Blessed Son, receive me, though

a sinner, where I hope that we ere long shall meet to sing the new song and remain for everlastingly happy, world without end.

BURGESS, George (Protestant Episcopal bishop of Maine):
I will lie down now.

BURGHLEY, William Cecil, Lord (counsellor to Queen Elizabeth; delivering his will to his steward):
I have ever found thee true to me, and I now trust thee with all.

BURKE, Robert O'Hara (explorer; starving in the Australian wilderness; notes):
I hope we shall be done justice to. We have fulfilled our task, but we have been aban—. We have not been followed up as we expected, and the depot party abandoned their post. King has behaved nobly. He has stayed with me to the last, and placed the pistol in my hand, leaving me lying on the surface as I wished.

BURN, Major-General Andrew (asked if he wished to see anyone in particular):
Nobody, nobody, but Jesus Christ: Christ crucified is the stay of my poor soul.

BURNETT, Frances Hodgson (author of *Little Lord Fauntleroy*):
With the best that was in me I have tried to write more happiness into the world.

BURNEY, Charles (musical historian):
All this will soon pass away as a dream.

BURNS, Sir George (shipowner):
Lord Jesus, come, come; I am waiting, I am ready. . . . Home, home. . . . Give me patience to wait Thy time, but Thou knowest what I suffer.

[36]

BURNS, Robert (referring to the legal agent who had written him a dunning letter):
That damned rascal, Matthew Penn!

BURR, Aaron:
Madame.

BURROUGHS, John (naturalist):
How far are we from home?

BURTON, Lady Isabel (after the last sacraments):
Thank God.

BURTON, Sir Richard F. (explorer and Orientalist; to his wife):
Quick, Puss, chloroform—ether—or I am a dead man!

BUSHNELL, Horace (preacher; benediction to his family):
Well, now, we are all going home together; and I say, the Lord be with you—and in grace—and peace— and love—and that is the way I have come along home.

BUSONI, Ferruccio (pianist; to his wife):
Dear Gerda, I thank you for every day we have been together.

BUTLER, Arthur John (translator; expressed a wish to be buried at Wantage):
where the larks sing.

BUTLER, Benjamin Franklin (attorney general):
I die a happy man—I die a happy man. . . . Rock of Ages, cleft for me.

BUTLER, Joseph (author of *The Analogy of Religion;* on his chaplain's calling his attention to John vi, 37):
True, and I am surprised that though I have read that Scripture a thousand times over, I never felt its virtue till this moment; and now I die happy.

BUTLER, Samuel (author of *Erewhon* and *The Way of All Flesh*):
Have you brought the check-book, Alfred?

BYRNE, Donn (novelist; killed in motor accident):
I think I'll go for a drive before dinner. Any one come along?

BYRON, George, Lord:
I want to go to sleep now.

C

CABRINI, Francesca ("Mother Cabrini"; asked what she would like for lunch):
Bring me anything you like. If I don't take it I may take something else.

CADOUDAL, Georges (royalist insurgent in the French Revolution; told on the scaffold to keep saying "Hail Mary, full of grace" to the hour of his death):
For what? Isn't this the hour of my death?

CAESAR, Augustus:
Live mindful of our wedlock, Livia, and farewell.

CAESAR, Julius (according to one version, alluded to Brutus's supposed paternity, crying in Greek):
Thou, too, Brutus, my son!

CALHOUN, John C.
The South! The poor South! God knows what will become of her!

CALLICRATES (struck by an arrow before his comrades advanced against the Persians at Plataea):
I grieve, not because I have to die for my country, but because I have not lifted my arm against the enemy, or done any deed worthy of me, much as I have desired to achieve something.

CALVIN, John:
Thou bruisest me, O Lord, but it is enough for me that it is Thy hand.

CAMBRONNE, Count Pierre (general under Napoleon):
Ah! mademoiselle, man is thought to be something, but he is nothing.

[39]

CAMBYSES (king of Persia):

I charge ye all, and especially such of you as are Achaemenids, that you do not tamely allow the kingdom to go back to the Medes. Recover it one way or another, by force or fraud; by fraud, if it is by fraud that they have seized on it; by force, if force has helped them in their enterprise. Do this, and then may your land bring you forth fruit abundantly, and your wives bear children, and your herds increase, and freedom be your portion for ever: but do it not—make no brave struggle to regain the kingdom—and then my curse be on you, and may the opposite of all these things happen to you—and not only so, but may you, one and all, perish at the last by such a fate as mine!

CAMBYSES' SISTER (stripping the leaves off a head of lettuce, she asked her brother which way it looked better; he answered, "When the leaves were on"):

But you have done as I did to the lettuce, and made bare the house of Cyrus.

CAMOENS, Luiz de (Portuguese epic poet; written):

Who ever heard tell that on such a tiny bed so great a calamity would have its fulfillment? And I—as if this had not been enough—align myself on its side; for the effort to withstand so many sorrows would appear as a kind of impudence. And so I shall conclude my life, and all will see how I was so attached to my country that I was not satisfied to die IN it, but to die WITH it.

CAMP, Major Henry Ward (at the battle of Richmond, waving his sword):

Come on, boys, come on!

CAMPAN, Mme. Henriette Genest (author of memoirs of Marie Antoinette; after ordering something):
How imperious one is when one no longer has time to be polite!

CAMPBELL, Thomas (poet; given drink):
Thank you—much obliged.

CAMPION, Edmund (English Jesuit martyr; asked what queen he prayed for):
Yes, for Elizabeth, your Queen and my Queen, unto whom I wish a long quiet reign with all prosperity.

CANIUS (lived under Caligula):
I have determined with myself to mark well, whether in this short pang of death my soul shall perceive and feel that he goeth out of my body. This point I fully intend to take heed of; and if I can I will surely bring you and the rest of my fellows word, what I felt, and what is the state of our souls.

CANNING, George (statesman):
Spain and Portugal.

CANOVA, Antonio (sculptor; said three times):
Pure and amiable spirit.

CAPEL, Arthur, Lord (English royalist; executed):
God Almighty stanch this blood, God Almighty stanch, stanch this issue of blood; this will not do the business, God Almighty find out another way to do it.

CARLOS, Don (of Austria):
God, be propitious to me, a sinner.

CARLYLE, Jane Welsh (letter to her husband Thomas—of a picture in a shop-window):

I will go back for it if you like, and can find a place for it on my wall. Yours ever, J. W. C.

CARLYLE, Thomas:
So this is Death—well . . .

CARNEGIE, Andrew (his wife said, "I hope you will rest well, Andrew"):
I hope so, Lou.

CARNOT, Sadi (president of France; assassinated; to the friends around him):
I am very touched by your presence, and I thank you for what you are doing for me.

CAROLAN, Turlough (Irish bard; called for a cup of his beloved usquebaugh):
It would be hard if two such friends should part at least without kissing.

CAROLINE, Queen (wife of George II):
Pray louder that I may hear.

CARROLL, Charles (of Carrollton; American Revolutionary leader):
Thank you, Doctor.

CARROLL, Lewis (C. L. Dodgson):
Take away those pillows—I shall need them no more.

CARSTARES, William (statesman and divine):
I have peace with God through our Lord Jesus Christ.

CARTER, Admiral Richard:
Fight the ship. Fight the ship as long as she can swim.

CARTERET, John, Earl Granville (when the preliminaries of the Treaty of Paris were brought him):
It has been the most glorious war and it is now the most honourable peace this nation ever saw.

CARUSO, Enrico:
Doro, I can't get my breath.

CARY, Alice (American poetess):
I want to go away.

CARY, Phoebe (Alice's sister; poetess):
O God, have mercy on my soul!

CASANOVA, Jacques:
I have lived as a philosopher; I die as a Christian.

CASAUBON, Isaac (theologian and classical scholar; the French Ambassador sent a nobleman to ask in what religion he professed to die):
Then you think, my lord, that I have been all along a dissembler in a matter of the greatest moment!

CASSIUS Longinus, Gaius (thinking, mistakenly, that Titanius had been taken by the forces of Antony)
Through too much fondness of life, I have lived to endure the sight of my friend taken by the enemy before my face.

CASTLEREAGH, Robert Stewart, Viscount (after cutting his throat, to the doctor):
Oh, Bankhead, it is all over.

CATHERINE of Siena, Saint:
No, I have not sought vainglory, but only the glory and praise of God!

CATHERINE of Alexandria, Saint:
O hope and salvation of them that believe, O honour and glory of virgins! Jesus, good King, I implore Thee that whosoever shall celebrate the memory of my passion, or shall call upon me at the moment of death or in any necessity, may obtain the benefit of Thy mercy!

CATHERINE de Medicis (learning that the name of her confessor was one that a prophecy said she should fear):
Ah! my God, I am dead!

CATHERINE of Aragon:
Lord, into Thy hands I commend my spirit.

CATHERINE Howard (Henry VIII's fifth queen; beheaded on conviction of adultery):
I die a Queen, but I would rather die the wife of Culpeper. . . . God have mercy on my soul. Good people, I beg you pray for me.

CATO, Marcus, the Elder (prophesied of Scipio):
The only wise man of them all is he,
The others e'en as shadows flit and flee.

CATO the Younger (to his freedman, before stabbing himself):
Shut the door.

CAUCHY, Augustin (mathematician) :
No, I do not suffer much. . . . Jesus, Mary, Joseph.

CAVELL, Edith (nurse; executed by Germans in World War I):
I know now that patriotism is not enough; I must have no hatred and no bitterness toward anyone.

CAVOUR, Count Camillo Benso di (Italian statesman):
Monk, monk, free church in a free state!

CAXTON, William (last written and printed):
God then give us his grace and find in us such an house that it may please him to lodge therein, to the end that in this world he keep us from adversity spiritual. And in the end of our days he bring us with him in to his Realm of heaven for to be partners of the glory eternal, the which grant to us the Holy Trinity. Amen.

[*44*]

CAZOTTE, Jacques (poet and royalist; guillotined) :
> *I die as I have lived, faithful to God and my King.*

CECILIA, Saint (to Bishop Urban):
> *I obtained three days' delay, that I might commend myself and all these to thy beatitude, and that thou mightest consecrate this my house as a church.*

CENCI, Beatrice (executed for the murder of her vicious father):
> *Jesus, Mary.*

CERVANTES, Miguel de:
> *Already my foot is in the stirrup. Already, great lord and master, the agonies of death are upon me, as I send you these lines. Yesterday they administered to me the last rites. Today I am writing this. Time is short, agony grows, hope lessens. Only the will to live keeps me alive. Would that life might last until I might kiss the feet of your Excellency! Seeing your Excellency back in Spain, hale and hearty, might restore me to life. But, if it be decreed that I must die, Heaven's will be done! May your Excellency know, at least, what my wish was, and know also that he had in me, a servant so faithful as to have wished to serve your Excellency even after death!*

CÉZANNE, Paul (in his delirium repeated the name of the curator of the Aix museum, who had steadfastly refused his pictures):
> *Pontier. Pontier.*

CHALAIS, Henry de Taleyrand de (master of the wardrobe and conspirator against Louis XIII; to the executioner, who proved clumsy and cruel):
> *Do not keep me in suspense.*

CHALMERS, Thomas (Scottish theologian and preacher):
> *A general good-night.*

[45]

CHAMBERS, Robert (publisher and author):
Quite comfortable—quite happy—nothing more!

CHAMFORT, Roch Nicolas (miscellaneous writer) :
Ah! my friend, at last I am about to leave this world, where the heart must be broken or be brass.

CHAMPIONNET, Jean (general):
My friends, take care to console my mother. Would that I had been able to die like Joubert! [who was killed in action]

CHANNING, William Ellery (Unitarian):
I have received many messages from the spirit.

CHAPMAN, John Jay (essayist; plucking at his wife's fingers):
I want to take it away, I want to take it away! ["What? the pillow?"] No, the mute, the mute. I want to play on the open strings.

CHARLEMAGNE:
Into Thy hands, O Lord, I commend my spirit.

CHARLES I (to Juxon):
Remember! . . . I go from a Corruptible to an Incorruptible Crown where no disturbance can be, but Peace and Joy for evermore.

CHARLES II:
Let not poor Nelly starve.

CHARLES V (Holy Roman Emperor):
It is time. . . . Ay, Jesus!

CHARLES V, called Charles the Wise (of France; after giving blessings and words of edification) :
Withdraw, my friends, withdraw and go away a little, so I can rest from the bother and labor I did not shirk.

CHARLES IX of France (to his Huguenot nurse):
Ah, my nurse, my dearest nurse, what blood and murders! Ah, I have had but wicked counsel! O my God, forgive me all that, and, so it please Thee, have mercy on me!

CHARLES XII of Sweden:
Don't be afraid.

CHARLES, Thomas (Welsh preacher; given Madeira with the hope it would prove useful):
Yes, if the Lord pleases.

CHARLOTTE Augusta (Princess of Wales; given hot wine and brandy by the doctors):
They have made me tipsy. . . .Stocky, Stocky! [Baron Stockmar]

CHARLOTTE Sophia (wife of George III; a servant, believing her unconscious, remarked, "This is a life of toil and trouble; but there is another life beyond it, in which none shall know trouble"):
Very true.

CHARMION (suicide with her mistress Cleopatra; asked by the messengers, "Was this well done of your Lady, Charmion?"):
Extremely well, and as became the descendant of so many kings.

CHATEAUBRIAND, René de (writer and statesman; hearing there was fighting in Paris):
I want to go there.

CHEKHOV, Anton (spoke first to the doctor in German, then took a glass of champagne that was offered him):
I am dying. . . . I haven't drunk champagne for a long time.

CHENIER, André (poet; guillotined; recited when he saw Roncher in the cart with him):
> *Yes, since I find a friend so true,*
> *My fortune has an aspect new.*

CHESTERFIELD, Lord (a visitor being ushered into his sick-chamber) :
> *Give Dayrolles a chair.*

CHESTERTON, Gilbert K.:
> *The issue is now clear. It is between light and darkness and every one must choose his side.*

CHICKERING, Hannah B. (Massachusetts prison reformer) :
> *Say only that I was at peace; more than this, if repeated, might indicate a deeper spiritual experience than I ever had.*

CHOATE, Joseph Hodges (lawyer and diplomat):
> *I am feeling very ill. I think this is the end.*

CHOATE, Rufus (congressman):
> *I don't feel well; I feel faint.*

CHOPIN, Frédéric (clutching the crucifix to his heart):
> *Now I am at the source of Blessedness!*

CHRISTINA, Queen of Sweden (requested a plain inscription) :
> *"Christina lived LXIII years."*

CHRISTODULE, Saint (declining burial elsewhere):
> *My children, do not be ungrateful towards the desert isle of Patmos, where we have labored so hard.*

CHISTOPHER, Saint (whose word was fulfilled):
> *I know, O king, that I shall be dead on the morrow. When I am dead, do thou, tyrant, make a paste of my blood, rub it upon thine eyes, and thou shalt recover thy sight!*

CHRYSIPPUS (Stoic; laughing after an ass had eaten up his figs):
Now give the ass a drink of pure wine to wash down the figs.

CHRYSOGONUS, Saint (to Diocletian):
I adore the one God in heaven, and I spurn thy proffered dignities as clay!

CHRYSOSTOM, Saint John:
Glory to God for all things.

CHUANG Tzu (follower of Lao-tzu; to the fears of his own followers, "lest the carrion kite should eat the body of our Master"):
Above ground, I shall be food for kites; below I shall be food for mole-crickets and ants. Why rob one to feed the other?

CHURCHILL, Charles (satirist):
What a fool I have been!

CHYTRÄUS, David (historian; died 1600):
I have concluded the history of this century and put the finishing touches to it, and not another word will I write.

CICERO, M. Tullius (stretching forward his head):
Here, veteran! if you think it right—strike!

CLARE, John (poet):
I have lived too long. . . . I want to go home.

CLAUDIUS, Matthias (German lyricist):
Lead me not into temptation and deliver me from evil. . . . Good night!

CLAY, Henry:
I believe, my son, I am going.

[49]

CLEMENCEAU, Georges (wanted to be):
buried standing, facing Germany.

CLEMENS, S. L. ("Mark Twain"):
Good-bye dear, if we meet—

CLEMENT, Jacques (Capuchin friar, slayer of Henry III of France; asked if he durst look an angry king in the face):
Yes, yes, yes, and kill him too.

CLEMMER, Mary (Ames) (American author; given water):
Thank you.

CLEOPATRA (seeing the asp among the figs):
So here it is.

CLEVELAND, Grover:
I have tried so hard to do right.

CLIFTON, Talbot (explorer):
Oh! I offer it.

CLIVE, Robert, Lord (taking out the penknife with which he killed himself; a lady had asked him if he would make her a pen):
To be sure.

CLONCURRY, Valentine Lawless, Lord (Irish agitator; to his physician):
Ah, Le Clerc, the closing scene!

CLOOTS, Anarcharsis (self-styled "Orator of the Human Race"; guillotined):
In the name of the earth, in the name of Humanity, do not confuse me in your memory with these common fellows! . . . No patched up peace!

COBBE, Frances Power (British philanthropist; letter).
I am touched by your affectionate words, dear

Blanche, but nobody must be sorry when that time comes, least of all those who love me.

COBDEN-SANDERSON, Thomas J. (bookbinder and printer; entry in journal):
Every day, every day, my Guide says to me, Are you ready?
And I say to my Guide, I am ready.
And my Guide says, March.
And to the end, one day more, I march.
Oh, every day, every day, am I ever on the ever-diminishing way, to the end, the end.

COCHIN, Augustin (student of social conditions; unfinished letter to Thiers):
It would be more manly to found the Republic because its name quiets the passions of the multitude, and we can present a braver front to Europe under that name than that of the Monarchy. But you cannot raise the dead to life. The Republic has been killed by her own children, the odious 1793, the foolish 1848. 1870 has carried her to the grave. She was killed by Robespierre and Marat, then by all the word-mongers, who have dealt in plots, in debts, and foolish actions, who have three times ascended this chariot of the people.

CODY, Buffalo Bill (of his foster-son):
I wish Johnny would come!

COFFIN, Charles Carleton (traveller and war correspondent):
If it were not for this pain I should get up and write.

COGHILL, George E. (American naturalist; as the nurse gave him a spoonful of peppermint water):
Why, that's what we used to give the babies.

COHAN, George M.:
Look after Agnes [his wife].

COKE, Sir Edward (lord chief justice):
Thy kingdom come, Thy will be done.

COLBATCH, Rev. Dr. John (opponent of Bentley at Cambridge; still remembering in his delirium his correction of Horace to a judge whose decision went against him):
ARROGAT, my lord.

COLBERT, General Auguste (scorning a warning to keep out of the line of fire):
You are then very much afraid today of dying?

COLE, Spencer Houghton (Baptist preacher):
I should like to finish my exposition of the 22nd of Revelation.

COLE, Thomas (landscape painter):
I want to be quiet.

COLERIDGE, Samuel Taylor (letter):
. . . I beg, expect, and would fain hope of them [his relatives] according to their means such a contribution as may suffice collectively for a handsome Legacy for that most faithful, affectionate and disinterested servant, Harriet Macklin [his nurse]. Henry can explain. I have never asked for myself. S. T. Coleridge.

COLIGNY, Gaspard de (leader of the Huguenots; he had been wounded before the assassin reached him):
Young man, you ought to consider my age and my infirmity. But you will not make my life shorter.

COLOMBINI, Giovanni (founder of the Jesuate order):
Father, into Thy hands I commend my spirit.

COLQUHOUN, Lady Janet (author of religious tracts; when her grandson was brought):
Where is he? I cannot see him.

COLT, Samuel:
It is all over now.

COLUMBA, Saint:
Dear children, this is what I commend with my last words—let peace and charity, that is mutual and sincere, reign always among you! If you act thus, following the example of the saints, God who strengthens the just will help you, and I, who shall be near Him, will intercede on your behalf, and you shall obtain of Him not only all the necessities of the present life in sufficient quantity, but still more the rewards of eternal life, reserved for those who keep His law.

COLUMBUS, Christopher:
Into Thy hands, O Lord, I commend my spirit.

COMBE, Andrew (physiologist and phrenologist):
Happy, happy.

COMBE, George (phrenologist):
From my present sensations, I should say I was dying —and I am glad of it.

CONDÉ, Henri de Bourbon, Prince de:
Hand me my chair; I feel extremely weak.

CONDER, Josiah (bookseller and author):
Amen.

CONFUCIUS:
No intelligent Monarch arises; there is not one in the kingdom that will make me his master. My time has come to die.

CONRAD, Joseph:
Here . . .

CONRADIN (of Swabia, last descendant of the imperial house of Hohenstaufen; executed):
O my mother! how deep will be thy sorrow at the news of this day!

CONSTANT de Rebecque, Benjamin (unable to finish correcting proofs for the final volume of his History of Religions):
The rest tomorrow.

CONTI, Princesse de (a niece of Mazarin):
Céphise [a maid]. My God!

COOK, Captain James (writing how the natives, who were to murder him, gathered around to welcome him):
We could not but be struck with the singularity of the scene; and perhaps there were few on board who ever lamented our having failed in our endeavours to find a northern passage homeward last summer. To this disappointment we owed our having it in our power to revisit the Sandwich Islands, and to enrich our voyage with a discovery which, though the last, seemed in many respects to be the most important that had hitherto been made by Europeans throughout the extent of the Pacific Ocean.

COOKE, Jay (banker; listened as the prayer for the dying was read):
That was the right prayer.

COOKE, Lt. W. W. (General Custer's adjutant; message written at Custer's direction to Capt. F. W. Benteen):
Benteen—Come on—Big Village—Be quick—Bring packs.

COOKMAN, Alfred (American Presbyterian clergyman):
My son, your pa has been all day long sweeping close by the gates of death. . . . How sweet and quiet everything seems; I feel like resting now.

COOPER, Sir Astley (surgeon):
Good-bye, God bless you!

COPLESTON, Edward (bishop of Llandaff):
I expect soon to die, and I die in the firm faith of the redemption wrought by God in man through Christ Jesus, assured that all who believe in Him will be saved.

COPLEY, John Singleton (portrait painter):
Happy, happy, supremely happy!

CORBET, Richard (divine):
Good night, Lushington.

CORBULO, Gnaeus Domitius (general recalled by Nero on suspicion of conspiracy; suicide):
Well deserved!

CORDAY, Charlotte (before mounting the tumbrel she cut off a lock of hair for the artist who had made her portrait):
Monsieur, I don't know how to thank you for your kindness. I have only this to offer you. Keep it as a remembrance of me.

COROT, Jean:
In spite of myself I go on hoping. . . . I hope with all my heart there will be painting in heaven.

CORYAT, Thomas (traveller; faint with fever in Persia):
Sack! Sack,—is there any such thing as sack? I pray you give me some sack!

COSIN, John (bishop of Durham) :
Lord.

COURTRIGHT, Jim (sharpshooter) :
Don't you pull a gun on me!

COWPER, William:
What does it signify?

COX, David (water-colorist):
God bless you.

CRABBE, George (poet):
All is well at last! . . . You must make an entertainment. . . . God bless you—God bless you!

CRAIGIE, Pearl Richards (pseudonym John Oliver Hobbes; telegram):
Excellent journey—crowded train—reached here by nine—fondest love—Pearl.

CRANE, Hart (American poet; as he jumped overboard):
Good-bye, everybody!

CRANE, Stephen (author of *The Red Badge of Courage*):
Robert— when you come to the hedge—that we must all go over—it isn't bad. You feel sleepy—and—you don't care. Just a little dreamy anxiety—which world you're really in—that's all.

CRANMER, Thomas (archbishop of Canterbury; at the stake, thrusting into the flames the hand that had signed his apostasy):
This hand having sinned in signing the writing must be the first to suffer punishment! This hand . . . hath offended . . . !

CRANTOR (Greek philosopher; asked where he wished to be buried):
Sweet in some corner of native soil to rest.

CRATES of Thebes (Cynic philosopher; made verses on himself):
You're going, noble hunchback, you are going
To Pluto's realms, bent double by old age.

CRAWFORD, F. Marion (novelist):
I love to see the reflection of the sun on the bookcase.

CREAM, Neil (convicted murderer; interrupted as the trap was sprung):
I am Jack—[the Ripper?]

CREIGHTON, Mandell (Anglican prelate and historian):
God.

CRITTENDEN, John J. (Kentucky legislator).
*Tom, come and raise me up, and arrange my pillow.
. . . That's right, Tom.*

CROKER, John Wilson (critic; to his servant as he was putting him into bed):
Oh, Wade!

CROLL, James (Scottish geologist; asking for a teaspoon of whisky):
I'll take a wee drop o' that. I don't think there's much fear o' me learning to drink now!

CROME, John (English landscape painter):
Hobbema, my dear Hobbema, how I have loved you!

CROMWELL, Oliver:
It is not my design to drink or sleep; but my design is, to make what haste I can to be gone.

CROMWELL, Thomas (on the scaffold) :
. . . The devil is ready to seduce us, and I have been seduced: but bear me witness that I die in the Catholic faith of the holy church, and I heartily desire you to pray for the King's grace, that he may long live with you in health and prosperity, and after him that his son prince Edward, that goodly imp, may long reign over you. And once again I desire you to pray for me, that so long as life remaineth in this flesh, I waver nothing in my faith.

CROSBY, Howard (American Presbyterian clergyman and author):
I place my hand in the hand of Jesus.

CROWFOOT (Isapwo Muksika, chief of the Blackfoot Confederacy):
A little while and I will be gone from among you, whither I cannot tell. From nowhere we come, into nowhere we go. What is life? It is a flash of a firefly in the night. It is a breath of a buffalo in the winter time. It is as the little shadow that runs across the grass and loses itself in the sunset.

CUMMINGS, Bruce (pseudonym W. N. P. Barbellion; biologist whose *Journal of a Disappointed Man* recorded the slow progress of his fatal disease):
The kindness almost everybody has shown the JOURNAL, and the fact that so many have understood its meaning have entirely changed my outlook. My horizon has cleared, my thoughts are tinged with sweetness, and I am content.

CUMMINS, George David (organizer of the Reformed Episcopal Church):
Jesus! precious Saviour!

CURIE, Madame Marie (to the doctor):
I don't want it. I want to be alone.

CURRAN, John P. (Irish orator and judge; letter) :
Dear Phillips,—Just got a note: Mrs. Godwin is sick; he'll dine here Sunday. If you prefer an invalid, come tomorrow.—You'd be more gratified on Sunday. UTRUM HORUM? Yours, J. P. Curran. Wednesday

CURTIUS, Ernst (classical philologist; last verses):
*As the bird with day's last gleam
Wearily sings itself asleep;*

> As it twitters in its dream,
> Ever fainter comes its peep.
> So MY songs scarce reach the ear,
> Overtaken by my night.
> But the loud ones will burst clear,
> When it comes—another light.

CUSHING, Harvey (surgeon; to his nephew, who had rearranged the patient's pillow):
> Pat, you have the 'touch'—you're a good doctor.

CUTHBERT, Saint:
> And know and remember, that if of two evils you are compelled to choose one, I would rather that you should take my bones, and leave these places, to reside wherever God may send you, than consent in any way to the wickedness of schismatics, and so place a yoke upon your necks. Study diligently, and carefully observe the Catholic rules of the Fathers, and practise with zeal those institutes of the monastic life which it has pleased God to deliver to you through my ministry. For I know, that, although during my life some have despised me, yet after my death you will see what sort of man I was, and that my doctrine was by no means worthy of contempt.

CUTLER, Benjamin C. (Brooklyn clergyman):
> Lift me up, lift me right up!

CUVIER, Clementine (daughter of the naturalist; to a friend):
> You know we are sisters for eternity— There is life, it is only THERE that there is life.

CUVIER, Baron Georges (having passed on a glass of lemonade to his daughter-in-law):
> It is very delightful to see those I love still able to swallow.

CYPRIAN, Saint (to the heathen judge who condemned him):

God be thanked.

CYRUS the Great:

And now, now it seems to me that my life begins to ebb; I feel my spirit slipping away from those parts she leaves the first. If you would take my hand once more, or look into my eyes while life is there, draw near me now; but when I have covered my face, let no man look on me again, not even you, my sons. But you shall bid the Persians come, and all our allies, to my sepulchre; and you shall rejoice with me and congratulate me that I am safe at last, free from suffering or sorrow, whether I am with God or whether I have ceased to be. Give all who come the entertainment that is fitting in honour of a man whose life on earth was happy, and so send them away.

Remember my last saying: show kindness to your friends, and then shall you have it in your power to chastise your enemies. Good-bye, my dear sons, bid your mother good-bye for me. And all my friends, who are here or far away, good-bye.

CYRUS the Younger:

Clear the way, villains, clear the way.

D

DA COSTA, Uriel (Portuguese philosopher; excommunicated by Amsterdam synagogue as atheist; written):

There you have the true story of my life. I have shown what role I played in this vain world-theater and in my unimportant and restless life. Now, fellow men, make your just and dispassionate judgment, speaking freely according to the truth, as becomes men who are really men. If you find something which arouses your sympathy, then realize and mourn the sad lot of Man, which you share. And let there be no confusion about this: the name that I bore as a Christian in Portugal was Gabriel da Costa; among the Jews—would that I had never got involved with them!—I was known, by a small change, as Uriel.

DAHLGREN, John A. (rear admiral in Union navy; to his wife):

Madeleine, I will take nothing more until you go to your breakfast, which you must require.

DALBERG, Karl von (last archbishop-elector of Mainz; proposing a toast):

Love! Life! ... God's will!

DAMIEN, Father (Joseph Damien de Veuster, the "Leper-priest of Molokai"):

Well! God's will be done. He knows best. My work with all its faults and failures, is in His hands, and before Easter I shall see my Saviour.

DAMIENS, Robert (would-be assassin of Louis XV; tortured):

My God, have pity on me! Jesus, deliver me.

[61]

DANKS, Hart Pease (composer of *Silver Threads Among the Gold;* unfinished note):
It is hard to die alone and—

D'ANNUNZIO, Gabriele (to the chauffeur):
Stop! . . . Turn home! . . . I'm bored . . . I'm bored!

DANTON, Georges Jacques (on the scaffold):
Show my head to the people, it is worth it.

DARIUS III (king of Persia; mourned that in his last extremity he was receiving benefits without being able to return them):
But Alexander, whose kindness to my mother, my wife, and my children I hope the gods will recompense, will doubtless thank you for your humanity to me. Tell him, therefore, in token of my acknowledgment, I give him this right hand.

DARNLEY, Henry Stuart, Lord (second husband of Mary, Queen of Scots; read the 55th psalm the evening of his murder):
It is not an open enemy that hath done me this dishonour, for then I could have borne it. It was even thou, my companion, my guide, and my own familiar friend.

DARWIN, Charles:
I am not the least afraid to die.

DAVID, Jacques Louis (when a print of his "Leonidas at Thermopylae" was brought him, indicated corrections with his cane):
Too dark. . . . Too light. . . . The dimming of the light is not well enough indicated. . . . This place is blurred. . . . However, I must admit, that's a unique head of Leonidas.

DAVIS, Jefferson (urged to take some medicine):
Pray excuse me. I cannot take it.

DAVIS, Richard Harding (war correspondent; written): *That France and her Allies succeed should be the hope and prayer of every American. The fight they are waging is for the things the real unhyphenated American is supposed to hold most high and most dear. Incidentally, they are fighting his fight, for their success will later save him, unprepared as he is to defend himself, from a humiliating and terrible thrashing. And every word and act of his now that helps the Allies is a blow against frightfulness, against despotism, and in behalf of a broader civilization, a nobler freedom, and a much more pleasant world in which to live.*

DAVIS, Thomas (Irish poet; letter): *In four days I hope to be able to look at light business for a short time.*

DAVIS, Varina Howell (wife of Jefferson Davis): *O Lord, in Thee have I trusted, let me not be confounded.*

DECATUR, Stephen (in a duel with another naval officer): *I am mortally wounded, I think.*

DEFFAND, Marquise du (urged to confess, said she would): *confess to my friend, the Duc de Choiseul.*

DEKKER, Edouard Douwes (pseudonym Multatuli; Dutch writer; playing chess by mail): *That you are still not crushed, I admit, but that will come a little later. And if this is too difficult for you, let it go, if you like: the game can wait.*

DE KOVEN, Reginald (composer of operettas; telegram to wife):

House sold out for Friday night, box office Vox Dei
Hurrah.

DE LANCEY, Sir William Howe (fallen at Waterloo):
Magdalene, my love, the spirits.

DELANY, Mary Granville (friend of Swift; told that the
doctors had ordered bark to be administered, looked dis-
tressed but bore with it):
*I have always had a presentiment that if bark were
given, it would be my death. You know I have at
times a great defluxion on my lungs; it will stop that
and my breath with it. . . . Oh, I never was reckoned
obstinate, and I will not die so.*

DEMONAX (Cynic philosopher; refusing to be concerned
about exposure to birds and dogs):
*I can see nothing out of the way in it, if even in
death I am going to be of service to living things.*

DE MORGAN, William (unfinished novel, *The Old Mad-
house*):
*Pinning her faith on this, she passed into the passage
where he ought to have been; the import of her
demeanour being, that her shrewder insight would at
once discern the whereabouts of—*

DEMOSTHENES (who had taken sanctuary at the temple
of Poseidon):
*Now, as soon as you please, you may commence the
part of Creon in the tragedy, and cast out this body
of mine unburied. But, O gracious Poseidon, I, for
my part while I am yet alive will rise up and depart
out of this sacred place; though Antipater and the
Macedonians have not left so much as thy temple
unpolluted.*

[64]

DENNIS, John (critic; hearing that someone had put out verses in his name):
> *By God, they could be no one but that fool S—'s.*

DENTON, John (member of the ill-fated Donner party, who died in the Sierran snow-fields; composed nostalgic poetry in his last moments):
> *I wish I could once more recall*
> > *That bright and blissful joy,*
> *And summon to my weary heart*
> > *The feelings of a boy.*
> *But now on scenes of past delight*
> > *I look and feel no pleasure,*
> *As misers on the bed of death*
> > *Gaze coldly on their treasure.*

DE QUINCEY, Thomas:
> *Sister! sister! sister!*

DESCARTES, René:
> *My soul, thou hast long been held captive; the hour has now come for thee to quit thy prison, to leave the trammels of this body; suffer, then, this separation with joy and courage.*

DESMOULINS, Camille (at the guillotine):
> *Thus, then, the first apostle of Liberty ends! Have this [a lock of Lucile's hair] sent to my mother-in-law! . . . O my poor wife!*

DESMOULINS, Lucile (reproving a fellow prisoner):
> *You insulted Antoinette when she was in the tumbrel; that does not surprise me. Had you not better keep a little of your courage to brave another queen, Death, to whom we are hastening?*

DE VEGA, Lope:
> *True glory is in virtue. Ah! I would willingly give*

*all the applause I have received to have performed
one good action more. . . . Jesus . . . Mary.*

DEWEY, Admiral George (in delirium):
*Gentlemen, the battle . . . is . . . done. The victory
. . . is . . . ours.*

DIAGHILEV, SERGEI (ballet master):
*Ah, Catherine. . . . How beautiful you look. . . . I am
ill—very ill indeed . . . I feel so hot . . . light-headed.*

DICKENS, Charles (as his sister-in-law tried to get him to
the sofa):
On the ground.

DICKINSON, Emily:
I must go in, the fog is rising.

DIDEROT, Denis (to his wife's remonstrance, as he took
an apricot):
*But what the devil do you think that that will do
to me?*

DIENECES (Spartan at Thermopylae; when told, "Such
was the number of the barbarians, that when they shot
forth their arrows the sun would be darkened by their
multitude"):
*Our Trachinian friend brings us excellent tidings.
If the Medes darken the sun, we shall have our fight
in the shade.*

DIESEL, Rudolf (letter):
Greetings and a kiss. In fondest love, Your Father.

DIGBY, Sir Everard (conspirator in the Gunpowder Plot;
when his heart was exposed by the executioner, who, according to the formula, cried, "Here is the heart of a traitor"):
Thou liest.

[66]

DIOGENES (the Cynic; asked how he wished to be buried, referred to the rise of the Macedonians):
On my face . . . Because after a little time down will be changed to up.

DISRAELI, Benjamin:
I have suffered much. Had I been a Nihilist, I should have confessed all . . . I had rather live, but I am not afraid to die

DIXON, Henry Hall (pen name The Druid, English sporting writer; told the end was at hand):
Oh, God, I thank Thee! I could not bear much more.

DODD, William (preacher, executed for forgery; written):
For this fraud I am to die; and I die declaring, in the most solemn manner, that however I have deviated from my own precepts, I have taught others, to the best of my knowledge, and with all sincerity, the true way to eternal happiness. My life, for some few unhappy years past, has been dreadfully erroneous; but my ministry has been always sincere. I have constantly believed, and I now leave the world solemnly avowing my conviction, that there is no other name under heaven by which we can be saved, but only the name of the Lord Jesus; and I entreat all who are here to join me in my last petition, that for the sake of that Lord Jesus Christ, my sins may be forgiven, and my soul received into His everlasting kingdom. June 23, 1777.

DODE de la Brunerie, Guillaume (general):
The doctors still assert that the enemy is retreating; I believe on the contrary that we are, as it were, on the eve of a battle. God knows what tomorrow will bring!

DODGE, Grace H. (philanthropist; regretted not having seen the "dear students" who had come as her guests):
And were they happy?

DOLET, Étienne (humanist; executed for heresy; imagining that the spectators were grieving):
This is not doleful for Dolet, but it means dole for the good people.

DOLLFUSS, Engelbert (Austrian chancellor; assassinated):
Children, you are so good to me. Why aren't the others? I have only desired peace—we have never attacked anybody—we have always had to defend ourselves. May God forgive them!

DOMINIC, Saint:
Let not my departure in the flesh trouble you, my sons, and doubt not that I shall serve you better dead than alive!

DONDEAUVILLE, Mme. de la Rochefoucauld, Duchess of (founder of the Society of Nazareth; "Do you love the good God?"):
Yes!

DONNE, John:
I were miserable if I might not die. . . . Thy Kingdom come, Thy Will be done.

DOSTIE, A. P. (anti-slavery patriot; mobbed):
I am dying. I die for the cause of Liberty. Let the good work go on.

DOUGLAS, General Sir Howard:
All that I have said about [against] armored ships will prove correct. How little do they know of the undeveloped power of artillery!

DOUGLAS, Stephen A. (asked if he had any word for his sons):

Tell them to obey the laws and support the Constitution of the United States.

DOUGLASS, Frederick (Negro lecturer and writer):
Why, what does this mean?

DOUMERGUE, Paul (editor; had just said that he refused to see the doctor for fear that):
he put me in the discard.

DOWSON, Ernest (poet; to Mrs. Robert Sherard):
You are like an angel from heaven. God bless you.

DOYLE, Sir Arthur Conan (to Lady Conan Doyle):
You are wonderful.

DRAPER, Daniel James (Methodist minister; in a shipwreck):
We may all make the port of heaven. . . . O God! may those that are not converted be converted now; hundreds of them! . . . In a few moments we must all appear before our Great Judge. Let us prepare to meet Him. . . . Rock of ages cleft for me.

DRAYTON, Michael (poet; wrote of his enduring love for Anne Rainsford):
So all my thoughts are pieces but of you,
Which put together make a glass so true,
As I therein no other's face but yours can view.

DREUX, Col. Charles D. (who fell at Newport News):
Boys, steady!

DREW, Samuel (Cornish metaphysician; told, "My dear sir, today, I trust, you will be with the Lord Jesus"):
Yes, my good sir, I trust I shall.

DREXEL, Anthony J., III (of the banking family; before a souvenir pistol he was showing a friend accidentally went off):
Here's one you've never seen before.

DRUSUS, Marcus Livius, the Younger (Roman tribune):
When will the republic find again a citizen like me?

DU BARRY, Madame:
Just a moment, Mr. executioner, only one moment more ... Help! help!

DUBOS, Jean Baptiste (abbé and historian):
Death is a law and not a punishment. Three things ought to console us for giving up life: the friends whom we have lost, the few persons worthy of being loved whom we leave behind us, and finally the memory of our stupidities and the assurance that they are now going to stop.

DUCOS, Jean Francois (French revolutionist; as he laid his head on the block) :
It is time that the convention decreed the inviolability of heads.

DUDLEY, John, Duke of Northumberland (adherent of Lady Jane Grey; bowing to the block):
I have deserved a thousand deaths.

DUFF, Captain George (before the battle of Trafalgar; to Mrs. Duff):
My Dearest Sophia, I have just had time to tell you we are just going into action with the combined (fleets). I hope and trust in God that we shall all behave as becomes us, and that I may yet have the happiness of taking my beloved wife and children in my arms. Norwich [who witnessed his father's death] is quite well and happy. I have, however, ordered him off the quarter deck. Yours ever and most truly, Geo. Duff.

DUMAS, Alexandre, père:
Tell me, Alexander, on your soul and conscience, do you believe that anything of mine will live?

DUNANT, Henri (founder of Red Cross):
I wish to be carried to my grave like a dog without a single one of your ceremonies which I do not recognize. I trust to your goodness faithfully to respect my last earthly request. I count upon your friendship that it shall be so. Amen. I am a disciple of Christ as in the first century, and nothing more.

DUNBAR, Paul Laurence (Negro poet; 23rd Psalm):
Through the valley of the shadow.

DUNCAN, Isadora:
Adieu, *my friends! I go to glory!*

DUNCAN, Joseph (governor of Illinois; asked if Christ was precious to him "at this hour"):
Ever precious, ever precious.

DUNDEE, John Graham of Claverhouse, Viscount (struck by a cannonball, asked):
How goes the day? ["Well for King James, but I am sorry for your lordship."] *If it goes well for him it matters the less for me.*

DUPANLOUP, Félix (bishop of Orléans; told that a prayer for him was about to be made to the Blessed Virgin):
Yes—yes.

DUPIN, Mme. Maurice (mother of George Sand):
Comb my hair.

DUPLEIX, Marquis Joseph François (colonial administrator; written):
I have sacrificed my youth, my fortune, my life, to enrich my nation in Asia. Unfortunate friends, too weak relations, devoted all their property to the success of my projects. They are now in misery and want.

I have complied with all the judiciary forms: I have demanded, as the last of the creditors, that which is due to me. My services are treated as fables, my demand is denounced as ridiculous, I am treated as the vilest of mankind. I am in the most deplorable indigence. The little property that remained to me has been seized. I am compelled to ask for decrees for delay in order not to be dragged to prison.

DU PONT, Alfred I.:
Thank you, doctors. Thank you, nurses. I'll be all right in a few days.

DURANTI, Jean E. (president of Toulouse parliament under Henri III; mobbed; to his wife):
Adieu, my beloved; what God has granted me—life, goods, honors—I am presently to be stripped of. Death is the end, but not the punishment of life; innocent of the charges imputed me, my soul is to appear at the tribunal of the sovereign Judge. Trust in Him; He will always help you . . . [to the mob] Yes, here I am. But what crime have I committed, what is the wrong, O people, I am guilty of in your eyes? . . . Lord God, receive my soul. Do not blame them for this wrong, for they know not what they do.

DUSE, Eleonora (Italian actress):
We must stir ourselves. Move on! Work! Work! . . . Cover me! . . . Must move on! Must work! Cover me.

DUVEEN, Joseph (art dealer for the wealthy):
Well, I fooled 'em for five years.

DWIGHT, Timothy (educator; as he stitched the cover on the manuscript of his essays on the Evidences of Divine Revelation):
There, I have done.

[72]

ε

EADS, James B. (engineer):
I cannot die; I have not finished my work.

EAGELS, Jeanne (actress):
I'm going to Dr. Caldwell's for one of my regular treatments.

EARHART, Amelia (letter to husband before last flight):
Please know that I am quite aware of the hazards. I want to do it because I want to do it. Women must try to do things as men have tried. When they fail, their failure must be but a challenge to others.

EASTMAN, George (inventor and industrialist; suicide note):
To my friends: My work is done. Why wait? G.E.

EASTMAN, Joseph B. (Interstate Commerce Commissioner and Defense Transportation director; letter):
I am glad to say that I seem to be making good progress, and from all prognostications I shall be back in circulation again before too long.

EATON, General William (asked, at sunrise, if he wished his head raised):
Yes, sir, I thank you.

EDDY, Mary Baker (written):
God is my Life.

EDGEWORTH, Richard Lovell (writer; father of Maria):
I die with the soft feeling of gratitude to my friends, and submission to the God who made me.

EDISON, Thomas A. (arousing from a coma):
It is very beautiful over there.

EDMUND or **Eadmund, Saint, the Martyr** (king of East Anglia; refusing to abjure his religion) :
Jesus, Jesus!

EDWARD, the Black Prince:
I thank Thee, O Lord, for all Thy benefits. With all my power I ask for Thy mercy that Thou wilt forgive me for all the sins that I, in my wrongdoing, have committed against Thee. And I ask with my whole heart the grace of pardon from all men whom I have knowingly or unwittingly offended.

EDWARD III (king of England):
Jesu.

EDWARD VI:
I am faint; Lord have mercy upon me, and take my spirit.

EDWARD VII:
No, I shall not give in; I shall go on; I shall work to the end.

EDWARDS, Edward (municipal library pioneer; to his landlady, after she had bathed his feet):
I am much obliged to you—very.

EDWARDS, Jonathan:
Trust in God and ye need not fear.

EGMONT, Lamoral, Count (fighter for Dutch freedom; executed):
Lord, into Thy hands I commit my spirit.

ELDON, John Scott, Lord (lord high chancellor; when someone remarked that it was a cold day):
It matters not to me, where I am going, whether the weather here be hot or cold.

ELIOT, Charles W. (educator):
I see Mother.

ELIOT, George:
Tell them I have great pain in the left side.

ELIOT, John (apostle to the Indians; to a friend):
You are welcome to my very soul. Pray retire into my study for me, and give me leave to be gone.

ELISABETH Christine (wife of Frederick the Great):
I know you will not forget me.

ELISABETH, Madame (sister of Louis XVI; her fichu fell off on the scaffold):
In the name of your mother, monsieur, cover me.

ELIZABETH, Saint:
The time is already arrived, wherein God has called those that are His friends to the heavenly espousals!

ELIZABETH, Queen (to the Archbishop of Canterbury, who was praying by her side the last night and who had been calling to her mind her great accomplishments as a monarch):
My lord, the crown which I have borne so long has given enough of vanity in my time. I beseech you not to augment it in this hour when I am so near my death.

ELIZABETH, Empress of Austria (stabbed):
Why, what has happened?

ELLIOTT, Ebenezer (the "Corn-Law rhymer"):
A strange sight, sir: an old man unwilling to die!

ELLIOTT, Henry Venn (divine):
Suffer me not . . . for any pains of death . . . to fall from Thee.

ELLIOTT, John Lovejoy (Ethical Culture leader):
The only things I have found worth living for, and working for, and dying for, are love and friendship.

ELLIS, Havelock:
You must go to bed, you are so tired and I feel better. Perhaps I may sleep a little. . . . I shall ring if I need you.

ELOI, Saint (bishop of Noyon):
And now, O Christ, I shall render up my last breath in confessing loudly Thy name; receive me in Thy great mercy, and disappoint me not in my hope; open to me the gate of life and render the Prince of Darkness powerless against me. Let Thy clemency protect me, Thy might hedge me, and Thy hand lead me to the place of refreshment and into the tabernacle Thou hast prepared for Thy servants and them that stand in awe of Thee.

EMERSON, Ralph Waldo (to Bronson Alcott):
Good-bye, my friend.

EMMET, Robert (Irish nationalist; asked by the hangman if he was ready):
Not—

ENGHIEN, Louis Antoine Henri de Bourbon-Condé, Duc d' (seized on Napoleon's orders; to the firing squad):
Let us go, my friends.

EPAMINONDAS (Theban conqueror of the Spartans; drawing the javelin from his wound):
Now it is time to die.

EPICURUS:
Now farewell; remember all my words.

ERASMUS:
Dear God.

ERICSSON, John (engineer and inventor):
I am resting. This rest is magnificent; more beautiful than words can tell!

ERRERA, Léo (Belgian anthropologist; reassuringly):
It is nothing. A little dizziness.

ERSKINE, Ralph (Scottish seceding divine and poet):
I shall be for ever a debtor to free grace. Victory, victory, victory!

ERSKINE, Thomas (of Linlathen; theologian):
You there! ... To the end ... O Lord my God ... Jesus ... Jesus Christ ... love ... the peace of God ... for ever and ever, for Jesus' sake, Amen and Amen.

ESSEX, Robert Devereux, Earl of (on the scaffold):
In humility and obedience to Thy commandment, in obedience to Thy ordinance, and to Thy good pleasure, O God, I prostrate myself to my deserved punishment. Lord be merciful to Thy prostrate servant. . . . Lord, into Thy hands I commend my spirit.

EUGENE, Prince of Savoy (Austrian general; breaking off a conference):
That is enough for today. We will reserve the rest for tomorrow—if I live that long.

EVANS, Christmas (Welsh preacher):
Good-bye—drive on.

EVARTS, Jeremiah (missionary):
Wonderful, wonderful, wonderful glory. We cannot understand—we cannot comprehend—wonderful glory —I will praise him, I will praise him. Who are in the room? Call all in—call all—let a great many come— I wish to give directions—wonderful—glory—Jesus reigns.

[77]

EVERETT, Edward (orator; letter to his daughter):
*I have turned the corner, and as soon as I can get a
little appetite, shake off my carking cough, and get
the kidneys to resume their action, and subdue the
numbness of my limbs, and get the better of my
neuralgic pain in the left shoulder, I hope to do
nicely.*

F

FAIRBANKS, Douglas:
I've never felt better.

FALLETTI, Marchesa Giulia, di Barolo (reformer of the Turin prisons):
May the will of God be done in me and by me in time and for eternity.

FAWCETT, Henry (English statesman):
The best things to warm my hands with would be my fur gloves. They are in the pocket of my coat in the dressing-room.

FAWCETT, John (Baptist theologian):
Come, Lord Jesus, come quickly. . . . O receive me to Thy children!

FENELON, François (author):
Lord, if I am still necessary to Thy people, I refuse not to labor for the rest of my days. Thy will be done!

FERGUSSON, Robert (poet admired by Burns; in a cell for the insane):
What ails ye? wherefore sorrow for me, sirs? I am very well cared for here—I do assure you. I want for nothing—but it is cold—it is very cold. You know, I told you, it would come to this at last—yes, I told you so. Oh, do not go yet, mother—I hope to be soon—oh, do not go yet—do not leave me!

FERRER, Francisco (Spanish revolutionary and educator):
I desire to be shot standing, without a bandage over

[79]

my eyes . . . [to the soldiers] Look well, my children,
it is not your fault. I am innocent. Long live the
School—

FESSENDEN, Reginald Aubrey (electrical engineer):
That was a nice little party. I'm sure this summer is
helping me, with all this rest and sunshine and the
sunshine lamps—I ought to be able to find out some-
thing that will be helpful not only to me, but to
others.

FICHTE, Johann Gottlieb (philosopher; when medicine
was brought):
Never mind that. I need no more medicine. I feel
that I am cured.

FIELD, Eugene (children's poet):
Good-night.

FIELD, Kate (lecturer and author):
The Amherst Eclipse Expedition!

FIELD, Marshall, II (merchant; suicide or accident):
I do not know how this happened. I can account for
it in no way. It was an accident. What are the chances
of my recovery, Doctor?

FILLMORE, Millard:
The nourishment is palatable.

FINUCANE, Wing Commander "Paddy" (over the radio
of his Spitfire as it lost altitude over the English channel):
This is it, chaps.

FISCHER, Adolph (Haymarket anarchist; as the hang-
man's cap was placed over his face):
Don't draw it so tight. I can't breathe. . . . Long live
Anarchy. . . . This is the happiest moment of my life.

FISK, WILBUR (first president of Wesleyan University; when his wife asked if he knew her):
Yes, love, yes.

FLAVUS, Subrius (conspirator against Nero; bidden to offer his neck resolutely):
I wish that your stroke may be as resolute.

FLECKER, James Elroy (poet)·
Lord, have mercy on my soul.

FLEMING, Marjory (the 8-year-old prodigy):
Oh mother, mother.

FLETCHER, Andrew, of Saltoun (Scottish patriot; asked by Lord Sunderland if there was anything he wished done):
I have a nephew who has been studying the law. Make him a judge when he is fit for it.

FOCH, Marshal Ferdinand:
Let us go.

FONTAINE-MARTEL, Mme. de (friend of Voltaire; having asked what time it was):
God be blessed! whatever the hour, there is always a rendezvous going on.

FONTENELLE, Bernard de (man of letters):
I do not feel anything but a certain difficulty of existing.

FONTON, Francis (forger; on the scaffold declared it was right in the Almighty to lead him home):
by a way which I knew not.

FOOT, Solomon (senator from Vermont):
What, can this be death? Is it come already? . . . I see it! I see it! The gates are wide open! beautiful! beautiful!

FOOTE, Rear-Admiral Andrew Hull:
We will have them, North and South. . . . The colored people. Yes, we will have them. . . . We must have charity—charity—charity.

FORREST, Edwin (letter):
God bless you ever, my dear and much valued friend.

FORRESTAL, James V. (Secretary of Defense; suicide; copied from the chorus to Sophocles' *Ajax*):
. . . Woe to the mother, in her close of day,
Woe to her desolate heart, and temples gray,
When she shall hear
Her loved one's story whispered in her ear!
'Woe, woe!' will be the cry,—
No quiet murmur like the tremulous wail—

FORSTER, Georg (traveller and writer; letter):
It's true, isn't it, my children, that two words are better than none? I haven't strength to write more. Good-bye. Keep away from illness. A kiss for my little darlings.

FOSTER, John (essayist; letter):
I commend you to the God of mercy, and very affectionately bid you—Farewell.

FOSTER, Stephen Collins (on a slip of paper found in his pocket):
Dear friends and gentle hearts.

FOTHERGILL, Samuel (Quaker):
All is well with me; through the mercy of God, in Jesus Christ, I am going to a blessed and happy eternity: my troubles are ended, mourn not for me.

FOX, Charles James (to his wife):
I die happy, but pity you. . . . It don't signify, my dearest, dearest Liz.

FOX, George:
> I am glad I was here [i.e., in the meeting of Friends].
> Now I am clear, I am fully clear! . . . All is well; the
> Seed of God reigns over all and over death itself. And
> though I am weak in body, yet the power of God is
> over all, and the Seed reigns over all disorderly spirits.

FOX, Henry, Baron Holland (British statesman; requested that if Mr. Selwyn called, he should be let in):
> If I am alive, I shall be glad to see him; and if I am
> dead, he would like to see me.

FOX, Henry Watson (missionary to South India):
> Jesus, Jesus must be first in the heart. ["He is the first
> in yours."] Yes, he is.

FOX, Margaret (wife of George; to her daughter):
> Take me in thy arms, I am in peace.

FRANCE, Anatole:
> Maman! [mother]

FRANCIS of Assisi, Saint:
> Welcome, sister Death!

FRANCKE, August Hermann (Pietist; his wife asked if his Saviour was still with him):
> Of that there is no doubt.

FRANKLIN, Benjamin (his daughter advised him to change his position in bed, that he might breathe more easily):
> A dying man can do nothing easy.

FRANZ Joseph (emperor of Austria):
> I thank thee, Ketterl.

FRASER, Simon, 12th Lord Lovat (Jacobite intriguer; quoted on the scaffold Horace and Ovid):
> It is sweet and proper to die for one's country.

Scarcely can I enumerate what we and our family have done.

FREDERICK the Great :
We are over the hill, we shall go better now.

FREEMAN, Edward A. (historian; entry in diary):
Very weak. Rail to La Encina and Alicante.

FRELINGHUYSEN, Theodore (American politician and educator):
All peace, more than ever before.

FRENCH, Daniel Chester (American sculptor; to his nurse):
You're very good to me.

FRERE, Sir Bartle (colonial administrator, recalled):
If they would only read the 'Further Correspondence' they would surely understand.—they must be satisfied.

FRICK, Henry Clay (industrialist):
That will be all; now I think I'll go to sleep.

FRIEDRICH Wilhelm I (of Prussia):
Lord Jesus, to Thee I live. Lord Jesus, to Thee I die; in life and in death Thou art my gain.

FROEBEL, Friedrich (founder of the kindergarten system; had himself put in front of an open window, though the doctor said this could accelerate his death):
My friend, I have peeked at lovely Nature all my life. Permit me to pass my last hours with this enchanting mistress.

FROHMAN, Charles (theatrical manager):
Why fear death? It is the most beautiful adventure of life. . . . Why fear death?

FROUDE, James Anthony (English historian):
Shall not the Judge of all the earth do right?

FRY, Elizabeth (prison reformer):
Oh! my dear Lord, help and keep Thy servant!

FULLER, Andrew (Baptist clergyman; in prayer):
Help me!

FULLER, Arthur Buckminster (Union chaplain, who fell at Fredericksburg; coming up with a musket in his hand):
Captain, I must do something for my country. What shall I do?

FULLER, Margaret (transcendentalist; shipwrecked):
I see nothing but death before me,—I shall never reach the shore.

FULLER, Melvin W. (U.S. Supreme Court Chief Justice):
I am very ill.

FURNIVALL, F. J. (English scholar; asked how he wished to be commemorated):
I want the Club.

FUSELI, Henry (painter):
Is it you, Samuel?

G

GADSDEN, Rev. Christopher Philip (of the South Carolina Gadsdens; arms raised):
I am reaching toward my inheritance.

GAINSBOROUGH, Thomas:
We are all going to heaven, and Van Dyck is of the company.

GALBA, Servius Sulpicius (Roman emperor):
Strike, if it be for the good of Rome.

GALLAUDET, Rev. Thomas H. (American teacher of the deaf and dumb):
I will go to sleep.

GAMBETTA, Léon (French statesman; awakened by a friend's falling in a faint on hearing that the illness would be fatal):
Good heavens! has he hurt himself?

GANDHI, Mahatma (shot):
Oh, God.

GARCIA, "Three Fingered" Jack:
I will throw up my hands for no gringo dog.

GARDINER, Capt. Allen F. (missionary; starving to death in Patagonia; letter):
My dear Mr. Williams, The Lord has seen fit to call home another of our little company. Our dear departed brother left the boat on Tuesday at noon, and has not since returned: doubtless he is in the presence of his Redeemer, whom he served so faithfully. Yet a little while, and through grace we may join that

blessed throng to sing the praises of Christ through-out eternity. I neither hunger nor thirst, though five days without food! Marvellous loving-kindness to me a sinner! Your affectionate brother in Christ,
Sept. 6, 1851   *Allen F. Gardiner*

GARDINER, James (colonel of dragoons; at Prestonpans in 1745):
> *Fire on, my lads, and fear nothing.* . . . *[waving his attendant to retreat] Take care of yourself.*

GARDINER, Stephen (English prelate; expressing remorse for his repudiation of the Roman supremacy):
> *I have denied with Peter, I have gone out with Peter, but not yet have I wept with Peter.*

GARFIELD, James Abram:
> *O Swaim, there is a pain here.* . . . *Oh! oh! Swaim.*

GARIBALDI, Giuseppe (two finches who knew him were playing on the window-sill):
> *Feed them when I am gone.*

GARNETT, Henry (executed as a conspirator in the Gun-Powder Plot):
> *Imprint the cross on my heart* . . . *Mary, mother of grace.*

GARRICK, David:
> *Oh! dear.*

GARRICK, Mrs. David (offered a cup of tea by one of the maids):
> *Put it down, hussy! Do you think I cannot help myself?*

GASPARIN, Count Agénor de (publicist; his wife wished to walk behind him as he ascended the steps):
> *No, you know I like to have you go before me.*

GASSENDI, Pierre (savant; when his confessor offered to recite the psalms out loud):

I pray you, say them softly, because speaking out loud disturbs me.

GATES, Sir John (statesman; to the executioner):

I forgive thee with all my heart. . . . I will see how meet the block is for my neck. I pray thee strike not yet, for I have a few prayers to say, and that done, strike on God's name, good leave have thou.

GAUGUIN, Paul (letter to a missionary):

Dear Monsieur Vernier: Would it be troubling you too much to ask you to come to see me? My eyesight seems to be going and I cannot walk. I am very ill. P.G.

GAVESTON, Piers (favorite of Edward II; to Lancaster):

Oh! noble Earl, spare me.

GEER, Baron Louis de (Swedish statesman):

My God, have pity on·me. Do not visit on me suffering beyond my strength. . . . O Christ! Thou hast suffered still more for me.

GELLERT, Christian M. (German poet; inquired how long he had to live, told perhaps an hour):

God be praised—only one more hour!

GEORGE IV (to his page):

Watty! What is this? It is death. They have deceived me.

GEORGE V (to the Privy Councillors; having difficulty signing his initials):

Gentlemen, I am sorry for keeping you waiting like this—I am unable to concentrate.

GEORGE, Henry:

Yes, yes, yes.

GERSON, Jean de (theologian):
> *My God, my creator, have mercy on Thy poor servant, Jean Gerson.*

GIANGER (son of Solyman the Magnificent; stabbing himself, refusing his brother's spoils—Mustapha's death having been arranged by Solyman):
> *Fie of thee, thou impious and wretched dog, traitor, murderer, I cannot call thee father—take the treasures, the horse and armour of Mustapha to thyself!*

GIBBON, Edward (to his valet):
> *Why are you leaving me?*

GIBBONS, Cardinal James:
> *I have had a good day.*

GIDE, André:
> *'Tis well.*

GILBERT, Mrs. Anne (Ann Taylor, writer of children's poetry; when her daughter assisted in arranging her hair gave her two kisses):
> *That's for thank you. . . . That's for good-night.*

GILBERT, Sir Humphrey (cheering his men):
> *We are as near to Heaven by sea as by land!*

GILBERT, W. S. (as he rescued a woman from drowning, only to drown himself):
> *Put your hands on my shoulders and don't struggle.*

GILDER, Richard Watson (poet and editor; writing of Tennyson):
> *He wrote some of his sagest and loveliest things in the last days—there seems to have been an otherworld light on these latest utterances. You see him standing serene in the afterglow, awaiting in tranquillity the natural end.*

GILFILLAN, George (Scottish Presbyterian clergyman and writer):
I am dying, doctor? ... The will of the Lord be done. ... Yes, I believe in God, in Christ.

GISSING, George (novelist):
Patience, patience. ... God's will be done.

GLADSTONE, W. E.:
Amen.

GODET, Frédéric (Swiss Protestant theologian; to his family):
I have carried you in my heart all my life, and I hope it will still be permitted to do the same up there.

GODWIN (earl; accused by Edward the Confessor of murdering his brother; choked):
So might I safely swallow this morsel of bread, as I am guiltless of the deed.

GODWIN, Fanny (Imlay) (illegitimate daughter of Mary Wollstonecraft; suicide note):
I have long determined that the best thing I could do was to put an end to the existence of a being whose birth was unfortunate, and whose life has only been a series of pains to those persons who have hurt their health in endeavouring to promote her welfare. Perhaps to hear of my death may give you pain, but you will soon have the blessing of forgetting that such a creature ever existed.

GODWIN, William (political philosopher; last words in diary):
Cough, snow.

GOEBBELS, Joseph:
Everything is over. My wife and I will commit suicide. You will burn our bodies. Can you do that? ... Here is a present for you [Hitler's photograph].

GOEBBELS, Magda:
>You see, we shall die an honorable death. If you
>should ever see Harald again [son from her first mar-
>riage, a war prisoner], give him our best and tell him
>we died an honorable death.

GOETHALS, Gen. George Washington (Panama Canal
builder):
>Let me stay here [New York]. If I stay here, I'll be
>much nearer to West Point.

GOETHE, Johann Wolfgang von:
>More light!

GOFFE, Thomas (divine and poet; warned by one Thomas
Thimble that his wife would break his heart):
>Oracle, oracle, Tom Thimble.

GOGOL, Nicholas (quoting the Old Testament):
>And I shall laugh a bitter laugh.

GOLDBERGER, Joseph (medical researcher; to his wife):
>Mary, don't leave me; you have always been my rock,
>my strength; Mary, we must have patience.

GOLDSMITH, Oliver (being asked if his mind was at
rest):
>No, it is not.

GOMPERS, Samuel (labor leader):
>God bless our American institutions. May they grow
>better day by day.

GOOD, John Mason (physician and writer):
>Which taketh away the sins of the world.

GORDON, General Charles ("Chinese Gordon"):
>Where is the Mahdi?

GORDON, Elizabeth, Duchess of (when it was repeated,
"My Beloved is mine, and I am His"):
>Yes.

GORETTI, Saint Maria ("The Martyr of Purity"; 11, stabbed resisting the advances of a 19-year old youth):
May God forgive him; I want him in heaven.

GOSSE, Sir Edmund (critic; letter before his operation):
You will think of me in this hour with sympathy and hope. There seems good reason to think I shall survive the shock. In any case I am perfectly calm, and able to enjoy the love which has accompanied me through such long years and surrounds me still.

GOUGH, John B. (temperance lecturer; on the platform):
Young man, keep your record clean.

GRADY, Henry W. (Southern editor and orator):
And the little children cried in the streets.

GRAHAM, Sir James (statesman; after a heart spasm):
Ah! I thought it was over then.

GRANDIER, Urbain (accused of having caused religious mania in Loudun; burnt):
My God, by the light I wait for you. . . . My God, forgive my enemies.

GRANT, Ulysses S.:
Water.

GRANVILLE, Augustus Bozzi (physician and Italian patriot):
Light, all light.

GRATTAN, Henry (Irish statesman; after dictating):
I die with a love of liberty in my heart, and this declaration in favour of my country in my head. . . . It will do. I should wish it to be read in the House; give my love to Plunket, he will do it.

GRAY, Lt. Bryant (of the Union Army):
Forward! march!

GRAY, Robert (bishop of Cape Town; when it was intimated that Holy Communion *tomorrow* would be too late):
Well, dear fellow, I am ready when you like.

GRAY, Thomas (to his niece):
Molly, I shall die!

GREBLE, Lt. Col. John T. (shot at the battle of Big Bethel or County Creek):
Sergeant! take command—go ahead.

GREEN, Joseph Henry (metaphysician; felt his own pulse):
Stopped.

GREGOIRE, Henri (bishop of Blois; delirious) :
Monsieur Baradère, I have been tormented for eight days; I see a whole population of blacks isolated on an island which serves as their refuge. They are going to die of hunger! ... I was told that some Protestants and Jews came to see me; although they are not of my church, I desire to make acknowledgments to them. . . . Let someone send theological books to Haiti. The poor Haitians! ... I see that my last hour is come. . . . Do not desert me in my last moments!

GREGORY VII, Pope:
I have loved righteousness and hated iniquity, and therefore I die in exile.

GRELLET, Stephen (Quaker missionary):
Not my will, but Thine be done.

GRENVILLE, Sir Richard (Elizabethan admiral):
Here die I, Richard Grenville, with a joyful and a quiet mind, for that I have ended my life as a good soldier ought to do, who has fought for his country, Queen, religion and honour. Wherefore my soul most

*joyfully departeth out of this body, and shall always
leave behind it an everlasting fame of a valiant and
true soldier, who hath done his duty, as he was bound
to do. But the others of my company have done as
traitors and dogs, for which they shall be reproached
all their lives, and leave a shameful name for ever.*

GREY, Lady Jane (having blindfolded herself, could not
find the block) :
*What shall I do? Where is it? . . .
Lord, into Thy hands I commend my spirit.*

GRIEG, Edvard:
Well, if it must be so.

GRIMSTON, Robert (British sportsman):
*I don't think I shall join you at dinner; but I will
punish your dinner for you—I will have a bit of your
fish.*

GRISWOLD, Rufus Wilmot (Poe's literary executor):
*Sir, I may not have been always a Christian, but I am
very sure that I have been a gentleman.*

GROENEVELD, Reinier, Seignior de (Dutch leader):
*O God! What a man I was once, and what am I now?
. . . Patience.*

GROTIUS, Hugo (Dutch jurist, statesman, and scholar):
*By understanding many things I have accomplished
nothing.*

GROVES, Anthony Norris (missionary):
*Now, my precious boy, I am dying; be a comfort to
your beloved mother, as your dear brothers Henry
and Frank have been to me. And may the Lord Himself bless you and make you His own. May the Lord
give you the peace and joy in Himself that He has*

given me, for these are true riches. What would thousands of gold and silver be to me now? Now I give you a father's blessing.

GUESCLIN, Bertrand Du (called "the Eagle of Brittany"):
Remember that your business is only with those who carry arms. The churchmen, the poor, the women and children are not your enemies. . . . I commend to the king my wife . . . my brother. . . . Farewell . . . I am at an end!

GUITEAU, Charles Julius (assassin of President Garfield; hanged):
Glory, hallelujah! Glory!

GUIZOT, François (French historian; his daughter said, "We shall meet again, my father"):
No one is more convinced of that than I am!

GUNTHER, John, Jr. (son of the journalist):
Mother . . . Father.

GURNEY, Joseph John (English Quaker philanthropist; to his wife):
I think I feel a little joyful, dearest.

GUSTAVUS Adolphus (fallen at Lützen; identifying himself to the cuirassiers):
I am the King of Sweden, who do seal the Religion and Liberty of the German nation with my blood.

GUTHRIE, James (Presbyterian divine; hanged):
The covenants, the covenants shall yet be Scotland's reviving!

H

HACKMAN, James (who killed Martha Ray, mistress of Lord Sandwich, on her refusal to marry him; scribbled to a friend before hanging):

> *Farewell for ever in this world! I die a sincere Christian and penitent, and everything I hope that you can wish me. Would it prevent my example's having any bad effect if the world should know how I abhor my former ideas of suicide, my crime . . . will be the best judge. Of her fame I charge you to be careful. My poor sister will . . .*

HADRIAN, the Emperor (to his soul):

> *O blithe little soul, thou, flitting away,*
> *Guest and comrade of this my clay,*
> *Whither now goest thou, to what place*
> *Bare and ghastly and without grace?*
> *Nor, as thy wont was, joke and play.*

HAIG, Douglas, Earl (British soldier; written):

> *I hope to see you on Tuesday at 10:30 A.M.*

HALDANE, James Alexander (first Congregational minister in Scotland; his wife said, "You are going to Jesus. How happy you will be soon"):

> *Oh, yes.*

HALDANE, Robert (brother of James; evangelist):

> *For ever with the Lord—for ever—for ever.*

HALE, Edward Everett (author of *The Man Without a Country*; entry in journal):

> *It was a lovely day and I spent all the time on the deck, from half past ten till five. Had a very good night.*

HALE, Nathan:
I only regret that I have but one life to lose for my country.

HALL, John Vine (author of *The Sinner's Friend*):
Passing away, passing away. . . . Jesus, Jesus! . . . He is, he is! . . . Pray . . . Amen.

HALLECK, Fitz-Greene (American poet; to his sister):
Maria, hand me my pantaloons, if you please.

HALLER, Albrecht (Swiss physician; felt his own pulse):
Now I am dying.

HALYBURTON, Thomas (theologian; to the ministers present):
Pray, pray.

HAMERTON, Philip Gilbert (essayist; written):
If I indulge my imagination in dreaming about a country where justice and right would always surely prevail, where the weak would never be oppressed, nor an honest man incur any penalty for his honesty— a country where no animal would ever be ill-treated or killed, otherwise than in mercy—that is truly ideal dreaming, because, however far I travel, I shall not find such a country in the world, and there is not any record of such a country in the authentic history of mankind.

HAMILTON, Patrick (Scotch martyr):
How long, Lord, shall darkness overwhelm this king-dom? How long wilt Thou suffer this tyranny of men? Lord Jesus, receive my spirit!

HAMILTON, William, Duke of (fell at Worcester for Charles II after having opposed Charles I; referring to the parable of the vineyard):
I believe that though in the last hour of the day I

*have entered into my Master's service, yet I shall
receive my penny.*

HAMLIN, Mrs. Henrietta A. L. (missionary in Turkey;
her mind wandering):
*What child is this? Is it little Carrie? . . . Yes! it is
little Carrie, and the room is full of them.*

HAMMOND, Henry (divine):
Lord, make haste.

HAMPDEN, John (Puritan leader) :
O Lord, save my country.

HANCOCK, John (Ohio school commissioner; letter):
I shall look forward to a pleasant time.

HANNA, Mark (politician; asked if he wanted a handker-
chief, joked):
*Yes, I would like one, but I suppose I cannot have it.
My wife takes them all.*

HANNIBAL (taking poison, by one account):
*Let us ease the Romans of their continual dread and
care, who think it long and tedious to await the death
of a hated old man. Yet Titus will not bear away a
glorious victory, nor one worthy of those ancestors
who sent to caution Pyrrhus, an enemy, and a conqueror too, against the poison prepared for him by
traitors.*

HANWAY, Jonas (traveller and philanthropist):
Christ . . .

HARDEN, Jacob S. (minister hanged for murder of his
wife):
*God have mercy upon me! Lord Jesus save me in
Heaven.*

HARDEN-HICKEY, Baron James A. (soldier of fortune; suicide note to wife) :

My dearest—No news from you, although you have had plenty of time to write; Harvey has written me that he has no one in view at present to buy my land. Well, I shall have tasted the cup of bitterness to the very dregs, but I do not complain. Good-bye. I forgive you your conduct toward me and trust you will be able to forgive yourself. I prefer to be a dead gentleman to a living blackguard like your father.

HARDING, Warren G.:

That's good. Go on. Read some more.

HARE, Robert Henry (Wesleyan minister):

There is a long, dreary lane in every life, called 'Suffering,' which I now seem to have entered.

HAROUN al-Rashid, Caliph:

Sahl, remember in a moment like this what the poet has said—'Descended from a race so great, I firmly bear the hardest fate.'

HARRINGTON, Calvin Sears (Latin professor):

As it was in the beginning, is now, and ever shall be, world without end. Amen.

HARRIS, Joel Chandler (creator of Uncle Remus):

I am about the extent of a tenth of a gnat's eyebrow better.

HARRISON, Benjamin:

Doctor . . . my lungs.

HARRISON, General Thomas (regicide; hanged, drawn, and quartered):

He hath covered my head many times in the day of battle. By God I have leaped over a wall; by God I have run through a troop; and by my God I will go through this death, and He will make it easy to me. Now into Thy hands, O Lord Jesus, I commit my spirit.

HARRISON, William Henry:
Sir, I wish you to understand the true principles of the government. I wish them carried out. I ask nothing more.

HARVEY, William Henry (botanist):
Yes, it has been a pleasant world to me.

HASSLER, Ferdinand Rudolph (engineer):
My children! My papers!

HASTINGS, Warren:
Surely at my age it is time to go. . . . God only can do me good . . . My dear, why wish me to live to suffer thus? none of you know what I suffer.

HAUFF, Wilhelm (German novelist and poet):
Father, into Thy hands I commend my immortal spirit!

HAUSER, Kaspar (German foundling possibly of noble birth; mysteriously stabbed):
Tired—very tired—a long journey—to take.

HAVELOCK, Sir Henry (soldier):
Come, my son, and see how a Christian can die.

HAVERGAL, Frances Ridley (writer of religious verse):
There, now it is all over! Blessed rest! [*trying to sing*] *He—*

HAWKER, R. S. (English poet):
His banner over me was love.

HAWTHORNE, Mrs. Nathaniel:
I am tired—too tired—I am—glad to go—I only— wanted to live—for you—and Rose. . . . Flowers— flowers.

HAYDN, Joseph:
Cheer up, children, I'm all right.

HAYDON, B. R. (English painter; suicide; entry in journal):
22nd.—God forgive me. Amen. Finis of B. R. Haydon.
"Stretch me no longer on this rough world." Lear.
End of Twenty-sixth Volume.

HAYES, Rutherford B. (referring to his deceased wife):
I know that I am going where Lucy is.

HAYNES, Rev. Lemuel:
I love my wife, I love my children, but I love my
Saviour better than all.

HAZLITT, William:
I have had a happy life.

HEARN, Lafcadio (author):
Ah—because of sickness!

HEBER, Reginald (prelate and hymn writer; wrote on the back of an address on confirmation):
Trichinopoly, April 3, 1826.

HECKER, Father Isaac Thomas (founder of Paulists; insisting on doing his own blessing) :
No, I will.

HECKEWELDER, John (Moravian church missionary to Ohio Indians):
Golgatha, Gethsemane.

HEINE, Heinrich:
Write—write! Paper . . . pencil!

HEMANS, Mrs. Felicia (author of "Casabianca"; after asking her son what book he was reading):
Well, do you like it?

HENDERSON, Alexander (moderator of Glasgow Assembly; declared himself, in writing):

most of all obliged to the grace and goodness of God, for calling me to believe the promises of the Gospel, and for exalting me to be a preacher of them to others, and to be a willing, though weak instrument in this great and wonderful work of Reformation, which I beseech the Lord to bring to a happy conclusion.

HENDERSON, Ebenezer (missionary):

My flesh and my heart faileth; but God is the strength of my heart, and my portion for ever.

HENLEY, Rev. John (as though gazing on a beatified vision):

Stay! stay! stay!

HENLEY, W. E. (poet; letter to Charles Whibley):

Dear Boy,—I'd give much to see you just now. When can you come? I can't get to town; being kind of broken-hearted; or I'd tryst you there. But I want your advice and (if I can get it) your help. And I want the first of these things soon. The sooner the better. W. E. H.

HENRIETTA Anne, Duchess of Orléans (daughter of Charles I and Henrietta Maria; asked by the abbé, "Madame, you believe in God, you hope in God, you love God?"):

With all my heart.

HENRY II (of England):

Shame, shame on a conquered king.

HENRY IV (told that the chamber in which he was sick was called Jerusalem):

Lauds be given to the father of heaven, for now I

know that I shall die here in this chamber, according to the prophecy of me declared, that I should depart this life in Jerusalem.

HENRY IV of France (stabbed to the heart by Ravaillac):
It is nothing.

HENRY IV, King of Germany and Holy Roman Emperor:
O how unhappy I am who squandered such great treasures in vain—how happy I could have been if I had given these things to the poor! But I swear before the eye of the All-Knowing that all my efforts have been only for the advancement of my church.

HENRY V of England:
Into Thy hands, O Lord—

HENRY VIII (said, in answer to an inquiry, that if he conferred with any learned man it would be Cranmer, but first he would):
take a little sleep; and then, as I feel myself, I will advise upon the matter.

HENRY, Prince of Wales (son of James I):
I would say somewhat, but I cannot utter it.

HENRY the Lion (Heinrich der Löwe, former Duke of Saxony and Bavaria):
God be merciful to me a sinner.

HENRY, Matthew (biblical commentator):
A life spent in the service of God and communion with Him is the most comfortable and pleasant life that any one can live in this world.

HENRY, Patrick:
Be thankful for the kind God who allows me to go thus painlessly.

HENRY, Philip (nonconformist divine):
O death, where is thy—

HERBERT, Edward, Lord Herbert of Cherbury (poet and philosopher; after asking what o'clock it was):
Then an hour hence I shall depart.

HERBERT, George (religious poet; after handing over his will):
I am now ready to die. Lord, forsake me not, now my strength faileth me: but grant me mercy for the merits of my Jesus. And now Lord, Lord, now receive my soul.

HERBERT, Sidney, Lord Herbert of Lea (statesman):
Well, this is the end. I have had a life of great happiness: a short one, perhaps; but an active one. I have not done all I wished; but I have tried to do my best.

HERDER, Johann Gottfried von (man of letters; regretting unfinished work, to the doctor):
My friend, my dearest friend, preserve me still, if that is possible.

HERRICK, Myron T. (ambassador to France; told he would "soon be all right"):
Do you really think so? Well, I will do my best.

HERVEY, James (devotional writer):
Lord, lettest now Thy servant depart in peace.

HERZL, Theodor (Zionist; to his son):
Your brethren are dispersed throughout the whole world. If you want to you will find them. I have found them too, because I have been looking for them. Think of it and don't forget that your people need young, healthy strength and that you are the heir of the name Herzl.

HESSUS, Helius Eobanus (German humanist):
I want to ascend to my Lord.

HEWITT, Abram S. (industrialist and political leader; taking out of his mouth the tube for oxygen that was sustaining him) :
And now I am officially dead.

HEY, Wilhelm (German author of poems for children; verses in gratitude to two men from his village who assisted him):
So you, my nurses dear,
In these last difficult days,
In bitter parting here
Show me your loving ways.
The love so tenderly given—
And yet such strength behind:
A brief foretaste of heaven
Is what it brings to mind.

HEYLIN, Peter (church historian; to a minister):
I know it is church-time with you, and I know this is Ascension Day. I am ascending to the Church Triumphant. I go to my God and Saviour, unto joys celestial, and to Hallelujahs eternal.

HICKOK, James Butler, "Wild Bill" (letter):
Agnes Darling: If such should be we never meet again, while firing my last shot, I will gently breathe the name of my wife—Agnes—and with wishes even for my enemies I will make the plunge and try to swim to the other shore. J. B. Hickok.

HILARY, Saint (bishop of Poitiers):
Soul, thou hast served Christ these seventy years, and art thou afraid to die? Go out, soul, go out!

HILL, Benjamin H. (senator from Georgia):
Almost home.

HILL, Ureli Corelli (founder of the Philharmonic Society of New York; suicide note) :
Ha, ha! I go, the sooner the better.

HILLARY, Richard (author of essays on flyings; as the plane rose above the aerodrome, was asked by radio-telephone, "Are you happy?"):
Moderately. I am continuing to orbit.

HILLMAN, Sidney:
I feel like hell. I'm going to lie down again.

HILTON, John (British broadcaster; as he managed to swallow a few drops of tea):
That was very good.

HILTZHEIMER, Jacob (18th-century Philadelphia diarist; entry referring to the epidemic that carried him off):
Deaths today, 66.

HIMMLER, Heinrich (suicide):
I am Heinrich Himmler.

HINDENBURG, Paul von:
It is all right, Sauerbruch, now tell Friend Hein [Matthias Claudius's euphemism for Death] he can come in.

HINGORO, Rahim (fanatic and murderous follower of Pir Pigaro, leader of the Hurs of India; hanged) :
Praise Pigaro.

HITLER, Adolf (close of his "Political Testament"):
Above all, I enjoin the government of the nation and the people to uphold the racial laws to the limit and to resist mercilessly the poisoner of all nations, international Jewry. Berlin, 29 April, 1945, 0400 hours. A. Hitler. [end of Personal Will]: My wife and I choose to die in order to escape the shame of overthrow or capitulation. It is our wish for our bodies

to be cremated immediately on the place where I have performed the greater part of my daily work during twelve years of service to my people.

HOBBES, Thomas:
I shall be glad to find a hole to creep out of the world at.

HOCHE, Lazare (French Revolutionary general):
Good-bye, my friends, good-bye; tell the government to keep a sharp eye in the direction of Belgium! Good-bye, my friends.

HODGE, Charles (Presbyterian clergyman):
Why should you grieve, daughter? To be absent from the body is to be with the Lord, to be with the Lord is to see the Lord, to see the Lord is to be like Him.

HODGSON, Francis (provost of Eton):
Charming ... God's mercy.

HOEFFLE, General Herman (Nazi commander in Slovakia; hanged):
Dear Germany.

HOFER, Andreas (Tyrolese patriot; before the firing squad):
Fire.

HOFFMAN, Eugene A. (dean of General Theological Seminary; bade farewell to his favorite retreat) :
Good-bye, Matapedia.

HOFMANNSTHAL, Hugo von (Austrian poet and playwright; letter—on his son's suicide):
Good friend, I sincerely hope it goes well with you. Yesterday afternoon a great misfortune visited our Rodauner House. During a bad, oppressive thunderstorm our poor Franz took his life with a shot in the temple. The motive for this dreadful deed lies darkly

deep: in the depths of character and of fate. There was no external motive. We had eaten together as usual, en famille. There is something infinitely sad and infinitely noble in the way the poor child went. He was never able to share his thoughts. So his departure was silent too.—Raymond is with us. In all friendship, Hugo von Hofmannsthal.

HOGG, James ("the Ettrick Shepherd," Scottish poet; complained of severe, continual hiccup):
It is a reproach to the faculty that they cannot cure the hiccup.

HOKUSAI:
If Heaven had only granted me five more years I could have become a real painter.

HOLCROFT, Thomas (miscellaneous writer; in pain) :
How tedious. My affections are strong.

HOLLAND, Henry Scott (theological writer; to his nurse):
Goodnight, dear.

HOLMES, Oliver Wendell (of the Supreme Court; as they moved the oxygen tent to him):
Lot of damn foolery.

HOLST, Gustav (English musician; written):
And I wish myself the joy of your Fellowship at Whitsuntide.

HOLTBY, Winifred (English novelist; announcing her intention to get married):
Not an engagement—just an understanding.

HÖLTY, Ludwig (German poet):
I am very ill. Send for Zimmermann. In fact, I think I'll die today.

HOOD, Edwin Paxton (Congregational divine and author):
> *O God! O God! my wife, my wife!*

HOOD, Thomas (poet):
> *Remember, Jane, I forgive all, all, as I hope to be forgiven.*

HOOK, Walter Farquar (dean of Chichester; letter):
> *I am old, 78, and very infirm. My contemporaries are passing away, and I expect soon to receive my summons. Pray for me.*

HOOKER, Richard (author of *Of the Laws of Ecclesiastical Polity*):
> *Good Doctor, God hath heard my daily petitions, for I am at peace with all men, and He is at peace with me; and from that blessed assurance I feel that inward joy which this world can neither give nor take from me: my conscience beareth me this witness, and this witness makes the thoughts of death joyful. I could wish to live to do the Church more service, but cannot hope it, for my days are past as a shadow that returns not.*

HOOKER, Thomas (founding father; told, "You are going to receive the reward of all your labours"):
> *Brother, I am going to receive mercy!*

HOPE, James (physician):
> *I thank God.*

HOPKINS, Gerard Manley (English Jesuit and poet):
> *I am so happy, I am so happy.*

HOPKINS, Harry (writing to Winston Churchill):
> *Do give my love to Clemmie and Sarah, all of whom I shall hope to see before you go back, but I want to*

have a good talk with you over the state of world affairs, to say nothing of our private lives.

HOPKINS, John Henry (Protestant Episcopal bishop of Vermont):
I feel easier.

HOPKINS, Samuel (Congregationalist friend of Jonathan Edwards; asked by a fellow minister, "Doctor, why do you groan? You know you have taught us that we must be willing even to be eternally lost"):
It is only my body; all is right in my soul.

HOUDETOT, Vicomtesse d' (née Perrinet de Faugnes):
I am sorry for myself.

HOUGHTON, Father John (prior of the London Charterhouse; refused to accept royal headship of the church; as the tormentor was in the act of tearing out his heart):
Good Jesu, what will you do with my heart?

HOUSMAN, A. E. (told by his doctor a "thoroughly naughty story"):
Yes, that's a good one, and tomorrow I shall be telling it again on the Golden Floor.

HOUSMAN, Robert (divine; given violets):
I shall never again see the spot where those flowers grew. Give him my best thanks for the present.

HOUSTON, Sam:
Texas—Texas—Margaret—

HOWARD, John (prison reformer; hearing that his son was getting better):
Is not this comfort for a dying father?

HOWE, Julia Ward (composer of "The Battle Hymn of the Republic"):
God will help me! . . . I am so tired.

HOWELLS, William Dean (writing about Henry James):
Our walks by day were only in one direction and in one region. We were always going to Fresh Pond, in those days a wandering space of woods and water where people skated in winter and boated in summer.

HUBBARD, Elbert (to a friend, when the German torpedo struck the "Lusitania"):
Well, Jack, they have got us. They are a damned sight worse than I ever thought they were!

HUDSON, William Henry (author of *Green Mansions*):
Good-bye.

HÜGEL, Baron Friedrich von (Roman Catholic theologian; to his nurse):
Pray for me.

HUGH of Lincoln, Saint (asked to pray God that his church might have a good pastor):
God grant it.

HUGO, Victor (to his grand-daughter):
Good-bye, Jeanne, good-bye.

HULL, Commodore Isaac (commanded "Old Ironsides"):
I strike my flag.

HUMBERT I (Umberto, king of Italy; assassinated):
I believe I have been hit.

HUMBERT, General Jean (French soldier):
I die far from my country, too far, alas! to rest one day in the cemetery of my village, beside my poor parents. There I should have wished to die. . . . Ah! my friends . . . Let the will of God—

HUMBOLDT, Alexander von (traveller and naturalist; when the blinds were opened):
How grand those rays! They seem to beckon Earth to Heaven.

HUME, David (letter):
> *I go very fast to decline, and last night had a small fever, which I hoped might put a quicker period to this tedious illness; but, unluckily, it has, in a great measure, gone off. I cannot submit to your coming over here on my account, as it is possible for me to see you so small a part of the day; but Doctor Black can better inform you concerning the degree of strength which may, from time to time, remain with me. Adieu.*

HUNT, Leigh:
> *I don't think I shall get over this.*

HUNT, Vincent (Leigh Hunt's son, as he drank a glass of water):
> *I drink the morning!*

HUNTER, William (anatomist):
> *If I had strength enough to hold a pen, I would write how easy and pleasant a thing it is to die.*

HUNTINGDON, Selina, Countess of (religious leader):
> *My work is done; I have nothing to do but to go to my Father.*

HUS, John (singing at the stake):
> *Christ, son of the living God, have mercy on me;*
> *Christ, son of the living God, have mercy on me;*
> *Christ, son of the living God, have mercy on me,*
> *Who art born of the virgin Mary.*

HUTCHINSON, Colonel John (Puritan):
> *'Tis as I would have it: 'tis where I would have it.*

HUTCHINSON, Thomas (Royal governor of Massachusetts):
> *Help me!*

HUTTON, William (geologist; asked if he sat easy):
O yes.

HUXLEY, T. H. (letter):
At present I don't feel at all like 'sending in my checks,' and without being oversanguine I rather incline to think that my native toughness will get the best of it—albuminuria or otherwise.—Ever your faithful friend, T. H. H.

HYDE, Anne, Duchess of York:
Truth! Truth!

I

IBÁÑEZ, Vincente Blasco (Spanish novelist) :
My garden . . . my garden!

IBSEN, Henrik (when someone remarked that his condition was improving):
Quite the contrary.

IGNATIUS, Saint (when he heard the lions roar):
I am the wheat or grain of Christ. I shall be ground with the teeth of wild beasts, that I may be found pure bread.

IMPEY, Sir Elijah (judge; having leaned hard upon a female servant who was assisting him to his bed):
Did I hurt you, my dear?

INGERSOLL, Robert:
I am better now.

IRVING, Edward (Scottish clergyman):
If I die, I die unto the Lord. Amen.

IRVING, Washington:
Well, I must arrange my pillows for another weary night! When will this end?

ISABELLA, Queen of Spain (to those in tears around her bed):
Do not weep for me, nor waste your time in fruitless prayers for my recovery, but pray rather for the salvation of my soul.

ITO, Prince Hirobumi (told of the identity of his assailant):
The fellow is a fool.

ITURBIDE, Gen. Augustin de (emperor of Mexico; before execution) :

> *I am no traitor! Such a stain will never attach to my children or to their descendants.*

J

JACKSON, Andrew:
Oh, do not cry. Be good children, and we shall all meet in Heaven.

JACKSON, Helen Hunt (author of *Ramona*; letter to President Cleveland):
Dear Sir: From my deathbed I send you message of heartfelt thanks for what you have already done for the Indians. I ask you to read my Century of Dishonor. *I am dying happier for the belief I have that it is your hand that is destined to strike the first steady blow toward lifting this burden of infamy from our country and righting the wrongs of the Indian race. With respect and gratitude, Helen Jackson.*

JACKSON, Gen. Thomas ("Stonewall"):
Let us cross over the river and rest under the shade of the trees!

JACOB:
I am to be gathered unto my people: bury me with my fathers in the cave that is in the field of Ephron the Hittite, in the cave that is in the field of Machpelah, which is before Mamre, in the land of Canaan, which Abraham bought with the field of Ephron the Hittite for a possession of a burying-place. There they buried Abraham and Sarah his wife; there they buried Isaac and Rebekah his wife; and there I buried Leah. The purchase of the field and of the cave that is therein was from the children of Heth.

JACOBI, Johann Georg (lyric poet; he wrote on New Year's Eve a poem about New Year's Day):
> *I shall not in fact see the New Year which I have just commemorated. . . . I hope, at least, it is not apparent in the poem how elderly I am.*

JACOBS, Friedrich (German classical philologist; recited Latin verse):
> *Who would wish, indeed, to prolong pain, the breath failing all too gradually? Better to die in death, than to drag out a dead life, the senses buried in the limbs.*

JAMES the Apostle (brother of John; kissing his fellow martyr):
> *Peace be to thee, brother.*

JAMES the brother of Jesus (by the Protestant interpretation; stoned):
> *O Lord God, Father, I beseech Thee to forgive them, for they know not what they do.*

JAMES the Dismembered, Saint:
> *O Lord of lords, Lord of the living and the dead, give ear to me who am half dead. I have no fingers to hold out to Thee, O Lord, nor hands to stretch forth to Thee. My feet are cut off and my knees demolished, wherefore I cannot bend the knee to Thee, and I am like to a house that is about to fall because its columns are taken away. Hear me, O Lord Jesus Christ, and deliver my soul from its prison!*

JAMES I (of England):
> *Come, Lord Jesus.*

JAMES II:
> *Into Thy hands I commend my soul, O Lord; lay not this great sin to their charge.*

JAMES V of Scotland (hearing of the birth of Mary Stuart, and referring to the crown):
> *The Devil go with it. It will end as it began. It came with a lass, and will go with a lass.*

JAMES, Henry, Sr. (philosopher):
> *I stick by Almighty God—He alone is, all else is death. Don't call this dying; I am just entering upon life.*

JAMES, Henry:
> *So here it is at last, the distinguished thing!*

JAMES, John Angell (Independent minister; to his physician):
> *Inasmuch as thou hast done it unto one of the least of these, thou hast done it unto Me.*

JAMES, William:
> *It's so good to get home!*

JANEWAY, Rev. Jacob J.:
> *I am tired of eating—I want to go home!*

JAY, John:
> *I would have my funeral decent, but not ostentatious. No scarfs—no rings. Instead thereof, I give two hundred dollars to any one poor deserving widow or orphan of this town, whom my children shall select.*

JAY, William (dissenting minister):
> *O, none of you know what it is to die.*

JEFFERIES, Richard (nature writer):
> *Yes, yes; that is so. Help, Lord, for Jesus' sake. Darling, good-bye. God bless you and the children, and save you all from such great pain.*

JEFFERSON, Thomas:
> *Is it the Fourth?*

JEFFREY, Francis, Lord (jurist and critic; wrote of a
dream he had of political journals):
*I read the ideal copies with a good deal of pain and
difficulty, owing to the smallness of the type, but
with great interest, and, I believe, often for more
than an hour at a time; forming a judgment of their
merits with great freedom and acuteness, and often
saying to myself 'this is very cleverly put, but there
is a fallacy in it, for so and so.'*

JEHORAM (king of Judah):
There is treachery, O Ahaziah.

JEROME of Prague (reformer; at the stake):
*O Lord God, Father Almighty, have mercy upon me,
and be merciful unto mine offences, for Thou knowest how sincerely I have loved Thy truth.*

JERROLD, Douglas (playwright and humorist; as his sons
took each hand):
This is as it should be.

JESUS CHRIST (combining the Gospels):
*My God! my God! why hast Thou forsaken me? . . .
Father, into Thy hands I commend my spirit. . . .
It is finished.*

JEWEL, John (bishop of Salisbury):
*O Lord, confound me not. This is my Today! This
day quickly let me come unto thee: This day let me
see the Lord Jesus.*

JEZEBEL (to Jehu, tauntingly):
Had Zimri peace, who slew his master?

JOAN of Arc, Saint:
*Ah Rouen! I have great fear that you are going to
suffer by my death! . . . Jesus, Jesus!*

JOFFRE, Marshal Joseph (to the priest):
I have not done much evil in my life, and I have sincerely loved my wife.

JOHN the Evangelist, Saint (going into his grave):
Thou hast invited me to Thy table, Lord; and behold I come, thanking Thee for having invited me, for Thou knowest that I have desired it with all my heart.

JOHN the Almoner, Saint:
I thank Thee, O my God, that Thy mercy has granted the desire of my weakness, which was that at my death I should possess naught but a single penny. And now this penny, too, can be given to the poor!

JOHN of the Cross, Saint:
Into Thy hands, O Lord, I commend my spirit.

JOHN the Abbot, Saint:
Never have I done my own will, and never have I taught others to do what I had not first done myself!

JOHN, King:
I commit my soul to God and my body to St. Alstane.

JOHN of Austria, Don (Spanish general; with a child's voice):
Aunt! Aunt! My lady Aunt!

JOHNSON, John G. (lawyer and art collector):
Good-night. I am going to sleep now.

JOHNSON, Dr. Samuel:
God bless you, my dear!

JOHNSON, Tom L. (Ohio politician):
It's all right. I'm so happy.

JOHNSON, Sir William (British agent to Iroquois; to his half-breed son, a Mohawk chieftain):
Joseph, control your people. I am going away.

JOHNSTON, Albert S. (Confederate general; "General, are you wounded?"):

Yes, and I fear seriously.

JOKAI, Maurus (Hungarian novelist):

I want to sleep.

JOLSON, Al:

This is it. I'm going, I'm going.

JONES, Henry Arthur (playwright; told that "Gertie" would be back):

I'm so glad.

JONES, Sir Henry (professor of Moral Philosophy at Glasgow):

The Lord reigneth. Let the earth rejoice.

JONES, John Paul (end of will):

I revoke all other testaments or codicils which I may have made before the present, which alone I stand by as containing my last will.

JORTIN, John (English ecclesiastic and historian; to a servant offering him food):

No, I have had enough of everything.

JOSEPH:

I die: and God will surely visit you, and bring you out of this land unto the land which he sware to Abraham, to Isaac, and to Jacob. God will surely visit you, and ye shall carry up my bones from hence.

JOSEPH II (of Germany; gave instructions that his epitaph should be):

Here lies Joseph, who was unsuccessful in all his undertakings.

Josephine (the Empress):

Bonaparte! ... Elba ... Marie-Louise!

JOYCE, James:
Does nobody understand?

JUDAS:
I have sinned in that I have betrayed the innocent blood.

JUDD, Rev. Sylvester (Unitarian author):
Cover me up warm, keep my utterance clear . . . I'm doing well.

JUDSON, Adoniram (Baptist missionary in Burma):
Brother Ranney, will you bury me? bury me?—quick! quick! . . . [of his wife, to the servant] Take care of poor mistress.

JUDSON, Mrs. Ann H. (missionary):
I feel quite well, only very weak.

JUGURTHA (king of Numidia; as the Romans cast him naked into the dungeon):
O Hercules! how cold your bath is!

JULIAN the Apostate:
Thou hast conquered, O Galilean!

K

KAFKA, Franz (Austrian novelist; afraid of infecting his sister):
> *Away, Elly—not so near, not so near.* . . . *Yes, that's good.*

KALAKAUA, David (king of the Hawaiian Islands; had his message recorded):
> *Tell my people I tried to restore our gods, our way of life* . . .

KANT, Immanuel:
> *It is enough.*

KARGE, Joseph (professor of Continental Languages and Literature at Princeton; had been reading of death while travelling):
> *I have but one desire concerning it—that it come suddenly and without warning.*

KATTE, Hermann von (executed for conspiracy with Frederick the Great when the latter was Crown Prince):
> *Death is sweet for a Prince I love so well.*

KAUFMANN, Angelica (artist; to her cousin, who began one of the hymns for the dying):
> *No, Johann, I will not hear that. Read me the 'Hymn for the Sick,' on page 128.*

KEAN, Edmund (delirious):
> *Give me another horse!* . . . *Howard.*

KEATS, John:
> *Severn—I—lift me up, for I am dying. I shall die easy. Don't be frightened! Thank God it has come.*

KEMBLE, John Philip (actor; to his wife):
Don't be alarmed, my dear, I have had a slight attack of apoplexy.

KEMP, Francis Adrian van der (autobiographer; letter):
Now I must close. I can scarcely distinguish one letter from another. Whatever may happen I know you remain unalterably my friend, as, so long as I draw breath, shall I be yours. Once again, farewell.

KEN, Thomas (bishop of Bath and Wells):
All glory be to God.

KENT, James (American jurist):
. . . Go, my children. My object in telling you this is that, if anything happens to me, you might know, and perhaps it would console you to remember, that on this point my mind is clear; I rest my hopes of salvation on the Lord Jesus Christ.

KEPLER, Johannes (asked by what means he hoped to be saved):
Solely by the merits of Jesus Christ, Our Saviour.

KERR, Michael C. (Speaker of the House of Representatives):
I stand upon my record.

KEYSERLING, William (Jewish philanthropist):
We must save Jewish lives.

KIDD, Captain William (before being hanged):
This is a very fickle and faithless generation.

KING, Thomas Starr (Unitarian clergyman; when his little son was brought):
Dear little fellow! He's a beautiful boy.

KINGSLEY, Charles (repeating the words of the Burial Service):
Thou knowest, O Lord, the secrets of our hearts; shut

not *Thy merciful ears to our prayer, but spare us,
O Lord most holy, O God most mighty, O holy and
merciful Saviour. Thou most worthy Judge Eternal,
suffer us not, at our last hour, for any pains of death,
to fall from Thee.*

KITCHING, Col. J. Howard (of the Army of the Potomac; to his sister, before operation):
> *It will all be over in a few minutes, darling, and we
> will have such a nice talk* afterward!

KLEBER, Jean Baptiste (Napoleon's commander in Egypt;
stabbed):
> *I have been assassinated!*

KLEIST, Heinrich von (German dramatist and poet; suicide letter to his sister):
> *I cannot die without, contented and serene as I am,
> reconciling myself with all the world and—before all
> others—with you, my dearest Ulrike. Give up the
> strong expressions which you resorted to in your letter
> to me: let me revoke them; truly, to save me, you
> have done all within the strength, not only of a sister,
> but of a man—all that could be done. The truth is,
> nothing on earth can help me. And now good-bye:
> may Heaven send you a death even half equal to
> mine in joy and unutterable bliss: that is the most
> heart-felt and profoundest wish that I can think of
> for you. Your Henry. Stimmung, at Potsdam, on the
> morning of my death.*

KLOPSTOCK, Friedrich (author of *Der Messias;* recited
the words of his ode "Der Erbarmer"):
> *Can a woman forget her child, that she should not
> have pity on the fruit of her womb? Yes, she may
> forget, but I will not forget Thee!*

KLOPSTOCK, Mrs. Meta (to her sister):
It is over! . . . The blood of Jesus Christ cleanse thee from all sin.

KLUGE, Field-Marshal Günther von (suicide note to Hitler):
I depart from you, my Führer, as one who stood nearer to you than you perhaps realized in the consciousness that I did my duty to the utmost. Heil, my Führer, Von Kluge, Field-Marshal. 18 August 1944.

KNIBB, William (missionary in Jamaica):
The service is over; you may go. . . . All is well.

KNILL, Richard (dissenting minister; to his daughter):
How are you, Mary?

KNOX, John:
Now it is come. . . . .

KOERNER, Theodor (German poet and patriot; killed in battle):
There I have one; but it doesn't matter.

KOSSUTH, Louis (Hungarian patriot who died in Turin; to his sister):
It grieves me that I have to perish in exile ["You are the most popular Hungarian."] Only your vanity holds this.

KRAUS, Christian Jacob (German professor of political science):
Dying is different from what I thought.

KRAUSE, William Henry (Irish divine):
I am so restless, I can hardly think; but the Lord's hand is not shortened.

KUANG-HSU (Chinese emperor; recording a wish that was not carried out):
We were the second son of the Prince Ch'un when

the Empress Dowager selected Us for the Throne. She has always hated Us. But for Our misery of the past ten years, Yuan Shi Kai is responsible and none other. When the time comes, I desire that Yuan be summarily beheaded.

KUSAKABE (Japanese revolutionary; said farewell on his way to execution with these two Chinese verses):
It is better to be a crystal and be broken,
Than to remain perfect like a tile upon the housetop.

L

LA BÉDOYÈRE, Charles Angélique Huchet, Comte de (arrested for treason after Waterloo; to the firing squad, as he showed his heart):
> *This is what you must not miss.*

LABOUCHÈRE, Henry, Baron Taunton (British statesman; when a spirit lamp overturned and flared up):
> *Flames? Not yet, I think.*

LACÉPÈDE, Bernard Delaville, Comte de (naturalist and writer; called for his unfinished manuscript and said to his son):
> *Charles, write in large letters the word END at the foot of the page.*

LACORDAIRE, Jean Baptiste (Dominican monk):
> *My God, my God! open to me! open to me!*

LAËNNEC, Théophile (physician, inventor of the stethoscope; taking off his rings and laying them upon the table):
> *It would be necessary soon that another do me this service. I do not want anyone to have the bother of it.*

LAFAYETTE, Marquis de:
> *What do you expect? Life is like the flame of a lamp; when there is no more oil—zest! It goes out, and it is all over.*

LAFAYETTE, Mme. de (to her husband):
> *Is it then true? you have loved me! How happy I am! Kiss me. . . . What a blessing! how happy I am to be yours!*

LA FOLLETTE, Robert M.:
I am at peace with all the world, but there is still a lot of work I could do. I don't know how the people will feel toward me, but I shall take to the grave my love for them which has sustained me through life.

LAGNY, Thomas Fantet de (mathematician; when almost entirely insensible, was asked, "What is the square of twelve?"):
One hundred and forty four.

LAHARPE, Jean François de (poet and critic; hearing the prayers for the dying):
My friend, I thank Heaven for having left me a consciousness free to realize how consoling and beautiful these are.

LAKANAL, Joseph (educator; to the doctor):
Your attentions will not save me; I feel that there is no more oil in the lamp.

LALANDE, Jérôme (astronomer):
Withdraw, I no longer have need of anything.

LAMB, Charles (letter):
Dear Mrs. Dyer—I am very uneasy about a Book, which I either have lost or left at your house on Thursday. It was the book I went out to fetch from Miss Buffam's while the tripe was frying. It is called "Phillips' Theatrum poetarum," but it is an English book. I think I left it in the parlour. It is Mr. Cary's book, and I would not lose it for the world. Pray, if you find it, book it at the Swan, Snow Hill, by an Edmonton stage immediately, directed to Mr. Lamb, Church Street, Edmonton, or write to say you cannot find it. I am quite anxious about it. If it is lost, I shall never like tripe again. With kindest love to Mr. Dyer and all, yours truly, C. Lamb.

LAMBALLE, Princesse de (torn to pieces; asked by the
French Revolutionary mob to cry, "Vive la nation!"):
Fie on the horror!

LAMBERT, John (martyr):
None but Christ, none but Christ.

LAMENNAIS, Félicité Robert de (priest and philosopher;
as the morning sun streamed into his chamber):
Let it come; it is coming for me.

LA MOTHE LE VAYER, François de (historiographer):
Well, what news have you of the great Mogul?

LANDIS, Carol (moving picture actress; suicide note):
*Dearest Mommie—I'm sorry, really sorry to put you
through this, but there is no way to avoid it—I love
you darling, you have been the most wonderful Mom
ever—and that applies to all our family. I love each
and every one of them dearly. Everything goes to you
—look in the files and there is a will which decrees
everything. Good-bye, my angel—pray for me—your
baby.*

LANDIS, Judge Kenesaw Mountain (asked his nurses to
say to those who called to inquire about his condition):
The Judge is doing all right.

LANDRU, Henri Desire (hanged for the murder of ten
women and a youth; to the prison chaplain when they
came for him):
*I am very sorry, but I must not keep these gentlemen
waiting.*

LANE, Franklin K. (Secretary of the Interior; manuscript
fragment):
*. . . But for my heart's content in that new land, I
think I'd rather loaf with Lincoln along a river bank.
I know I could understand him. I would not have to*

learn who were his enemies, what theories he was
committed to, and what against. We could just talk
and open out our minds, and tell our doubts and
swap the longings of our hearts that others never
heard of. He wouldn't try to master me nor to make
me feel how small I was. I'd dare to ask him things
and know that he felt awkward about them, too. And
I know I would find, I know I would, that he had hit
his shin on those very stumps that had hit me. We'd
talk of men a lot, the kind they call the great. I would
not find him scornful. Yet boys that he knew in New
Salem would somehow appear larger in their souls,
than some of these that I had called the great. His
wise eyes saw qualities that weighed more than smart-
ness. Yes, we would sit down where the bank sloped
gently to the great stream and glance at the picture of
our people, the negroes being lynched, the miners'
civil war, labor's hold ups, employers' ruthlessness,
the subordination of humanity to industry,-

LANIER, Sidney (American poet; offered a drop of cor-
dial):
   I can't.

LAPLACE, Pierre Simon, Marquis de:
   What we know is of small amount; what we do not
   know is enormous.

LARCOM, Lucy (author and educator):
   Freedom.

LA SALLE, Jean Baptiste de, Saint (asked if he accepted
with joy his sufferings)
   Yes. I adore in all things the designs of God in my
   regard.

LATIMER, Bishop Hugh (to his companion at the stake,
Bishop Ridley):

> *Be of good comfort, Master Ridley, and play the man;*
> *we shall this day light such a candle by God's grace in*
> *England as (I trust) shall never be put out.*

LAUD, William (Archbishop of Canterbury; before being beheaded):
> *Lord, I am coming as fast as I can. I know I must pass*
> *through the shadow of death before I can come to*
> *Thee. But it is but* umbra mortis, *a mere shadow of*
> *death, a little darkness upon nature. But Thou by*
> *Thy merits and passion hast broke through the jaws*
> *of death. So, Lord, receive my soul and have mercy*
> *upon me, and bless this kingdom with peace and*
> *plenty and with brotherly love and charity, that there*
> *may not be this effusion of Christian blood amongst*
> *them, for Jesus Christ his sake, if it be Thy will.*

LAURENCE, Saint (who was broiled alive on a gridiron):
> *This side is now roasted enough, turn up, O tyrant*
> *great; assay whether roasted or raw thou thinkest the*
> *better meat.*

LAURIER, Sir Wilfrid (Canadian prime minister):
> *It is finished.*

LAVAL, Pierre (executed):
> *Vive la France.*

LAWRENCE, D. H.
> *I am better now.*

LAWRENCE, Sir Henry (soldier and Indian administrator; asked as an epitaph):
> *'Here lies Henry Lawrence, who tried to do his duty.'*
> *This text I should like: 'To the Lord our God belong*
> *mercies and forgivenesses, though we have rebelled*
> *against Him.' Is it not in Daniel? It was on my dear*
> *wife's tomb.*

LAWRENCE, Captain James:
Don't give up the ship. Blow her up.

LAWRENCE, T. E. (of Arabia; telegram):
Lunch Tuesday wet fine Cottage one mile north Bovington Camp. Shaw.

LEAR, Edward (nonsense poet; to his manservant):
My good Giuseppe, I feel that I am dying. You will render me a sacred service in telling my friends and relations that my last thought was for them, especially the Judge and Lord Northbrook and Lord Carlingford. I cannot find words sufficient to thank my good friends for the good they have always done me. I did not answer their letters because I could not write, as no sooner did I take a pen in my hand than I felt as if I were dying.

LE CLERC du Tremblay, François (Father Joseph, adviser to Richelieu):
Render an account, render an account.

LECOUVREUR, Adrienne (actress; asked by the priest to repent, pointed to the bust of the Comte de Saxe):
There is my universe, my hope, my deity.

LEE, Charles (Revolutionary general; in delirium):
Stand by me, my brave grenadiers.

LEE, John Doyle ("official assassin" of the Mormon Church; letter):
. . . I hope to meet the bullets with manly courage. I declare my innocence. I have done nothing wrong. I have a reward in Heaven, and my conscience does not accuse me. This to me is a consolation. I place more value upon it than I would upon an eulogy without merit. If my work be finished on earth, I ask God in Heaven, in the name of His Son Jesus Christ,

to receive my spirit, and allow me to meet my loved ones who have gone behind the veil. The bride of my youth and her faithful mother; my devoted friend and companion, N. A.; my dearly beloved children, with whom I parted in sorrow, but shall meet in joy— I bid you farewell. Be true to each other. Live faithful before God, that we may meet in the mansion that God has prepared for His servants. Remember the last words of your most true friend on earth, and let them sink into your aching hearts. I leave my blessing with you. Farewell. John Doyle Lee.

LEE, Robert E.:
Strike the tent. . . . Tell Hill that he must come up.

LEEUWENHOEK, Anton van (pioneer microscopist):
Hoogvliet, my friend, be so good as to have those two letters on the table translated into Latin . . . Send them to London to the Royal Society.

LEGER, Saint (as four swordsmen were leading him away to be beheaded):
There is no need to weary yourselves longer, brothers! Do here the bidding of him that sent you!

LEHAR, Franz:
Now I have finished with all earthly business—high time, too. . . . Yes, yes, my dear child, now comes death.

LEICHHARDT, Dr. Ludwig (Australian explorer; lost; letter):
. . . The soil is pebbly and sound, richly grassed, and, to judge from the Myalls, of the most fattening quality. I came right on Mount Abundance, and passed over a gap in it with my whole train. My latitude agreed well with Mitchell's. I feel that the absence of

water on Fitzroy Downs will render this fine country to a great extent unavailable. I observe the thermometer daily at 8 a. m. and 8 p. m., which are the only convenient hours. I have tried the wet thermometer, but am afraid my observations will be very deficient. I shall, however, improve on them as I proceed.

The only serious accident that has happened was the loss of a spade, but we are fortunate enough to make it up on this station. Though the days are still very hot, the beautiful clear nights are cool, and benumb the mosquitoes, which have ceased to trouble us. Myriads of flies are the only annoyance we have.

Seeing how much I have been favoured in my present progress, I am full of hopes that our Almighty Protector will allow me to bring my darling scheme to a successful termination. Your most sincere friend, Ludwig Leichhardt.

LENCLOS, Ninon de (French lady of fashion; composition at 85):
Let no vain hope strike me at the core;
I'm ripe for death—have business here no more.

LEO X, Pope:
Jesus.

LEOPARDI, Giacomo:
I can't see you any more.

LEOPOLD I of Belgium:
Don't leave me.

LEOPOLD II:
I am hot.

LEPELLETIER de Saint-Fargeau, Louis Michel (politician; assassinated on eve of execution of Louis XVI):
I am cold.

LESPINASSE, Julie de (famous for her liaisons):
Am I still alive?

LEWIS, Ellis (Pennsylvania chief justice):
I believe I am dying now.

LEWIS, Sinclair (to his Italian secretary):
Alec, I beg it of you, help me. I am dying.

LEY, Dr. Robert (awaiting trial as war criminal; suicide note):
Farewell, I can't stand this shame any longer. Physically nothing is lacking; the food is good; it is warm in my cell; the Americans are correct and partially friendly. Spiritually, I have reading matter and write whatever I want. I receive paper and pencil. They do care more for my health than is necessary, and I may smoke and receive tobacco and coffee. I may walk at least twenty minutes every day. Up to this point everything is in order, but the fact that I should be a criminal—that is what I can't stand.

LIEUTAUD, Joseph (physician to the French king; when his colleagues proposed different remedies):
Ah, I shall die well enough without all that!

LIEVEN, Madame Dorothea de (note to her friend Guizot):
I thank you for twenty years of affection and happiness. Don't forget me. Good-bye, good-bye.

LIGNE, Prince Charles von (Austrian soldier):
Close the doors! Away with it! There is the monster, the Grey Comrade.

LINDSAY, Vachel (suicide; delusions of persecution):
They tried to get me; I got them first.

LINDSEY, Rev. Theophilus (Unitarian):
God's will is best.

LINTON, Mrs. Linn (novelist and miscellaneous writer; letter):

> *I am very forlorn at the present moment, and wish I was at Malvern. Oh, don't I just!*

LISLE, Sir George (English royalist; put to death at Colchester):

> *Oh how many do I see here about me, whose lives I have shed in hot blood: and now must mine be taken away in cold blood most barbarously! Sure the like was never heard of among the Goths and Vandals, or the veriest barbarians in the world in any age. But what dare not those rebels and traitors do, that have imprisoned, and could willingly cut the throat of their King? for whose deliverance from his enemies and peace to this distracted kingdom, these my last prayers shall be presented. Now then rebels and traitors do your worst to me. . . . Jesus.*

LISZT, Franz:

> *Tristan.*

LIVINGSTONE, David (in his journal):

> *Knocked up quite, and remain=recover sent to buy milch goats. We are on the banks of R. Molilamo.*

LODGE, Henry Cabot (letter to President Coolidge):

> *The doctors promise prompt recovery. I shall be back in Washington well and strong, and I trust that I shall be able to be of some service to you when I get there.*

LODY, Carl (German spy of World War I):

> *My dear Ones, I have trusted in God and He has decided. My hour has come, and I must start on the journey through the Dark Valley like so many of my comrades in this terrible War of Nations. May my life be offered as a humble offering on the altar of*

the Fatherland. A hero's death on the battlefield is certainly finer, but such is not to be my lot, and I die here in the Enemy's country silent and unknown, but the consciousness that I die in the service of the Fatherland makes death easy. The Supreme Court-Marshal of London has sentenced me to die for Military conspiracy. Tomorrow, I shall be shot in the Tower. I have had just Judges, and I shall die as an Officer, not as a spy. Farewell. God bless you. "Hans."

LONDON, Jack (written):
I leave California Wednesday following. Daddy.

LONG, Senator Huey P. (assassinated):
I wonder why he shot me.

LONGFELLLOW, Henry W. (when his sister arrived from Portland):
Now I know that I must be very ill, since you have been sent for.

LOPEZ, Francisco (Paraguayan dictator):
I die with my country!

LOTHAR I (Clotaire, king of the Franks):
What manner of king is He above who thus doeth to death such great kings?

LOUIS I (on hearing that one of his sons had revolted against him):
I pardon him, but let him know that it is on his account that I am dying.

LOUIS I de Bourbon-Condé (at the battle of Jarnac, to D'Argence, who told him, "Hide your face"):
Ah, D'Argence, D'Argence! you will not be able to save me.

LOUIS II de Bourbon-Condé:
In Thy justice free me.

LOUIS IX, Saint (Psalm):
> *I will enter into Thy house; I will adore in Thy holy temple and will confess Thy name.*

LOUIS XI (Te Deum):
> *Lord, in Thee have I trusted, let me never be confounded.*

LOUIS XIII (to his confessor):
> *Dinet! thoughts arise which trouble me!*

LOUIS XIV (to his domestics):
> *Why do you weep? Did you think I was immortal?*

LOUIS XV (asked if he was suffering much):
> *Oh, much!*

LOUIS the Dauphin (son of Louis XV and Maria Leszczyńska; taking the hand of the Bishop of Verdun):
> *Lay it on my heart; you have never left it . . . [when the doctor took his pulse] Ah! take the bishop's. What fortitude he has!*

LOUIS XVI:
> *People, I die innocent! Messieurs, I am innocent of all that I am accused of. I hope that my blood may cement the happiness of the French people!*

LOUIS XVII (10-year old son of Louis XVI; in prison):
> *I suffer much less. The music is so beautiful. . . . Listen, listen, in the midst of all those voices I recognize my mother's!*

LOUIS XVIII (gave his blessings):
> *Adieu! may Providence be with you.*

LOUISE, Madame (daughter of Louis XV):
> *Hurry! At a gallop! To paradise!*

LOUISE, Queen of Prussia (to her husband, Frederick William III):

Do not fear, dear friend, I am not going to die. . . .
I am dying, Jesu! Make it short!

L'OUVERTURE, Toussaint (Haitian Negro liberator;
letter to his keeper):
Nothing can compare with the humiliation to which
you subjected me today. You have taken away my
watch and the money I had in my pocket. I hereby
serve notice on you that these objects are my personal
property and that I will call you to account for them
on the day I am executed, when I shall expect you to
remit them to my wife and children.

LOWELL, Amy (poet):
Pete, a stroke. . . . Get Eastman.

LOYOLA, Saint Ignatius (sending his secretary to the
pope):
Tell him that my hour has come, and that I ask his
benediction. Tell him that if I go to a place where
my prayers are of any avail, as I trust, I shall not fail
to pray for him, as I have indeed unfailingly, even
when I had most occasion to pray for myself.

LUCAN (suicide under Nero; quoted from his epic *Phar-*
salia):
He was torn asunder, and his blood gushed out, not
trickling as from a wound, but raining on all sides
from his severed arteries; and the free play of the life
coursing through the different limbs was cut off by
the water. No other victim's life escaped through so
wide a channel . . .

LUCAS, Sir Charles (royalist; taken prisoner at Colchester
and executed):
Now, rebels, do your worst.

LUCY, Saint:
I make known to you that peace is restored to the

*Church! This very day Maximian has died, and Dio-
cletian has been driven from the throne. And just as
God has bestowed my sister Agatha upon the city of
Catania as its protectress, so He has this moment
entitled me to be the patroness of the city of Syracuse.*

LUNA, Alvaro de (favorite of John II of Castile; executed; informed that the post and hook he saw were to at-
tach his head thereto):
*It does not matter what they do with my body and
head after my death.*

LUTHER, Martin (asked if he would "stand steadfast by
Christ and the doctrine you have preached"):
Yes.

LYON, Mary (American educator):
*I should love to come back to watch over the semi-
nary, but God will take care of it.*

LYTTELTON, George, Lord (man of letters):
Be good, be virtuous, my lord; you must come to this.

M

MABIE, Hamilton W. (American editor and essayist):
I have had a quiet but very happy Christmas.

MACCABAEUS, Judas:
If our time be come, let us die manfully for our brethren, and let us not stain our honour.

McCLELLAN, General George B.:
Tell her [his wife] I am better now.

McCORMICK, Cyrus Hall (inventor of the mechanical reaper):
It's all right. It's all right. I only want Heaven.

McGUFFEY, William Holmes (author of primary readers):
Oh that I might once more speak to my dear boys! But Thy will be done.

McINTYRE, O.O. (newspaper columnist; to his wife):
Snooks, will you please turn this way? I like to look at your face.

MacKENNA, Stephen (English novelist; letter from hospital):
Dear Peggy,—I cannot resist: tho' I meant to see no one, not never no more. But you mustn't bring me anything whatever: I abhor grapes, am worried by flowers, can't read magazines. I'm greatly touched by your goodness, Peggy. Probably you could come any hour, simply arranging things over telephone with the Sister—you know the ropes. But Regular Visiting Fixtures: Sunday 2-3½. Tuesd. and Frid. 5-6. I wept when I got you—S.M.K. What a howling swell of an address you have acquired. "God save us" [in Irish].

MACKENZIE, Sir Morell (laryngologist; referring to his brother, a doctor):
Yes, send for Stephen.

McKINLEY, William:
We are all going; we are all going; we are all going. . . . Oh, dear.

MACKINTOSH, Sir James (Scottish philosopher):
Happy.

McLOUGHLIN, John (Oregon pioneer; asked, "Comment allez-vous?"):
To God.

MADISON, Dolly:
My poor boy!

MAETERLINCK, Maurice (to his wife):
For me this is quite natural. It is for you that I am concerned.

MAGINOT, André (to Premier Laval):
For me, this is the end, but you—continue!

MAHAN, A. T. (writer on sea power; contemplating a tree outside his window):
If a few more quiet years were granted me, I might see and enjoy these things, but God is just and I am content.

MAHOMET:
O Allah! be it so!

MAHLER, Gustav:
Mozart!

MAINTENON, Madame de (mistress and second wife of Louis XIV; being asked to bless her daughters) :
I am not worthy.

M'KAIL, Hugh (Scots Covenanter; on the scaffold):
And now I leave off to speak any more to creatures,

*and begin my intercourse with God, which shall nev-
er be broken off: farewell, father and mother, friends
and relations; farewell the world and all delights;
farewell meat and drink; and sun, moon, and stars;
welcome God and Father, welcome sweet Jesus
Christ, the Mediator of the new covenant; welcome
blessed Spirit of grace, and God of all consolation;
welcome glory; welcome eternal life; and welcome
death. . . . O Lord, into Thy hands I commit my
spirit, for Thou hast redeemed my soul, O Lord God
of truth.*

MALHERBE, François de (poet and critic; stopping his
confessor's inelegant and trivial description of heaven):
*Don't speak of it any more. Your bad style leaves me
disgusted.*

MANDRIN, Louis (brigand; before execution):
*Ah! what a moment, great God, and one that I ought
to have foreseen!*

MANN, Horace (to his wife):
Sing to me, if you have the heart.

MANNING, Henry Edward, Cardinal (to Sir Andrew
Clark):
*Is there any use in your coming tomorrow? . . . Then
mind you come, Sir Andrew, at nine tomorrow.*

MANSFIELD, Katherine (short story writer):
I believe . . . I'm going to die.

MANSFIELD, Richard (actor):
God is love.

MARAT, Jean Paul (stabbed in his bath by Charlotte
Corday; to his mistress):
Help, my dear, help!

MARC, Chevalier de Montreal (decapitated by order of Rienzi; when he felt the executioner putting the axe on his neck to size up the jointure of his bones):
You are not setting it in the right place.

MARCONI, Guglielmo:
I'm feeling awfully ill.

MARGARET, Saint, of Antioch (to the executioner):
Brother, draw thy sword now, and strike!

MARGARET, Saint (falsely accused of adultery; letter):
I am of noble birth, and was called Margaret in the world; but in order safely to cross the sea of temptation, I called myself Pelagius, and was taken for a man. I did this not for a lie and a deception, as my deeds have shown. From the false accusation I have gained virtue, and have done penance albeit I was innocent. Now I ask that the holy sisters may bury me, whom men have not known; and that my death may show forth the innocence of my life, when women acknowledge the virginity of one whom slanders accused as an adulterer.

MARGARET of Angoulême or Navarre (Renaissance writer):
Jesus! Jesus! Jesus!

MARGARET of Austria (regent of the Netherlands; letter to her nephew, the future Charles V):
. . . I have made you my universal and sole heir, recommending you to fulfil the charges in my will. I leave you your countries over here which, during your absence, I have not only kept as you left them to me at your departure, but have greatly increased them, and restore to you the government of the same, of which I believe to have loyally acquitted myself,

in such a way as I hope for divine reward, satisfaction from you, monseigneur, and the goodwill of your subjects; particularly recommending to you peace, especially with the Kings of France and England. And to end, monseigneur, I beg of you for the love you have been pleased to bear this poor body, that you will remember the salvation of the soul, and the recommendation of my poor vassals and servants. Bidding you the last adieu, to whom I pray, monseigneur, and give you prosperity and a long life. From Malines, the last day of November 1530.—Your very humble aunt, Margaret.

MARGARET of Scotland:
Fie on the life of this world! Speak not to me of it any more.

MARIANNE, Mother, of Molokai:
Now, Sister, to my room.

MARK, the Evangelist, Saint:
Into Thy hands I commend my spirit.

MARLBOROUGH, John Churchill, Duke of (asked if he would like to go to bed):
Yes.

MARQUETTE, Père:
Jesus, Mary.

MARRYAT, Captain Frederick (novelist of sea life; dictated):
After years of casual, and, latterly, months of intense thought, I feel convinced that Christianity is true, and the only religion that can be practised on this earth; that the basis of Christianity is love; and that God is love. To attempt to establish any other creed will only, in the end, be folly. But Christianity must

be implanted in the breast of youth; there must be a bias towards it given at an early age. It is now half-past nine o'clock. World, adieu!

MARSH, John (pioneer; to Mexican robbers):
Do you want to kill me?

MARTI, José (Cuban patriot; unfinished letter):
There are some affections which involve such delicate points of honor—

MARTIN of Tours, Saint (thought he saw the Devil near him):
Why standest thou here, horrible beast? Thou hast no share in me. Abraham's bosom is receiving me.

MARVELL, Rev. Andrew (father of the poet; on impulse flung his walkingstick onto the bank as he boarded a ferry that was to go down in midstream):
Ho for heaven!

MARY Queen of Scots:
Lord, into Thine hands I commend my spirit.

MARY I:
When I am dead and opened you shall find Calais lying upon my heart.

MARY II (her mind wandering, she asked Archbishop Tenison to look behind the screen which stood near her bed):
For Dr. Radclyffe has put a Popish Nurse upon me; and she is always listening to what is said about me; that woman is a great disturbance to me.

MASANIELLO, Tommaso (leader of revolt at Naples against Spanish viceroy; murdered by his own soldiers):
Ah! traitors! ingrates!

MATA HARI (real name Gertrud Margarete Zelle; to the officer of the firing squad):
Thank you, monsieur.

MATHER, Cotton:
Is this dying? Is this all? Is this all that I feared, when I prayed against a hard death? O! I can bear this! I can bear it! I can bear it! . . . I am going where all tears will be wiped from my eyes.

MATHER, Increase (told by son Cotton, "This day thou shalt be in Paradise. Do you believe it, Sir, and rejoice in the views and hopes of it?"):
I do! I do! I do!

MATHEWS, Charles (comedian):
I am ready.

MATURIN, Father Basil (lost on the Lusitania; handing in a little child as the last boat was lowered):
Find its mother.

MAURICE, Frederick Denison (English theologian):
The knowledge of the love of God—the blessing of God Almighty, the Father, the Son, and the Holy Ghost, be amongst you—amongst us—and remain with us for ever.

MAURY, Matthew Fontaine (American naval officer and oceanographer):
Are my feet growing cold? Do I drag my anchors? . . . All's well.

MAXIMILIAN (emperor of Mexico; executed) :
I die in a just cause. I forgive all, and pray that all may forgive me. May my blood flow for the good of this land. Long live Mexico! . . . Men!

MAZARIN, Cardinal:
Ah! blessed Virgin, have pity on me and receive my soul.

MAZZINI, Giuseppe (Italian patriot):
Yes! Yes! I believe in God!

MEADE, General George Gordon:
I am about crossing a beautiful wide river, and the opposite shore is coming nearer and nearer.

MEDICI, Lorenzo de (being asked, on taking a morsel of food, how he relished it)
As a dying man always does.

MELANCHTHON (asked if he wished anything):
Nothing but heaven, and therefore do not ask me such questions any more . . . [restored from a faint] Ah, what are you doing? Why do you disturb my sweet repose? Let me rest unto the end, for it will not last very long . . . [asked if he heard the psalm that was read] Yes.

MELVILLE, Herman (cried out with Billy Budd):
God bless Captain Vere!

MENDELSSOHN, Felix (asked how he felt):
Weary, very weary.

MERCIER, Désiré Joseph (Belgian cardinal; after the Profiscere):
Now there is nothing more to be done, except to wait.

MERGENTHALER, Ottmar (inventor of Linotype):
Emma, my children, my friends, be kind to one another.

MEREDITH, George (referring to the consulting physician):
I am afraid Sir Thomas thinks very badly of my case.

METCHNIKOFF, Élie (Russian bacteriologist):
You remember your promise? You will do my post-mortem? and look at the intestines carefully, for I think there is something there now.

MEW, Charlotte (English poet; suicide):
Don't keep me, let me go.

MEYNELL, Alice (poet and essayist):
This is not tragic. I am happy.

MICHELANGELO:
In your passage through this life remember the sufferings of Jesus Christ.

MICHELET, Jules (French historian; the physician ordered his linen to be changed):
Linen, doctor, you speak of linen. Do you know what linen is?—the linen of the peasant, of the worker. . . . Linen, a great thing. . . . I want to make a book of it.

MIDDLETON, Richard (English poet and story writer; suicide note):
Good-bye! Harry. I'm going adventuring again, and thanks to you I shall have some pleasant memories in my knapsack. As for the many bitter one, perhaps they will not weigh so heavy now as they did before. "A broken and contrite heart, oh Lord, thou shalt not despise." Richard.

MILL, John Stuart (informed he would not recover):
My work is done.

MILLAY, Edna St. Vincent (written):
It is 5:30, and I have been working all night. I am going to bed. Good morning—E. St. V. M.

MILLER, Henry (theater manager; to his son Gilbert):
Gilbert—poor Dodd.

MILLER, Hugh (Scottish geologist and man of letters; letter to his wife before shooting himself):

Dearest Lydia,— My brain burns, I must have walked; and a fearful dream rises upon me. I cannot bear the horrible thought. God and Father of the Lord Jesus Christ, have mercy upon me. Dearest Lydia, dear children, farewell. My brain burns as the recollection grows. My dear wife, farewell. Hugh Miller.

MILLER, Joaquin (Western poet):

Take me away; take me away.

MIRABEAU, Comte de (Revolutionary leader; wanted drugs):

Are you not my doctor and my friend? Did you not promise to save me from the pain of such a death? Do you wish me to carry away regret for having given you my confidence?

MITCHELL, Silas Weir (physician and author; delirious, combated death on the Civil War battlefield again):

That leg must come off—save the leg—lose the life!

MITFORD, Mary Russell (English novelist; letter):

Today I am better; but if you wish for another cheerful evening with your old friend, there is no time to be lost.

MOHAUPT, Juliana (niece of the German author Stifter; drowned herself at 17, fifteen years after her mother's death; written):

I am going to my mother in the great Service.

MOLENEUX, Thomas (constable of Chester in the reign of Richard II; caught by his enemies refreshing himself in a river, made a request that was not granted):

Suffer me to come up and let me fight either with thee or some other, and die like a man.

MOLIÈRE (protested there was no need for alarm):
Still, go call my wife.

MOLTKE, Helmuth von (Prussian soldier; "Uncle Helmuth, are you ill?"):
What?

MONCEY, Marshal Bon Adrien Jeannot de, Duc de Conegliano (soldier in Revolutionary and Napoleonic armies):
Let everyone fulfill and close his course like me.

MONICA (mother of St. Augustine):
Lay this body wherever it may be. Let no care of it disturb you: this only I ask of you that you should remember me at the altar of the Lord wherever you may be.

MONMOUTH, the Duke of:
Prithee, let me feel the axe. . . . I fear it is not sharp enough.

MONTAGU, Lady Mary Wortley (poet and letter writer):
It has all been very interesting; it has all been very interesting.

MONTCALM, Marquis de:
I have no more orders to give. I am busy with more important affairs, and the time which remains to me is short . . . I die content. I leave the affairs of the king my master in good hands; I have always had a high opinion of M. de Lévis.

MONTEZ, Lola (British dancer and adventuress):
I am very tired.

MONTEZUMA (Aztec emperor; told Cortes he hoped his children would be allowed some portion of their rightful inheritance):

Your lord will do this, if it were only for the friendly
offices I have rendered the Spaniards, and for the
love I have shown them—though it has brought me
to this condition! But for this I bear them no ill-will.

MONTFORT, Simon de (medieval English statesman
and soldier; killed at Evesham):
It is God's grace.

MONTMORENCY, Duc Anne de (French soldier):
Do you think a man who has known how to live hon-
ourably for eighty years does not know how to die
for a quarter of an hour?

MONTMORENCY, Duc Henry II de (executed for revolt
against Richelieu):
Give a good stroke. Sweet Saviour, receive my soul.

MONTROSE, James Graham, Earl of (adherent of
Charles I; hanged):
May God have mercy on this afflicted kingdom.

MOODY, Blair (Michigan senator):
I feel better.

MOODY, Dwight L. (evangelist; doubtful about hypo-
dermic injection):
Doctor, I don't know about this. Do you think it
best? It is only keeping the family in anxiety.

MOORE, Sir John (fallen in battle; rumored to be en-
gaged to Lady Hester Stanhope):
Stanhope—remember me to your sister.

MORE, Hannah (English religious writer):
Joy.

MORE, Sir or Saint Thomas (to the executioner):
Pluck up thy spirits, man, and be not afraid to do
thine office. My neck is very short; take heed there-
fore thou strike not awry, for saving of thine honesty.

MOREAU, Jean Victor (general of Revolutionary and Napoleonic armies; exiled):
> *Say to the Emperor that I go to the tomb with the same feelings of veneration, of respect and devotion, that he inspired in me the first time I saw him. . . . I have nothing to reproach myself with.*

MOREHEAD, John A. (Lutheran leader; on the day of his wife's burial):
> *Will you do me a favor? Will you kindly ask my physician how long before I shall join my Nellie?*

MORGAN, J. Pierpont:
> *Don't baby me so!*

MORIALE or Monreale, Fra (Italian freebooter; on the scaffold, to the people):
> *I die for your poverty and my wealth.*

MORRIS, William (letter to Lady Burne-Jones):
> *Come soon. I want a sight of your dear face.*

MORSE, Samuel F. B. ("This is the way we doctors telegraph"):
> *Very good.*

MORTON, Oliver P. (Indiana statesman):
> *I am dying, I am worn out.*

MOULE, Handley Carr Glyn (bishop of Durham; told, "The Lord Jesus is with thee"):
> *I know it.*

MOZART, Wolfgang Amadeus (of his "Requiem"):
> *Did I not tell you that I was writing this for myself?*

MUHLENBERG, William Augustus (founder of St. Luke's Hospital, New York):
> *Good morning.*

MUNRO, Hector Hugh (pseudonym Saki; short story

writer; in a shallow crater during the attack on Beaumont Hamel, November, 1916):
Put that bloody cigarette out.

MÜNSTERBERG, Hugo (psychologist):
By spring we shall have peace!

MURAT, Joachim (king of Naples):
Soldiers, do your duty. Aim for the heart; but spare the face.

MURGER, Henri (author of *Scenes de la Vie de Bohème*):
..No more music, no more commotion—no more Bohemia!

MURPHY, Arthur (playwright; repeated the lines of Pope):
>*Taught, half by reason, half by mere decay,*
>*To welcome death, and calmly pass away.*

MURRIETA, Joaquin (desperado in California):
It is enough. Shoot no more. The job is finished. I am dead.

MUSSET, Alfred de:
Sleep! At last I am to sleep.

MUSSOLINI, Benito (to the man who was aiming at him):
But . . . but . . . Mr. Colonel . . .

MUSSORGSKY, Modest Petrovich:
It's the end. Woe is me!

ℕ

NAPOLEON:
France! ... Army! ... Head of the army! ... Josephine!

NAPOLEON II:
Call my mother. Call my mother. ... Take the table away. I don't need anything any more ... Poultices.

NAPOLEON III:
Were you at Sedan?

NARVAEZ, Ramon Maria (Spanish patriot; to his confessor):
I do not have to forgive my enemies, because I killed them all.

NEANDER, Johann (German Protestant church historian and theologian):
I am weary, let us go home! ... Good-night!

NELSON, Horatio:
God and my Country!

NERO:
The sound of swift-footed steeds strikes upon mine ears! Jupiter!—What an artist is lost to the world!— What an artist! ... [to a servant who attempted to stanch his wound] *Too late! Is this your loyalty?*

NEVIN, Ethelbert (composer of songs; to his wife):
Anne, I'm dying, and I don't want to leave you.

NEWELL, Harriet (missionary in India):
Oh the pains, the groans, the dying strife. How long, O Lord, how long!

NEWTON, John (English divine):
I am satisfied with the Lord's will.

NEY, Marshal Michel (refusing the blindfold):
Don't you know, Sir, that a soldier does not fear death . . . Frenchmen, I protest against my condemnation. My honour . . .

NICHOLAS, Saint:
Into Thy hands . . .

NICHOLAS II of Russia (hearing his sentence of death):
What?

NICOLL, Sir William Robertson (pseudonym Claudius Clear, Scottish man of letters):
I believe everything that I have written about immortality.

NIEBUHR, Barthold Georg (philologist; given medicine he knew was only used in extreme cases):
What essential substance is this? Am I so far gone?

NIJINSKY, Waslaw:
Mamasha [mother].

NODIER, Charles (French man of letters):
It is very hard, my children, I no longer see you. . . . Remember me—love me always.

NOTHNAGEL, Hermann (clinician; report on his condition):
Paroxysms of angina pectoris, with extremely violent pains. Pulse and attacks completely different, sometimes slow, about 56-60, entirely regular, very intense, then again accelerated, 80-90, rather even and regular, finally completely arhythmic, entirely unequal, now palpitating, now slow, with differing intensity. The first sensations of these attacks date several—

three or four—years back, in the beginning rather weak, becoming slowly more and more definite. Proerly speaking, attacks with sharp pains have appeared only within the last five or six days. Written on July 6, 1905, late in the evening, after I had three or four violent attacks.

O

OATES, Lawrence E. G. (on the ill-fated Scott expedition
to the South Pole, walked alone in the blizzard to die
rather than be a drag on his comrades):
> *I am just going outside and may be some time.*

O'BRIEN, William (Irish nationalist):
> *Well, the night is so long and dreary, I think I will
> wait up a little longer.*

O'CONNELL, Daniel (Irish national leader):
> *My dear friend, I am dying . . . Jesus . . . Jesus . . .
> Jesus.*

OGILVY, Margaret (Barrie's mother):
> *God . . . love.*

OLGIATTI, Girolamo (one of the assissins of Galeazzo
Sforza; executed):
> *My death is untimely, my fame eternal, the memory
> of the deed will last for aye.*

OLIPHANT, Laurence (mystic):
> *More light.*

OLIPHANT, Margaret O. W. (Scottish novelist):
> *I seem to see nothing but God and our Lord.*

O'NEILL, Eugene, Jr. (son of the playwright; Greek
scholar; suicide note):
> *Never let it be said of O'Neill that he failed to empty
> a bottle. Ave atque vale.*

OPIE, Amelia (novelist and poet; message for those who
were inquiring):
> *Tell them, I have suffered great pain; but I think on*

Him who suffered for me. Say that I am trusting in
my Saviour, and ask them to pray for me.

O'REILLY, John Boyle (poet and editor):
Yes, Mamsie dear, I have taken some of your sleeping
medicine. I feel tired now, and if you will let me lie
down on that couch I will go to sleep right away. . . .
Yes, my love! Yes, my love!

ORLÉANS, Charlotte Elisabeth, Duchess of (sister-in-law
of Louis XIV; letter):
Thank God, I am prepared to die, and I only pray
for strength to die bravely. It is not bad weather, although today a fine rain is setting in. But I do not
think any weather will help me. Many complain of
coughs and colds, but my malady lies deeper. Should
I recover, you will find me the same friend as ever.
Should this be the end, I die with full faith in my
Redeemer.

ORLÉANS, Louis Philippe Joseph, Duc d' ("Philippe-
Égalité"; to the executioner's assistant, who wanted to
draw off his boots):
You can do that more easily to my dead body. Come
—be quick.

OSLER, Sir William (treated a doctor friend as if he were
still a child):
Nighty-night, a-darling!

OTHO, Marcus Salvius (Roman emperor; before falling
on his sword, to one of his freedmen):
Go then and show yourself to the soldiers, lest they
should cut you to pieces for being accessory to my
death.

OUGHTRED, William (mathematician; hearing of the
restoration of Charles II):

[160]

*And are ye sure he is restored? Then give me a glass
of sack to drink his Sacred Majesty's health.*

OUIDA (pseudonym of Louise de la Ramée, English novelist; letter):

*I have been very ill these days, and my maid is of
opinion that I shall never get well. The weather is
intensely cold; and at St. Remo it is so warm and
brilliant, it is odd there should be so great a difference. Excuse this rough word; I am ill and cannot
write well.*

OUTLAW, Bass (gunfighter):

*Go gather my friends around me, for I know that I
must die*

OWEN, John (non-conformist divine; told by Rev. William Payne that the first sheet of his *Meditations on the
Glory of Christ* had just passed through the press):

*I am glad to hear it; but, O brother Payne! the long-
wished-for day is come at last, in which I shall see that
glory in another manner than I have ever done, or
was capable of doing, in this world.*

OWEN, Robert (pioneer in socialism):

Relief has come.

OWEN, Wilfred (World War I poet; at the front, to his
men):

Well done! . . . You are doing very well, my boy.

OZANAM, Frédéric (French historian):

My God! my God! have mercy on me!

$\mathcal{P}$

PADEREWSKI, Ignace Jan (asked if he would care for some champagne):
Please.

PAGE, Thomas Nelson (novelist and diplomat):
Here Alfred, take this spade.

PAINE, Thomas (the doctor remarked, "Your belly diminishes"):
And yours augments.

PALM, Johann Philipp (German bookdealer; published pamphlet attacking Napoleon; shot; letter to his wife and children):
My Heart's Treasure and my Dearly Beloved Children! By man but not by God abandoned, the military court of this place has pronounced judgment against me after only two examinations. I was questioned as to whether I had circulated certain political writings. I replied, what I knew to be true, that at most only in some incidental way by mail were these distributed—but without my will and knowledge. Whereupon I was condemned to death, without attorney for my defence. I asked for one, but none was forthcoming. However, there will be one for me before God. To you, dear wife, I say a thousand thanks for your love. Trust in God, and do not forget me. I have nothing in the world to say, but farewell, you and the children, God bless you and them. My regards to Mr. and Mrs. Schwägerin and all my friends, whom I thank for their goodness and love. Once more, farewell. Yonder we shall meet again. Your hus-

band, and children's father, Johann Palm. Braunau, in prison, August 26, 1806, a half hour before my death.

PALMER, Courtlandt (founder of the Nineteenth Century Club):

I want you to say that you have seen a free-thinker die without fear of the future, and without changing his opinion.

PALMER, William (the Rugeley poisoner; as he stepped on the trap of the gallows):

Are you sure it's safe?

PALMERSTON, Lord:

That's Article ninety-eight; now go on to the next.

PANCRATIUS, Saint (14, to the Emperor Diocletian):

In body I am a child, but I bear a man's heart: and by the grace of my Master Jesus Christ, thy threats seem as vain to me as this idol which stands before me. And as for the gods whom thou desirest me to adore, they are naught but impostors, who sully the women of their own household, and spare not their own kin. If thine own slaves today behaved as these gods, thou wouldst be in haste to put them to death. And it wonders me much that thou dost not blush to adore such gods!

PARKER, Theodore (Unitarian clergyman; letter):

My dear John Ayers, So I shall still call you. Will you come over tomorrow and see us; just after your dinner time. Bring me a last year's apple if you can, or any new melon.

PARNELL, Charles Stewart:

Kiss me, sweet Wifie, and I will try to sleep a little.

PARRY, Sir William Edward (Arctic explorer):

The chariots and horses!

PASCAL, Blaise:
May God never abandon me!

PASCIN, Jules (artist; wrote in blood on the wall of his studio before hanging himself):
Adieu Lucy.

PASTEUR, Louis (offered a cup of milk):
I cannot.

PATMORE, Coventry (English poet; as he embraced his wife):
I love you, dear, but the Lord is my Life and my Light.

PATON, Captain J. (covenanter; on the scaffold):
Farewell, sweet scriptures, preaching, praying, reading, singing, and all duties. Welcome, Father, Son, and Holy Spirit. I desire to commit my soul to Thee in well-doing. Lord, receive my spirit.

PATTISON, Dorothy Wyndlow ("Sister Dora"; philanthropist):
I have lived alone, let me die alone, let me die alone.

PATTISON, William (starving poet; note):
Sir,—If you was ever touched with a sense of humanity, consider my condition: what I am, my proposals will inform you; what I have been, Sidney College, in Cambridge, can witness; but what I shall be some few hours hence, I tremble to think! Spare my blushes!—I have not enjoyed the common necessaries of life for these two days, and can hardly hold to subscribe myself, Yours, etc.

PAUL, Saint (written: 2nd Epistle to Timothy):
Do thy diligence to come before winter. Eubulus greeteth thee, and Pudens, and Linus, and Claudia,

and all the brethren. The Lord Jesus Christ be with thy spirit. Grace be with you. Amen.

PAULINUS, Saint (bishop of Nola):
Thy word is a lantern unto my feet, and a light unto my paths.

PAVLOVA, Anna:
Get my "Swan" costume ready.

PAYNE, John (English poet and translator):
Have you got the sheets? . . . Did you get the pillow-cases?

PAYSON, Edward (American Congregational divine):
Faith and patience, hold out!

PEACE, Charles (English criminal; on the scaffold):
What is the scaffold? A short cut to Heaven!

PEACOCK, Thomas Love (English novelist and lyricist; refusing to leave his beloved library, though there was some danger from fire):
By the immortal gods, I will not move!

PEARSON, Charles Henry (education minister in Victoria):
My life has been faulty, but God will judge me by my intentions.

PEEL, Sir Robert (to Lady Peel, before mounting his horse):
Julia, you are not going without wishing me "good-bye," or saying those sweet words: "God bless you"?

PEERSON, Anthony (martyr; pulled the straw to him and laid a good deal upon the top of his head):
This is God's hat; now am I dressed like a true soldier of Christ, by whose merits only I trust this day to enter into His joy.

PÉGUY, Charles (French writer; killed at first battle of the Marne):
Keep firing.

PELAGIA, Saint:
Hast thou a bishop? . . . Let him pray the Lord for me, for he [Veronus] is a true apostle of Christ!

PELLICO, Silvio (Italian writer and patriot; pressing his hands on his heart):
Here my God is.

PENN, Gulielma (wife of William):
I have cast my care upon the Lord. My dear Love to all Friends.

PENN, Springett (a son of William; when the doctor came):
Let my father speak to the doctor, and I'll go to sleep.

PENROSE, Boies (Pennsylvania politician; to his Negro valet):
See here, William. See here. I don't want any of your damned lies. How do I look? Am I getting any better? The truth now. . . . All right, William. When you go to church tomorrow—pray for me, too.

PENRUDDOCK, Col. John (royalist; kissing the axe):
I am like to have a sharp passage of it, but my Saviour hath sweetened it unto me. If I would have been so unworthy as others have been, I suppose I might by a lie have saved my life, which I scorn to purchase at such a rate: I defy temptations and them that gave them me. Glory be to God on high, on earth peace, good will towards men, and the Lord have mercy upon my poor soul. Amen.

PEPONILA (wife of the rebellious Gaul Sabinus; pleading with Vespasian for mercy for her family) :
These little ones, Caesar, I bore and reared in the

monument [where her husband had hidden] that we might be a greater number to supplicate you.

PERCEVAL, Spencer (statesman; assassinated in the lobby of the house of Commons):
Oh! I am murdered.

PERICLES:
No Athenian, through my means, ever wore mourning.

PETACCI, Claretta (Mussolini's mistress):
Mussolini must not die!

PÉTAIN, Marshal Henri (to his wife):
Do not weep, do not grieve.

PETER, Saint (to his wife, as she was led out to die):
Oh thou, remember the Lord.

PETER Martyr, Saint:
Lord, into Thy hands I commend my spirit.

PETER the Great (written):
Give back all to . . .

PETER III (strangled):
It was not enough then to prevent my reigning over Sweden, and to tear from my head the crown of Russia! they must have my life besides!

PETER, Prince (brother of Prince Henry the Navigator):
Oh, body of mine! I feel that you can do not more; and you my spirit, why should you tarry here? . . . Fight on, comrades! And you, you villains, do your worst!

PETERS, Hugh (executed as regicide; to the sheriff, when a fellow prisoner was quartered before his eyes):
Sir, you have here slain one of the servants of God

*before mine eyes, and have made me to behold it, on
purpose to terrify and discourage me; but God hath
made it an ordinance to me for my strengthening and
encouragement.*

PHILIP II of Spain (asking for a sacred taper):
Give it to me; it is time now.

PHILLIPS, David Graham (American novelist; shot by
a paranoiac):
*I could have won against two bullets but not against
six.*

PHILOPOEMEN (Greek general; he learned from the
man who brought him the poison that some of his men
had escaped):
*It is well that we have not been every way unfortu-
nate.*

PHOCION (general; as he was led away to death, a friend
exclaimed what an unworthy treatment this was):
*Yes, but not surprising—this is what usually happens
at Athens to her great men.*

PIKE, Albert (American poet; written in Hebrew):
Peace, peace, peace.

PILKINGTON, George Lawrence (Ugandan pioneer):
*Thank you, my friends, you have done well to take
me off the battlefield; and now give me rest.*

PIRANDELLO, Luigi:
The hearse, the horse, the driver, and—enough!

PITMAN, Sir Isaac (inventor of phonetic shorthand):
*To those who ask how Isaac Pitman passed away, say,
Peacefully, and with no more concern than in passing
from one room into another to take up some further
employment.*

PITT the Elder, William, Earl of Chatham:
*Go, my son, go whither your country calls you: let
her engross all your attention; spare not a moment,
which is due to her service, in weeping over an old
man, who will soon be no more.*

PITT the Younger, William (referring to Austerlitz):
My country! How I leave my country!

PIUS IX, Pope (as they said the Proficere):
Yes, depart.

PIZARRO, Francisco:
Jesu.

PLATT, Orville H. (Connecticut senator):
You know what this means, Doctor, and so do I.

PLOTINUS:
*I am making my last effort to return that which is
divine in me to that which is divine in the universe.*

PLOWMAN, Max (poet; letter to an editor):
*Good wishes to you very sincerely. Do come & see
us here someday—even tho' we are bunged up at the
moment. And let me know if the enclosed needs re-
vision. Yours ever, Max P.*

PLUMB, Preston B. (Kansas senator; note to his former
private secretary):
*Dear Frank: Please come to my room tomorrow
(Sunday) about ten o'clock. Yours truly. P. B. P.*

POE, Edgar Allan:
Lord help my poor soul.

POLK, James K. (to his wife):
I love you, Sarah. For all Eternity—I—love—you.

POLYCARP, Saint:
. . . I give Thee thanks that thou hast vouchsafed to

grant me this day, that I may have my part among the number of the martyrs in the cup of Christ, unto the resurrection of eternal life, both of body and soul, through the operation of Thy Holy Spirit; among whom I shall this day be received into Thy sight for an acceptable sacrifice: and as Thou hast prepared and revealed the same before this time, so Thou hast accomplished the same, O Thou most true God, which canst not lie. Wherefore I in like case for all things praise Thee, and bless Thee, and glorify Thee by our everlasting Bishop, Jesus Christ, to whom be glory evermore. Amen.

POMPADOUR, Madame de:
Stay a little longer, Monsieur le Curé, and we will depart together.

POOLE, William (leader of the foreigner-hating Native American or Know-Nothing party; shot in a saloon):
I die a true American!

POPE, Alexander:
There is nothing that is meritorious but virtue and friendship, and indeed friendship itself is only a part of virtue.

PORCARO, Etienne (Italian patriot; hanged):
O my people, your deliverer dies today!

PORTER, Noah (lexicographer):
Go call your mother—wake her up—I want to consult with her.

PORTER, William Sydney (pseudonym O. Henry):
Turn up the lights. I don't want to go home in the dark.

PORTEUS, Beilby (bishop of London):
O, that glorious sun!

POTTER, Beatrix (creator of the Peter Rabbit stories; letter):

> *I write a line to shake you by the hand, our friendship has been entirely pleasant. I am very ill with bronchitis. With best wishes for the New Year.*

PRESCOTT, William Hickling (American historian; amused that his wife was able to recall the name of a diplomat he had forgotten):

> *How came you to remember?*

PRESTON, John (Puritan divine):

> *I feel death coming to my heart, my pain shall now be quickly turned into joy.*

PRIESTLEY, Joseph (chemist; after dictating some emendations for a posthumous publication):

> *I have now done.*

PROTASIUS, Saint:

> *I bear thee no anger, count, for I know that thou art blind in thy heart, but rather do I pity thee, for thou knowest not what thou dost. Cease not to torture me, that I may share with my brother the good countenance of our Master!*

PROUST, Marcel (his brother asked, "Am I hurting you?"):

> *Yes, Robert dear, you are.*

PUCCINI, Giacomo:

> *My poor Elvira! My poor wife.*

PULITZER, Joseph (to a reader):

> *Softly, quite softly.*

PURCELL, Henry (English composer; will):

> *... And I do hereby constitute and appoint my said loving wife my sole executrix of this my last will and testament, revoking all former wills. Witness my*

[*171*]

*hand and seal this 21st day of Nov. anno 1695. And
in the 7th year of the reign of King William the
Third.*

PUSEY, Edward B. (Anglican theologian):
My God.

PUSHKIN, Alexander:
Life is ended. It is difficult to breathe. I am choking.

Q

QUARLES, Francis (poet):

O sweet Saviour of the world, let Thy last words upon the cross be my last words in this world: Into Thy hands, Lord, I commend my spirit. And what I cannot utter with my mouth, accept from my heart and soul.

QUEZON, Manuel L. (Philippine statesman; hearing over the radio the news that MacArthur's liberation forces had just landed at Sansapor in Dutch New Guinea):

Just 600 miles!

QUIJANO, Gen. Alfredo Rueda (involved in the Mexican Revolution of 1927; shot; asked the firing squad to move closer, and when they did so):

Still a little closer . . . [to newspaper correspondents] Good-bye, good-bye.

QUIN, James (actor; wished the "last tragic scene" were over but hoped he should):

be able to go through it with becoming dignity.

R

RABELAIS, François:
Draw the curtain: the farce is ended.

RADCLIFFE, Anne (English romantic novelist; on receiving nourishment):
There is some substance in that.

RADCLIFFE, Sir James, Earl of Derwentwater (English Jacobite; to the executioner):
I am but a poor man; there's ten guineas for you; if I had more, I would give it you; I desire you to do your office so as to put me to the least misery you can.

RADCLIFFE, John (physician; letter to his sister):
...I have nothing further than to beseech the Divine Being who is the God of the living to prosper you and all my relations with good and unblameable lives, that when you shall change the world you are now in for a better, we may all meet together in glory and enjoy these ineffable delights which are promised to all that love Christ's coming. Till then, my dear, dear Milly, take this as a last farewell from your most Affectionate and Dying Brother, J. Radcliffe. N. B. The Jewels and Rings in my gilt cabinet, by my great scrutore, not mentioned in my will, I hereby bequeath to you.

RALEIGH, Sir Walter (to the executioner):
What dost thou fear? Strike, man, strike!

RALSTON, William Chapman (Comstock Lode speculator):
Keep these for me. There are valuable papers in my pocket.

RANDOLPH, John (of Roanoke; note):
Dying. Home ... Randolph and Betty, my children, adieu! Get me to bed at Chatham or elsewhere, say Hugh Mercer's or Minor's. To bed I conjure you all.

RAVAILLAC, François (murderer of King Henry IV of France; given a conditional absolution that if he were concealing any accomplices he should be damned eternally):
I receive absolution upon this condition.

RAVEL, Maurice (regarding himself in a mirror and pointing to the bandages about his head):
I look like a Moor.

RAY, John (naturalist):
When you happen to write to my singular friend Dr. Hotton I pray tell him I received his most obliging and affectionate letter for which I return thanks and acquaint that I am not able to answer it.

READE, Charles (novelist):
I have no hope but in God. God only can create; and God only can recreate.

RÉCAMIER, Madame Jeanne (society beauty):
We shall meet again!

REED, Major Walter (told he had been recommended for promotion to the rank of colonel):
I care nothing for that now.

REMINGTON, Frederic (painter and sculptor of the West; told an operation for appendicitis was called for):
Cut her loose, Doc.

RENAN, Ernest (religious philosopher):
Remove that sun from off the Acropolis!

RENOIR, Pierre:
I am still progressing.

REYNOLDS, Sir Joshua:
I know that all things on earth must have an end, and now I am come to mine.

REYNOLDS, Stephen (English essayist; telegram):
Reference my letter of last night. Have got influenza myself now. Stop. Pretty sure unable to come to London next week.

RHODES, Cecil John:
Turn me over, Jack.

RIBBENTROP, Joachim von (hanged as war criminal):
God save Germany! My last wish is that Germany rediscover her unity and that an alliance be made between East and West and that peace reign on earth.

RICE, Grantland (end of last sports column):
Willie, at least, has a golden start.

RICHARD III:
I will die King of England. I will not budge a foot. . . . Treason! Treason!

RICHELIEU, Cardinal (asked to forgive his enemies):
I have had no enemies save those of the State.

RICHELIEU, Louis, Duc de (dying on the eve of the French Revolution):
What would Louis XIV have said!

RICHMOND, Leigh (English clergyman):
It will be all confusion . . . The church! There will be such confusion in my church!

RICHTER, Jean Paul (murmuring and finding that he was not understood):
We'll let it go.

RIDLEY, Bishop Nicholas (at the stake; the fire under him being poorly made):

> *Let the fire come unto me, I cannot burn. Lord, have mercy upon me.*

RILKE, Rainer Maria (German lyric poet; letter):

> *My dear, dear Supervielle, gravely ill, painfully, miserably, humbly ill, I find myself again a moment in the comforting knowledge that even there, in that untenantable and inhuman plane, your message and all the influences it brings could reach me. I think of you, poet, friend, and in so doing I still think of the world —poor shard of a vessel that remembers being of the earth. (But how it abuses our senses and their "dictionary," the pain that turns their pages!) R.*

RIZAL, José (national hero of the Filipinos):

> *O Father, how terrible it is to die! How one suffers! Father, I forgive every one from the bottom of my heart; I have no resentment against any one: believe me, your reverence!*

ROBERTSON, Frederick W. (author of sermons; when they sought to change his position):

> *I cannot bear it. Let me rest. I must die. Let God do His work.*

ROBERTSON, W. Graham (British author; end of last instructions):

> *I should like the ashes to be buried or otherwise disposed of at the crematorium, with no tombstone nor inscription to mark the place of burial. No funeral, no mourning, no flowers. By request. If these arrangements are carried out one may perhaps manage to die without making a public nuisance of oneself. W. Graham Robertson.*

ROBERTSON, James (missionary in Northwest Territory):
I am done out.

ROBERTSON, Thomas William (dramatist):
Good-bye, my son, and God bless you. Come and see me tomorrow. If I don't speak to you, don't be frightened, and don't forget to kiss your father.

ROBESPIERRE, Maximilien de (when the garter that was constricting him was loosened):
Thank you, sir.

ROBINSON, Edwin Arlington:
We'll have our cigarettes together. . . . Good-night.

ROBINSON, Henry Crabb (man of letters; entry in diary):
He [Matthew Arnold] thinks of Germany as he ought, and of Goethe with high admiration. On this point I can possibly give him assistance, which he will gladly— But I feel incapable to go on.

ROB ROY (nickname of Robert MacGregor; having successfully got through a last interview with a foeman):
Now all is over—let the piper play 'We Return No More.'

ROCHESTER, John, Earl of (lyric poet):
Has my friend [Gilbert Burnet] left me? Then I shall die shortly.

RODGERS, Commodore John:
Butler, do you know the Lord's Prayer? . . . Then repeat it for me.

RODIN, Auguste:
And people say that Puvis de Chavannes is not a fine artist!

RODIN, Mrs. Auguste (Rose):
I don't mind dying, but it's leaving my man. Who will look after him? What will happen to the poor thing?

RODNEY, George Brydges (English admiral):
I am very ill indeed.

ROHAN - CHABOT, Louis François Auguste, Duc de (archbishop of Besançon):
I am nothing, nothing, less than nothing!

ROLAND, Madame (guillotined):
O Liberty, how you are mocked!

ROLAND de la Platière, Jean Marie (Girondist; suicide note):
Whoever thou art that findest me lying, respect my remains: they are those of a man who consecrated all his life to being useful; and who has died as he lived, virtuous and honest. Not fear, but indigation, made me quit my retreat, on learning that my Wife had been murdered. I wished not to remain longer on an Earth polluted with crimes.

ROMAINE, William (divine):
Holy, Holy! Holy blessed Jesus, to Thee be endless praise!

ROMMEL, General Erwin (chose suicide):
I have spoken to my wife and made up my mind. I will never allow myself to be hanged by that man Hitler. I planned no murder. I only tried to serve my country, as I have done all my life, but now this is what I must do. In about half an hour there will come a telephone call from Ulm to say that I have had an accident and am dead.

ROOSEVELT, Franklin D.:
I have a terrific headache!

ROOSEVELT, Theodore:
Please put out the light.

ROSA, Salvator (Italian painter and poet):
*To judge by what I now endure, the hand of death
grasps me sharply.*

ROSCOMMON, Wentworth Dillon, Earl of (poet; quoted
from his own version of "Dies Irae"):
*My God, my father, and my friend,
Do not forsake me in my end.*

ROSSETTI, Christina (poet):
*I love everybody. If ever I had an enemy I should
hope to meet and welcome that enemy in heaven.*

ROSSETTI, Dante Gabriel:
*Then you really think I'm dying. At last you think
so; but I was right from the first.*

ROSSETTI, Mrs. Dante Gabriel (suicide note):
My life is so miserable I wish for no more of it.

ROSSINI, Gioacchino (murmured his wife's name):
Olympe.

ROTHSCHILD, Meyer Amschel (called his five sons and
enjoined them to be faithful to the law of Moses, to remain
united to the end, and undertake nothing without consulting their mother):
*Observe these three points, and you will soon be rich
among the richest, and the world will belong to you.*

ROTHSTEIN, Arnold (gambler; shot; asked by police
"Who did it?"):
*I won't tell and please don't ask me any more ques-
tions.*

ROUSSEAU, Jean Jacques:
See the sun, whose smiling face calls me; see that immeasurable light. There is God! Yes, God Himself, who is opening His arms and inviting me to taste at last that eternal and unchanging joy that I had so long desired.

ROYER-COLLARD, Pierre Paul (French philosopher and politician):
There is nothing substantial in the world but religious ideas. Never give them up, or if you do, come back to them.

RUBINSTEIN, Anton (pianist and composer):
I am suffocating. A doctor! Quick! A doctor!

RUBINSTEIN, Nicholas (brother of Anton; pianist):
Oysters! Nothing, Helen Andreyevna, will do me so much good as a dozen cold oysters. And an ice afterward.

RUDOLF of Habsburg, Crown Prince of Austria (suicide at Mayerling; letter to his wife):
Dear Stephanie, You are freed henceforward from the torment of my presence. Be happy, in your own way. Be good to the poor little girl who is the only thing I leave behind. Give my last greetings to all my acquaintances, especially to Bombelles, Spindler Latour, Nowo, Gisela, Leopold, etc., etc. I face death calmly; death alone can save my good name. With warmest love from Your affectionate Rudolf.

RUNYON, Damon (journalist; note to his friends):
You can keep the things of bronze and stone, and give me one man to remember me just once a year.

RUSH, Benjamin (Revolutionary leader; to his son):
Be indulgent to the poor.

RUSSELL, Charles, Lord Russell of Killowen (judge):
My God, have mercy upon me.

RUSSELL, John, Lord Amberley (father of Bertrand):
It is all done. . . . Good-bye my little dears for ever.

RUTHERFORD, Samuel (Scottish theologian):
Glory, glory dwelleth in Immanuel's land!

RUTHVEN, Alexander (stabbed for his part in the Gowrie conspiracy against James VI of Scotland):
Alas! I had na wyte [blame] of it!

RYLAND, John (Baptist minister):
No more pain.

S

SACCO, Nicola:
Vive Il Anarchismo! . . . *Farewell my wife and child and all my friends! Good—good-evening, gentlemen.* . . . Addio, Mamma mia, addio, Mamma mia.

SAINT-EDME, Bourg (French man of letters; suicide note for his children):
. . . At four o'clock or at 4:15 I will carry out my design, if everything goes right. I am not afraid of death, since I am seeking it, since I desire it! But prolonged suffering would be frightful. I walk; all ideas vanish. I think only of my children. The fire is dying out. What a silence all around! Four o'clock. I hear the chimes. Soon comes the moment of sacrifice. I put my snuff-box in my desk-drawer. Good-bye my dearest daughters! God will pardon my sorrows. I put my spectacles in the drawer. Good-bye, once more, good-bye, my darling children! . . . My last thought is yours—for you are the last flutterings of my heart.

SAINT-GAUDENS, Augustus (sculptor; as he lay watching a sunset):
It's very beautiful, but I want to go farther away.

SAINT-PIERRE, Charles, Abbé de (writer on social questions; told the priest, after he had consented to and gone through the last ceremonies for the family's sake):
I am only to be reproached for this action. I do not believe a word of all this. It was a vile concession for the family and for the house, but I wanted to be the confessor of the truth all my life.

SAINT-SIMON, Henri de (socialist):
The future belongs to us.

SALADIN (hearing the passage, "He is God, than whom there is no other God,—who knoweth the unseen and the seen,—the Compassionate, the Merciful"):
True.

SAMSON:
Let me die with the Philistines.

SAND, George (Baronne Dudevant):
Let green things . . .

SANDERSON, F. W. (English schoolmaster; asked, after a lecture, if he was "not too tired to answer" a few questions):
No—no.

SANDERSON, Robert (bishop of Lincoln):
My heart is fixed, O God, my heart is fixed where true joy is to be found.

SANDOZ, Jules Ami (pioneer):
The whole damn sandhills is deserted. The cattlemen are broke, the settlers about gone. I got to start all over—ship in a lot of good farmers in the spring, build up—build—build—

SAN MARTÍN, José de (South American soldier and statesman; to his brother-in-law):
Mariano—back to my room.

SANTO-IRONIMO, Caserio (who stabbed President Carnot):
Courage, comrades, long live Anarchy!

SAPPHO (poem to her daughter):
For it is not right that in the house of song there be mourning. Such things befit not us.

SARPI, Father Paul (Italian prelate and historian; what was understood to be a prayer for the prosperity of Venice):

> *Mayst thou last for ever.*

SARSFIELD, Patrick, Earl of Lucan (Irish soldier; fallen in French service at Landen):

> *Would to God this were shed for Ireland!*

SAUCKEL, Fritz (hanged as war criminal):

> *I pay my respect to American officers and American soldiers but not to American justice.*

SAUL:

> *Stand, I pray thee, upon me, and slay me; for anguish is come upon me, because my life is yet whole in me.*

SAUNDERS, Laurence (martyr; embracing the stake):

> *Welcome the cross of Christ! Welcome everlasting fire!*

SAVAGE, Richard (poet and adventurer; to his gaoler):

> *I have something to say to you, sir . . . 'Tis gone!*

SAVINA, Saint:

> *O Lord, Who hast ever preserved me in chastity, suffer me not longer to be wearied with journeying! Command me not to go beyond this place! Let my body here find rest! I commend to Thee my servant, who has borne so much for me, and let me be worthy to see my brother in Thy Kingdom, whom I have not seen here!*

SAVINIANUS, Saint:

> *Fear not to strike me down; and do ye bear away some drops of my blood to the emperor, that he may receive his sight, and acknowledge the power of God!*

SAVONAROLA, Girolamo:

> *The Lord hath suffered so much for me.*

SAXE, Maurice, Comte de (French marshal):
Doctor, life is but a dream. Mine has been beautiful, but it has been brief.

SCARRON, Paul (comic writer):
Ah, my children, you cannot cry for me as much as I have made you laugh.

SCHILLER, Friedrich von:
Judex! (the judge).

SCHIMMELPENNINCK, Mary Anne (English author):
Rejoice with me, rejoice with me! I am entering my Father's house. . . . Do you not hear the voices? and the children's are the loudest!

SCHLEGEL, Friedrich von (unfinished lecture; written):
But the consummate and perfect knowledge—

SCHLEIERMACHER, Friedrich (theologian and philosopher):
In this love and communion we are, and ever will remain united. . . . Now I can no longer remain here. . . . Place me in another position.

SCHMITT, Lt. Aloysius Herman (chaplain of the "Oklahoma" at Pearl Harbor; insisted on being last through the porthole—and then his shoulders wedged):
Go ahead, boys, I'm all right.

SCHREINER, Olive (author of *The Story of an African Farm;* letter):
. . . I long to see the stars and the veld: one day I will go up to Matjesfontein just for one day, if I can find anyone to take me. It doesn't seem to me this is Africa. A Happy New Year, my dear one.

SCHUBERT, Franz:
Here, here is my end!

SCHULTZ, "Dutch" (real name Arthur Flegenheimer; delirious with another gangster's bullet in him):

> Turn your back to me, please, Henry. I am so sick now. The police are getting many complaints. Look out. I want that G-note. Look out for Jimmy Valentine, for he's a pal of mine. Come on, come on, Jim. O.K., O.K., I am all through. I can't do another thing. Look out, mama. Look out for her. You can't beat him. Police, Mama, Helen, mother, please take me out. I will settle the indictment. Come on, open the soap duckets; the chimney sweeps. Talk to the sword. Shut up. You got a big mouth. Please help me get up. Henry! Max! Come over here. French Canadian bean soup. I want to pay. Let them leave me alone.

SCHUMANN, Clara:

> You two must go to a beautiful place this summer.

SCHURZ, Carl (American politician):

> It is so simple to die.

SCHWIND, Moritz von (German painter; asked how he felt):

> Excellent!

SCOTT, Captain Robert Falcon (diary found by searching party):

> Every day we have been ready to start for our depot 13 miles away, but outside the door of the tent it remains a scene of whirling drift. I do not think we can hope for any better things now. We shall stick it out to the end, but we are getting weaker, of course, and the end cannot be far. It seems a pity, but I do not think I can write more. Last Entry: For God's sake look after our people.

SCOTT, Sir Walter (to his family):

> God bless you all; I feel myself again.

SCOTT, General Winfield:
Peter, take good care of my horse.

SCRIPPS, E. W. (newspaper publisher):
Too many cigars this evening, I guess.

SECUNDUS, Saint (when boiling pitch and resin was poured into his mouth):
How sweet are Thy words to my palate! more than honey to my mouth.

SELWYN, George Augustus (bishop of Lichfield):
It is all light.

SENECA, Lucius Annaeus (as, bleeding, he entered a pool of heated water, with which he sprinkled the nearest of his slaves):
I offer this liquid as a libation to Jupiter the Deliverer.

SERMENT, Mlle. Louise Anastasie (called "The Philosopher"; lines):
Soon the light of the skies
Will be gone from my eyes;
Soon the black night will creep,
Bringing smooth dreamless sleep.
Gone—the struggle and strife
Of the sad dream of life!

SERRA, Junipero (Spanish missionary in America):
Now I shall rest.

SERVETUS, Michael (at the stake):
Jesus Christ, thou Son of the eternal God, have mercy upon me!

SETON, Elizabeth Ann (founder of Sisters of Charity):
Jesus—Mary—Joseph.

SEUME, Johann Gottfried (German poet; asked if he wanted anything):
> *Nothing, dear Weigel. I only wanted to tell you that you shouldn't be annoyed if I should say some things I wouldn't say in a different situation. I take a guilt with me. You I cannot repay. My eyes grow dim.*

SEVERUS, Septimius (Roman emperor):
> *Make haste, if there is anything more for me to do.*

SEWARD, William Henry (statesman; asked by his daughter-in-law if he had anything to say to them):
> *Nothing, only 'Love one another.'*

SFORZA, Galeazzo, Duke of Milan (assassinated):
> *Oh God!*

SHACKLETON, Sir Ernest (explorer; told to take it easy):
> *You are always wanting me to give up something. What do you want me to give up now?*

SHAFTESBURY, Anthony Ashley Cooper, 7th Earl of (philanthropist; handed something by his valet):
> *Thank you.*

SHARP, Cecil (British musician; given an injection and told he would feel no more pain):
> *Never again.*

SHARP, William (pseudonym Fiona Macleod; Scottish poet and man of letters):
> *Oh, the beautiful 'Green Life' again! Ah, all is well.*

SHAW, George Bernard (to the nurse):
> *Sister, you're trying to keep me alive as an old curiosity, but I'm done, I'm finished, I'm going to die.*

SHEPPARD, Jack (English robber; hanged):
> *Of two virtues I have ever cherished an honest pride:*

*never have I stooped to friendship with Jonathan
Wild, or with any of his detestable thief-takers; and,
though an undutiful son, I never damned my
mother's eyes.*

SHERIDAN, Richard Brinsley:
*Tell her [Lady Bessborough] that my eyes will look
up to the coffin-lid as brightly as ever.*

SHERMAN, John (recognizing his daughter):
Oh, Mamie.

SHERWOOD, Mrs. Mary Martha (English writer of juvenile books):
*God is very good. Remember this, my children, that
God is love. He that dwelleth in love dwelleth in
God, and God in him.*

SICKINGEN, Franz von (German knight; to the priest):
*I have confessed God in my heart. He is the one to
give absolution and administer the Sacrament.*

SIDNEY, Sir Philip:
*I would not change my joy for the empire of the
world.*

SIMON (a monk; drank poisoned wine in order to get
King John of England to drink it):
*If it shall like your princely majesty, here is such a
cup of wine as ye never drank a better before in all
your lifetime; I trust this wassail shall make all England glad.*

SISERA (general; to Jael, before being slain in his sleep
by her with a hammer and nail):
*Stand in the door of the tent; and it shall be, when
any man doth come and enquire of thee, and say,
'Is there any man here?' that thou shalt say, 'No!'*

SIWARD, Earl of Northumberland (Danish warrior in England):

Shame on me that I did not die in one of the many battles I have fought, but am reserved to die with disgrace the death of a sick cow! At least put on my armour of proof, gird the sword by my side, place the helmet on my head, let me have my shield in my left hand, and my gold-inlaid battle-axe in my right hand, that the bravest of soldiers may die in a soldier's garb.

SMEDLEY, Rev. Edward (poet):

Be—always—thankful.

SMITH, Adam:

I believe we must adjourn this meeting to some other place.

SMITH, Alfred E. (to the priest):

Start the Act of Contrition.

SMITH, Captain E. J. (of the "Titanic"; declining to be helped into a lifeboat to which he had just swum with a child):

Let me go.

SMITH, Joseph (founder of the Mormon Church):

Is there no help for the widow's son? . . . Oh Lord, my God!

SMITH, Sydney (English humorist; told jokingly that he had probably drunk a dose of ink by mistake):

Then bring me all the blotting paper there is in the house.

SNYDER, Ruth (electrocuted murderess):

Oh, Father, forgive them, for they know not what they do! . . . Father, forgive me—oh, Father, forgive me! . . . Father, forgive them, Father, oh Father, forgive them . . .

SOCRATES:
Crito, I owe a cock to Asclepius; will you remember to pay the debt?

SOLEYMAN (Egyptian impaled for his assassination of General Kléber):
There is no God but God, and Mahomet is his prophet.

SOMERSET, Henry Beaufort, Duke of (beheaded):
Lord Jesus, save me.

SOPHIA, Saint (lying down upon the grave of her three martyred daughters):
I yearn, my dearest children, to be with you!

SOPHONISBA (daughter of Hasdrubal of Carthage; sent poison by her husband to save her from falling into the hands of the Romans):
I accept the wedding gift, nor is it displeasing, if my husband can give his wife nothing better. Say this, however, that it would have been a more honorable death if my wedding and my funeral had been further apart.

SPENCER, Herbert:
Now I take this step for the benefit of those who are to be my executors; my intention being that after death this my body shall be conveyed by sea to Portsmouth.

SPENGLER, Peter (martyr; "a very lean man"):
It is all one, for shortly I must have forsaken this skin, which already hangeth to my bones. I know well that I am a mortal, and a corruptible worm, and have nothing in me but corruption. I have long time desired my latter day, and have made my request that I might be delivered out of this mortal body, to be

joined with my Saviour Christ. I have deserved,
through my manifold sins committed against my
Saviour Christ, my cross; and my Saviour Christ hath
borne the cross, and hath died upon the cross; and
for my part I will not glory in any other thing but
only in the cross of Jesus Christ.

SPIES, August (one of the Haymarket anarchists):
Our silence will be more powerful than the voices
they are going to strangle today.

SPIESSHEIMER, Johann (called Suspinianus; Viennese
humanist; writing to another humanist Johann Brassican):
That you have not visited me in my grievous and
deadly sickness—what even strangers do—will be no-
ted at the appointed time. Through my man-servant
I informed myself of your situation and sent you
wine and other good things. By your behavior you
have marked out yourself as a sneak and intriguer,
and I shall see that our posterity knows about it.
What is another man to you? In order that you may
be aware of my intention, even when my hand is a
corpse's, I am putting it in writing. Let it be good-
bye, then. It goes badly with me, but I am what I
always was.

STAEL, Madame de (asked if she thought she would be
able to sleep):
Deeply and profoundly.

STAFFORD, William Howard, Viscount (beheaded for
treason; asked by the still hesitating headsman if he for-
gave him):
I do.

STANFORD, Mrs. Leland (wife of the capitalist):
May God forgive me my sins.

STANISLAS I of Poland (of the bathrobe in which he caught fire):

You gave it to me to warm me, but it has kept me too hot.

STANISLAVSKY, Konstantin (director of the Moscow Art Theater; asked by his nurse if he wished to "say something" to his sister in a letter the nurse was writing):

I've lots to say to her, not just something. But not now. I'm sure to get it all mixed up.

STANLEY, Sir Henry Morton (the explorer; as Big Ben struck four):

Four o'clock? How strange! So that is Time! Strange! . . . Enough.

STANTON, C. P. (sitting by the camp-fire, after having three times led the way across Donner Pass in the snow and come back to rescue more):

Yes, I am coming soon.

STANTON, Elizabeth Cady (plea sent to Theodore Roosevelt):

Abraham Lincoln immortalized himself by the emancipation of four million Southern slaves. Speaking for my suffrage coadjutors, we now desire that you, Mr. President, who are already celebrated for so many honorable deeds and worthy utterances, immortalize yourself by bringing about the complete emancipation of thirty-six million women.

STEDMAN, Edmund Clarence (poet and editor):

Twenty-seven letters! What is the use!

STEIN, Gertrude:

What is the question? . . . What is the question? . . . If there is no question, there is no answer.

STEINMETZ, Charles Proteus (electrical engineer):
All right. I'll lie down.

STEPHEN, Saint (the first martyr):
Lord, lay not this sin to their charge.

STEPHENS, Alexander H. (Georgia statesman):
But I carried it individually by six hundred majority.

STERNE, Laurence:
Now it is come.

STEVENSON, Robert Louis:
My head, my head!

STEWART, Sir John (colonel; found it necessary to issue a declaration asserting the legitimacy of his surviving son):
. . . I Sir John Stewart of Grantully do solemnly declare, before God, that the forementioned Lady Jane Douglas, my lawful spouse, did, in the year 1748, bring to the world my two sons, Archibald and Sholto, and I firmly believe the children were mine, as I am sure they were hers. Of the two sons, Archibald is the only in life now. I make this declaration as stepping into eternity, before the witnesses aforementioned, James Bisset, minister of the gospel at Caputh, and James Hill, minister at Gurdie, John Stewart of Dalgoos, Esq., justice of peace, Joseph Anderson tenant in Slogen-hole. Jo. Stewart.

STOLBERG, Count Friedrich Leopold (poet; to the doctor):
Tell me, will it truly all be over tomorrow or the next day? . . . Praise God! Thanks, thanks! I thank you with all my heart. Jesus Christ be praised.

STONE, Lucy (suffragist):
Make the world better!

STOWE, Harriet Beecher (to the Irish nurse):
I love you.

STRAFFORD, Thomas Wentworth, Earl of (on the scaffold):
I do as cheerfully put off my doublet at this time as ever I did when I went to bed. [refusing blindfold, jestingly] Nay, for I will see it done.

STRATHCONA and Mount Royal, Donald Alexander Smith, Baron (Canadian administrator):
O God of Bethel, by whose hand Thy people still are fed.

STRAUS, Mrs. Isidore (on the ill-fated "Titanic," refused to leave her husband for a lifeboat):
We have been together for forty years and we will not separate now.

STRAUSS, Johann (told to "go to sleep"):
I will, whatever happens.

STRAW, Jack (confession at the gallows):
Against the same day that Wat Tyler was killed, we purposed that evening (because that the poor people of London seemed to favor us) to set fire in four corners of the city and so to have burnt it, and to have divided the riches at our pleasures amongst us.

STREICHER, Julius (hanged as war criminal):
Heil Hitler!

STRINDBERG, August (pressing the Bible to his breast):
Everything is atoned for.

STROZZI, Filippo II (Florentine intriguer against Medicis; suicide note in prison, and line from Virgil carved with his sword):
If I have not known how to live, I shall know how to die. . . . May some avenger rise from my bones!

STUART, General J. E. B.:
I am resigned, if it be God's will.

SUDBURY, Simon of (archbishop of Canterbury; still alive after being smitten on the neck by one of the John Ball rioters):
Aha, it is the hand of God.

SULLIVAN, Sir Arthur:
My heart! my heart!

SUMNER, Charles:
My book, my unfinished book! . . . You must take care of the Civil Rights Bill,—my bill, the Civil Rights Bill,—don't let it fail! . . . Tell Emerson how much I love and revere him.

SUN YAT-SEN:
Peace . . . struggle . . . save China.

SURRATT, Mary E. (hanged for complicity in assassination of Lincoln; to those standing by on the scaffold):
Please don't let me fall.

SUTTER, John (pioneer in California):
Next year, next year they will surely—

SWEDENBORG, Emanuel:
Dat be good, me tank you; God bless you.

SWETCHINE, Madame Sophie Soymonof (mystic; at 5:30 a.m.):
It will soon be time for mass. They must raise me.

SWIFT, Rigby (justice; letter):
My dear Chief, Your most kind and sympathetic letter has been a wonderful tonic and I already feel much better. Yours very faithfully, Rigby Swift.

SYDNEY, Algernon (republican martyr; answering the headsman's questions, "Are you ready, sir?" and "Will you rise again?"):

> Not till the general resurrection—strike on!

SYNGE, John Millington (Irish dramatist):

> It is no use fighting death any longer.

T

TABOR, Horace A. W. (Colorado Silver King; to his wife, who died there in abject poverty thirty-six years later):
Hang on to the Matchless [mine]. It will make millions again.

TAFT, Senator Robert A. (to his wife):
Well, Martha! . . . Glad to see you looking so well.

TAIT, Archibald Campbell (archbishop of Canterbury; note to Queen Victoria) :
A last memorial of twenty-six years of devoted service: with earnest love and affectionate blessing on the Queen and her family.—A. C. Cantuar.

TALLEYRAND, Charles Maurice de (told that the Archbishop of Paris "would willingly give his life for you"):
He can find a much better use for it.

TALMA, François Joseph (French tragedian):
The worst is I cannot see.

TAMERLANE (referring to his son):
I would like nothing except to see Shah Rurh again. But that is—impossible.

TANEY, Roger B. (chief justice):
Lord Jesus receive my spirit.

TASSO, Torquato:
Into Thy hands, O Lord . . .

TAYLOR, Bayard (versifier and translator):
I want—I want, oh, you know what I mean, that stuff of life!

TAYLOR, Jeremy (prelate and author; responsible for cathedral of Dromore):

Bury me at Dromore.

TAYLOR, Zachary:

I am about to die. I expect the summons very soon. I have tried to discharge my duties faithfully; I regret nothing, but I am sorry that I am about to leave my friends.

TEKAKWITHA, Catherine ("Lily of the Mohawks"; protegée of the Jesuits):

I am leaving you. I am going to die. Remember always what we have done together since first we met. If you change I shall accuse you before the tribunal of God. Take courage, despise the discoursings of those who have not the Faith. If they ever try to persuade you to marry, listen only to the Fathers. If you cannot serve God here, go to the Mission at Lorette. Don't give up your mortifications. I shall love you in Heaven. I shall pray for you. I shall aid you.

TENNYSON, Alfred, Lord:

I have opened it.

TERESA of Avila, Saint:

Oh, my Lord! my Lord, and my Bridegroom, the longed-for hour has come, the hour in which I shall see Thee! Lord, now is the time to arise and go!—the good time which I welcome, which is Thy will; the hour when I must leave my exile, and my soul shall enjoy the fulfilment of all her desire!

TERRY, Ellen (actress):

Up to the skies ... down to the—

THACKERAY, William Makepeace (revised these last words in *Denis Duval*):

And my heart throbbed with an exquisite bliss.

[*200*]

THAYER, William Sydney (physician):
This is the end—and I am not sorry.

THEODORA, Saint (to the child that she, having been disguised as a monk, was falsely accused of being the father of):
Sweet my son, the end of my life approaches, and I leave thee to God, Who shall be thy Father and thy Helper. Sweetest son, persevere in fasting and prayer, and serve thy brethren devoutly!

THEODORE, Saint:
With my Christ I was, and am, and will be!

THEODORIC the Goth (disappearing on a strange coal-black steed):
I am ill-mounted. This must be the foul fiend on which I ride. Yet will I return, if God wills and Holy Mary.

THEOPHRASTUS (to his disciples):
Farewell, and may you be happy. Either drop my doctrine, which involves a world of labor, or stand forth its worthy champion, for you will win great glory. Life holds more disappointment than advantage. But, as I can no longer discuss what we ought to do, do you go on with the inquiry into right conduct.

THERAMENES (Athenian statesman and general; of his accuser, as he drank the hemlock):
This to the health of the lovely Critias!

THERESA, Maria (when the Dauphin Louis remarked to his mother it was raining):
Yes, it is indeed frightful weather for a journey as long as the one before me.

THOMAS the Apostle, Saint:
I adore, but not this metal; I adore, but not this graven image; I adore my Master Jesus Christ in Whose name I command thee, demon of this idol, to destroy it forthwith!

THOMAS, Theodore (orchestra conductor):
I have had a beautiful vision—a beautiful vision.

THOMPSON, "Big Bill" (Mayor of Chicago; referring to his affairs):
Everything is all set, Jim. . . . That's right. That's right.

THOREAU, Henry David:
moose . . . Indian.

THRALE, Hester Lynch (Piozzi) (friend of **Dr. Johnson**):
I die in the trust and the fear of God.

THRASEA Paetus (senator and Stoic; suicide under Nero):
We pour out a libation to Jupiter the Deliverer. Behold, young man, and may the gods avert the omen, but you have been born into times in which it is well to fortify the spirit with examples of courage.

THRING, Edward (schoolmaster; entry in diary):
And now to bed; sermon finished, and a blessed feeling of Sunday coming.

THURLOW, Edward (lord chancellor):
I'm shot if I don't think I am dying.

TIMROD, Henry ("laureate of the Confederacy"):
I shall soon drink of the river of eternal life.

TOJO, Hideki, Premier (hanged as a war criminal; poem):
Oh, look, see how the cherry blossoms fall mutely.

TOLAND, John (deist; asked if he wanted anything):
I want nothing but Death.

TOLSTOY, Leo:
I do not understand what I have to do.

TOPLADY, Augustus M. (hymn-writer):
Can you and my friends give me up? . . . Oh, what a blessing it is that my dear friends are made willing to give me up into the hands of my dear Redeemer, and to part with me. It will not be long before God takes me—nay, I feel that I am dying: no mortal man could live after experiencing the glories which God has manifested to my soul.

TORAL, Leon (assasin of President Obregon):
Long live—

TRAUBEL, Horace (author and socialist):
I am tired, damned tired.

TREE, Sir Herbert Beerbohm (of a part in the play he was planning to produce):
I shall not need to study the part at all; I know it already.

TROBRIAND, Gen. Régis de (of the Army of the Potomac; letter):
You will understand, dear Bonnaffon, that in such condition it is out of question for me to receive any visit, or even to designate any possible time of meeting, as by that time it is as likely that I may be underground as on it. Farewell then or "au revoir," as the case may turn. Anyhow I remain, Yours faithfully,
R. de Trobriand.

TROLLOPE, Frances (mother of Anthony; novelist):
Poor Cecilia! [daughter]

TROMP, Martin Harpertzoon (Dutch admiral):
Take courage, children. Act so that my end will be glorious, as my life has been.

TROTSKY, Leon
Please say to our friends I am sure of the victory of the Fourth International. Go forward!

TSUHMU, Lt. Commander Sakuma (in command of Japanese submarine that sank in Hiroshima Bay, 1910; note found when vessel was raised):
12:30 I feel great pain in breathing. I thought I had blown out gasoline, but I have been intoxicated by gasoline. Commander Nakano ... It is now 12:40 ...

TURENNE, Henri de La Tour d'Auvergne, Vicomte de (marshal of France; warned at Sasbach to withdraw from the line of fire):
Then I will gladly come, for I particularly wish not to be killed just now.

TURGENEV, Ivan S. (letter to Tolstoy):
... I can neither walk, nor eat, nor sleep. It tires me even to mention all this. My friend, great writer of the Russian land, heed my request. Let me know whether you receive this sheet, and permit me once more closely, closely to embrace you, your wife, and all yours. I can no more. I am tired.

TURNER, Joseph M. W. (English landscape painter):
The sun is God.

TUSSAUD, Madame (to her two sons):
I divide my property equally between you, and implore you, above all things, never to quarrel.

TWEED, William Marcy, "Boss":
Tilden and Fairchild—they will be satisfied now.

TYLER, John:
Doctor, I am going. . . . Perhaps it is best.

TYNDALE, William:
Lord! open the king of England's eyes.

TYNDALL, John (physicist; his wife gave him accidentally an overdose of chloral):
Yes, my poor darling, you have killed your John! . . . Let us do all we can. Tickle my throat. Get a stomach pump. . . . Yes, I know you are all trying to rouse me.

TYNG, Rev. Dudley Atkins (who inspired a hymn when he said earlier, "Father, stand up for Jesus"; was asked if he was happy):
Oh! perfectly, perfectly.

TZU-HSI (Chinese empress):
Never again allow a woman to hold the supreme power in the State. It is against the house-law of Our dynasty and should be forbidden. Be careful not to allow eunuchs to meddle in government matters. The Ming dynasty was brought to ruin by eunuchs, and its fate should be a warning to my people.

U

USSHER, James (archbishop of Armagh):
But Lord in special forgive my sins of omission.

V

VALDÉS, Gabriel de la Concepción (pseudonym Placido; Cuban poet; the firing squad had merely wounded him):
Good-bye, world! . . . Good-bye, Cuba . . . There is no mercy for me. . . . Fire here.

VALENTINO, Rudolph:
Don't pull down the blinds! I feel fine. I want the sunlight to greet me.

VANDERBILT, Cornelius:
I'll never give up trust in Jesus. How could I let that go?

VANE, Sir Harry (on the scaffold):
Father, glorify Thy servant in the sight of men, that he may glorify Thee in the discharge of his duty to Thee and to his country.

VAN GOGH, Vincent:
Now I want to go home.

VANINI, Lucilio (philosopher; burned as atheist and magician):
There is neither God nor devil: for if there were a God, I would pray him to send a thunderbolt on the Council, as all that is unjust and iniquitous; and if there were a devil, I would pray him to engulf it in the subterannean regions; but since there is neither one nor the other, there is nothing for me to do.

VANZETTI, Bartolomeo:
I want to thank you, I want to thank you for everything you have done for me, warden. . . . I wish to

tell you, all of you, that I am innocent. I have never done a crime. Maybe, oh yes, maybe sometimes I done some sin, but not a crime. I am innocent of all crime, not only of this, but of all, of all. I am an innocent man. . . . I wish to forgive some people for what they are now doing to me.

VARGAS, G. D. (president of Brazil; suicide letter):
I fought against the looting of the people. I have fought barebreasted. The hatred, infamy and calumny did not beat down my spirit. I gave you my life. Now I offer my death. Nothing remains. Serenely I take the first step on the road to eternity and I leave life to enter history.

VEBLEN, Thorstein (economist; note):
It is also my wish, in case of death, to be cremated, if it can be conveniently done, as expeditiously and inexpensively as may be, without ritual or ceremony of any kind; that my ashes be thrown loose into the sea, or into some sizable stream running to the sea; that no tombstone, inscription, or monument of any name or nature, be set up in my memory or name in any place or at any time; that no obituary, memorial, portrait, or biography of me, nor any letters written to or by me be printed or published, or in any way reproduced, copied or circulated.

VESPASIAN (struggling to get on his feet):
An Emperor ought to die standing.

VETSERA, Mary (in suicide pact with Rudolf at Mayerling; letter to Marie Larisch):
Dear Marie, Forgive me all the trouble I have caused. I thank you so much for everything you have done for me. If life becomes hard for you, and I fear it will

after what we have done, follow us. *It is the best thing you can do. Your Mary.*

VICTOR EMMANUEL II (of Italy; to the doctor):
How much longer will it last? I had some important things to attend to.

VICTORIA, Queen:
Bertie [*her name for the new king*].

VIDOCQ, François Eugène (detective; to the priest):
You, you . . . my only physician.

VIGNY, Alfred de:
Pray for me, pray to God for me.

VILLARS, Louis Hector, Duc de (marshal of France; told that the Duke of Berwick had just perished by a cannon ball):
I had always contended that that man was born luckier than I!

VINCENT de Paul, Saint:
Jesus.

VITELLIUS (slain in civil war; to the insults of a tribune):
Yet I was your Emperor.

VOLTAIRE (taking his old valet's hand):
Adieu, my dear Morand, I am dying.

W

WAGNER, Richard:
Call my wife and the doctor.

WAIBLINGER, Wilhelm (German poet):
Addio!

WALKER, James J. (at first resisted his nurse's order to lie back, but then learned she was a Democrat):
In that case, I shall abide by the wishes of a fair Constituent.

WALLACE, Gen. Lew (author of *Ben Hur;* to his wife):
We meet in Heaven.

WARD, Sam:
I think I am going to give up the ghost.

WARWICK, Mary Rich, Countess of (pietist):
Ladies, if I were but one hour in Heaven, I would not be again with you, well as I love you.

WASHINGTON, Booker T. (former slave):
Take me home. I was born in the South, I have lived and labored in the South, and I wish to die and be buried in the South.

WASHINGTON, George:
'Tis well.

WASSERMANN, Jakob (his companion's name):
Marta.

WATERFORD, Louisa, Marchioness of:
Oh darling Adelaide, goodness and beauty, beauty and goodness, those are ever the great things!

WATSON, Thomas E. (Georgia senator):
I am not afraid—I am not afraid to die.

WATT, James (to the friends assembled around his bed):
*I am very sensible of the attachment you show me,
and I hasten to thank you for it, as I feel that I am
now come to my last illness.*

WATTS, Isaac (hymn-writer; asked if he experienced the
comfort of the words, "I will never leave thee, nor forsake
thee"):
I do.

WAYNE, "Mad Anthony":
*This is the end. . . . I am dying. . . . I can't bear up
much longer. . . . Bury me here on the hill—by the
flagpole.*

WEBB, Mary (novelist; told they would all have tea together in the afternoon):
That will be nice.

WEBER, Carl Maria von:
Now let me sleep.

WEBSTER, Daniel:
I still live . . . poetry . . .

WEBSTER, Noah (lexicographer):
*I have struggled with many difficulties. Some I have
been able to overcome, and by some I have been overcome. I have made many mistakes, but I love my
country, and have labored for the youth of my country, and I trust no precept of mine has taught any
dear youth to sin.*

WEED, Thurlow (journalist and politician):
I want to go home!

WELLINGTON, Duke of:
Do you know where the apothecary lives? . . . Then send and let him know that I should like to see him. I don't feel quite well and I will lie still till he comes.

WELLS, H. G. (to the nurse):
Go away. I'm all right.

WESLEY, John:
Farewell.

WHATELY, Richard (English logician and theologian; objecting to his chaplain's reading Anglican version of Philippians iii, 21, "Who shall change our vile body," the chaplain repeated from memory the literal translation, "This body of our humiliation"):
That's right, not vile—*nothing that He made is vile.*

WHITE, Joseph Blanco (British theological writer):
Now I die.

WHITE, Henry Kirke (poet; letter from Cambridge to his brother):
Our lectures began on Friday, but I do not attend them until I am better. I have not written to my mother, nor shall I while I remain unwell. You will tell her, as a reason, that our lectures began on Friday. I know she will be uneasy, if she do not hear from me, and still more so, if I tell her I am ill. I cannot write more at present, than that I am your truly affectionate brother, H. K. White.

WHITEFIELD, George:
I am dying.

WHITGIFT, John (archbishop of Canterbury):
In behalf of the Church of God.

WHITMAN, Walt:
Shift, Warry.

WHITNEY, William C. (politician):
Don't get angry, nurse. I love my son and daughter. It does me good to chat with them.

WHITTIER, John Greenleaf (in response to a question from his niece):
I have known thee all the time.

WICKSTEED, Philip Henry (Dante scholar):
Hurrah, hurrah!

WIELAND, Christoph Martin (German poet):
To be or not to be.

WILBERFORCE, William (English philanthropist and antislavery crusader; his son had said, "You have your feet on the Rock"):
I do not venture to speak so positively, but I hope I have.

WILD, Jonathan (end of alleged last speech, but he had taken laudanum and may not have said anything; on the scaffold):
There is little occasion to mention my religion, since I always thought every religion the offspring of the brain of some politician and denied the existence of that Being who is the basis and foundation of all religion and society. If I merit any pity from you, as you are men, I desire your prayers as you are Christians, the last favor that I have to ask in this world. I die in full persuasion that there is an Eternal Being and that Jesus Christ died for my sins, of Whom I humbly ask forgiveness and to Whom I commend my soul.

WILDE, Sir William (surgeon; father of Oscar; his two sons were having a noisy party):
Oh, those boys, those boys!

WILHELM I, Kaiser (hearing the minister say, "I trust in the Lord, my soul likewise, and I hope in His word"):
That was beautiful.

WILHELM II:
I am sinking.

WILLARD, Frances (educator and reformer):
How beautiful it is to be with God!

WILLIAM the Conqueror:
I commend myself to our blessed Lady, Mary the mother of God, that she by her holy intercession may reconcile me to her son, our Lord Jesus Christ.

WILLIAM II (to Walter Tirel, who shot, but not the deer):
Shoot, Walter, shoot—as if it were the devil.

WILLIAM III:
Can this last long? ... Bentinck.

WILLIAM the Silent (founder of Dutch Republic; asked, "Do you trust your soul to Jesus Christ?"):
Yes.

WLLIAMS, Alfred (English poet; to his dying wife):
My dear! This is going to be a tragedy for us both.

WILLIAMS, Horace (American philosopher; the nurse asked his name):
Horace Williams.

WILLIAMS, John Sharp (Mississippi senator):
I've done things that seemed at the time worth doing. I think that if a man can get to my age and, looking back, believe a majority of things he did were worth the effort, he has nothing to regret.

WILLKIE, Wendell (note):
I enjoyed our talk this morning very much. Frankly,

I cannot answer your ultimate question [whom he would support] yet because I have not fully decided.

WILSON, Edward (physician lost on the antarctic expedition of Scott; letter to wife):

... God knows I am sorry to be the cause of sorrow to anyone in the world, but everyone must die—and at every death there must be some sorrow. All the things I had hoped to do with you after this Expedition are as nothing now, but there are greater things for us to do in the world to come. My only regret is leaving you to struggle through your life alone, but I may be coming to you by a quicker way. I feel so happy now in having got time to write to you. One of my notes will surely reach you. Dad's little compass and Mother's little comb and looking-glass are in my pocket. Your little testament and prayer book will be in my hand or in my breast pocket when the end comes. All is well.

WILSON, Woodrow (his wife's name):
Edith.

WINDOM, William, (secretary of the Treasury; speech):
Give us direct and ample transportation facilities under the American flag, and controlled by American citizens; a currency sound in quality and adequate in quantity; an international bank to facilitate exchanges, and a system of reciprocity carefully adjusted within the lines of protection—and not only will our foreign commerce again invade every sea, but every American industry will be quickened, and our whole people feel the impulse of a new and enduring prosperity.

WIRZ, Captain Henry (stockade commander convicted of mistreatment of Union prisoners at Andersonville, Georgia; to the hangman):

*This is too tight; loosen it a little. I am innocent.
I will have to die sometime. I will die like a man.
My hopes are in the future.*

WISHART, George (Scottish martyr; on being asked by
the executioner for forgiveness, kissed him):
*Come hither to me. . . . Lo, here is a token that I for-
give thee. My heart, do thine office.*

WITT, Cornelius de (Dutch official; brother of John; to
the mob that tore them to pieces):
*What do you want me to do? Where do you want me
to go?*

WITT, John de (Dutch statesman; to the angry mob):
What are you doing? This is not what you wanted.

WOLCOT, John (pseudonym Peter Pindar; satirist; asked
if anything could be done for him):
Bring me back my youth.

WOLFE, Charles (author of the poem "The Burial of Sir
John Moore"):
*Close this eye, the other is closed already; and now
farewell!*

WOLFE, General James:
*Who run? . . . Go one of you, my lads, with all speed
to Colonel Burton, and tell him to march Webb's
regiment down to the St. Charles River, and cut off
the retreat of the fugitives to the bridge. Now God
be praised, I die happy.*

WOLLSTONECRAFT, Mary (Godwin) (feminist; died
giving birth to the future Mary Shelley; of her husband):
He is the kindest, best man in the world.

WOLSEY, Thomas, Cardinal:
*Master Kingston, farewell. I can no more, but wish
all things to have good success. My time draweth on*

fast. I may not tarry with you. And forget not, I pray you, what I have said and charged you withal, for when I am dead ye shall peradvanture remember my words much better.

WOOD, Grant (American painter; his sister's name):
Nan.

WOOLF, Virginia (suicide note to her husband):
I have a feeling I shall go mad. I cannot go on any longer in these terrible times. I hear voices and cannot concentrate on my work. I have fought against it but cannot fight any longer. I owe all my happiness to you but cannot go on and spoil your life.

WOOLLCOTT, Alexander (stricken at a broadcast):
Go back in there. Never mind me. Go back in there.

WOOLMAN, John (Quaker preacher and abolitionist; written):
I believe my being here is in the wisdom of Christ. I know not as to life or death.

WOOLSTON, Thomas (English deist):
This is a struggle which all men must go through, and which I bear not only patiently but with willingness.

WOOLTON, John (bishop of Exeter):
A bishop ought to die standing.

WORDSWORTH, William (having been told by his wife, with reference to their dead daughter, "William, you are going to Dora;" when a niece was drawing the curtains twenty-four hours later):
Is that Dora?

WRIGHT, Joseph (English philologist):
Dictionary.

WYATT, Sir Thomas (conspirator; son of the poet):

Then let every man beware how he taketh any thing in hand against the higher powers! Unless God be prosperable to his purpose it will never take good effect or success, whereof you may now learn of me, and I pray God I may be the last example in this place, for that or any other life. And where it is said and noised abroad that I should accuse the lady Elizabeth and the lord Courtney, it is not so, good people, for I assure you, neither they nor any other now yonder in hold was privy of my rising before I began, as I have declared no less to the queen's council, and that is most true.

WYCHERLEY, William (upon his young wife's promise not to deny him one last request):

My dear, it is only this, that you will never marry an old man again.

WYLIE, Elinor (American poet; after a glass of water had been brought):

Is that all it is?

X

XAVIER, St. Francis (Te Deum):
In Thee, O Lord, have I hoped, let me never be confounded!

XIMENES (Jimenez) de Cisneros, Cardinal (Spanish minister; from the Psalm):
In Thee, O Lord, have I hoped.

Υ

YANCEY, "Cap'n Bob" (Virginia attorney):
*I will just lie here for a few minutes—I will stay here
a little while, just to please you—don't leave me, little
lady. I love to watch your bright young face. Two
things in this world I have always loved—a bright
young face and—walking in the sunshine.*

YANCEY, William Lowndes (politician):
*I am dying; all is well; it is God's will. . . . Sarah
[his wife's name].*

YEATS, Jack B. (artist; father of the poet; spoken to a
friend):
*Remember, you have promised me a sitting in the
morning.*

YEATS, William Butler (letter):
*In two or three weeks—I am now idle that I may rest
after writing much verse—I will begin to write my
most fundamental thoughts and the arrangement of
thought which I am convinced will complete my studies. I am happy and I think full of an energy I had
despaired of. It seems to me that I have found what
I wanted. When I try to put all into a phrase I say
'Man can embody truth but he cannot know it.' I
must embody it in the completion of my life. The
abstract is not life and everywhere drags out its con-
tradictions. You can refute Hegel but not the Saint
or the Song of Sixpence.*

YOUNG, Brigham:
I feel better.

YSAYE, Eugene (Belgian violinist; after his Fourth Sonata was played for him):

Splendid . . . the finale just a little too fast.

Z

ZEISBERGER, David (Moravian missionary in America):
The Saviour is near! perhaps He will soon call and take me home!

ZENO of Citium (founder of the Stoic school; striking the ground with his hand when he tripped):
I come, I come, why dost thou call for me?

ZENZABURO, Taki (an officer of the Prince of Bizen; hara-kiri):
I, and I alone, unwarrantably gave the order to fire on the foreigners at Kobe, and again as they tried to escape. For this crime I disembowel myself, and I beg you who are present to do me the honour of witnessing the act.

ZEPPELIN, Count Ferdinand von:
I have perfect faith.

ZIMMERMANN, Johann Georg von (Swiss physician and philosopher):
Leave me to myself, I am dying.

ZINZENDORF, Count Nicholas Lewis von (religious leader):
Now, my dear son, I am going to the Saviour, I am ready, I am quite resigned to the will of my Lord, and He is satisfied with me. If he is no longer willing to make use of me here, I am quite ready to go to Him; for there is nothing more in my way.

ZOLA, Emile:

I feel sick. My head is splitting. . . . No, don't you see the dog is sick too. We are both ill: it must be something we have eaten. It will pass away. Let us not bother them.

ZWEIG, Stefan (Austrian biographer and novelist; suicide letter):

. . . After I saw the country of my own language fall, and my spiritual land—Europe—destroying itself, and as I reach the age of sixty, it would require immense strength to reconstruct my life, and my energy is exhausted by long years of peregrination as one without a country. Therefore, I believe it is time to end a life which was dedicated only to spiritual work, considering human liberty and my own as the greatest wealth in the world. I leave an affectionate goodbye to all my friends.

ZWINGLI, Ulrich (fallen at the battle of Kappel):

You can kill the body, but you cannot kill the soul.

SOURCES

Where the source is a biography, in English, of the person quoted, whose name appears, in some form, in the main title, the title is not given: author, place of publication, and date being a sufficient identification. Titles of biographies in French, German, Italian, and Spanish are at least partly given. The compiler has translated occasionally from the Greek and Latin also, but generally has relied on such English versions of the ancients as were conveniently at hand. B=Boston; E= Edinburgh; L=London; N=New York; P=Paris; Ph=Philadelphia.

ABBOT: Arthur Onslow (Guildford, 1777), 154.

ABBOTT: *Dictionary of National Biography*, I, 29.

ABD - ALLAH BEN - ZOBAIR: M. Quatremère, *Mémoire Historique sur la Vie d'* (P, 1832), 166.

ABDALRAHMAN III: Edward Gibbon, *Decline and Fall of the Roman Empire*, Ch. LII.

ABERDEEN: E. B. Elliott (L,1868), 361.

ABERNETHY: George Macilwain (N, 1853), 408.

ABIMELECH: Judges, IX, 54.

ACCORAMBONI: Domenico Gnoli, *Vittoria Accoramboni* (Florence, 1870), 326.

ACHARD: Abbé de Jumièges (Marquis de Fortia), *Vie de* (P, 1830), 42-43.

ADAM: John G. Lockhart, *Memoirs of the Life of Sir Walter Scott* (B, 1901), I, 28.

ADAMS, Abigail: Dorothie Bobbé (N, 1929), 326.

ADAMS, Alice: Henry Phelps Johnston, *Nathan Hale* (N, 1901), 202·

ADAMS, H.: Harold Dean Cater (B, 1947), cvi.

ADAMS, J.: J. Q. and Charles Francis Adams (Philadelphia, 1871), II, 405.

ADAMS, Dr. J.: M. E. B[rown] and H. G. B[rown] (N, 1900), 261-62.

ADAMS, J. Q.: Bennett Champ Clark (B, 1932), 418.

ADDAMS: James H. Linn (N, 1935), 421.

ADDISON: Edward Young, *Conjectures on Original Composition* (in *The Great Critics*, ed. James

308.

ANNE, Queen: M. R. Hopkinson (N, 1934), 359

ANNE of Austria: Jean de La Varende, *Anne d'Autriche* (P, 1938), 275-76.

ANSELM: Martin Rule (L, 1883), II, 405.

ANTOINETTE: John Carber Pulache (N, 1920), 309.

ANTONINUS: Pauly - Wissowa, *Real-Encyclopädie der Classischen Altertumswissenschaft*, II, 2504.

ANTONY, Saint: S. Baring-Gould, *Lives of the Saints* (E, 1914), I, 271-72.

ANTONY, Mark: Arthur Weigall (N, 1931), 466.

AQUINAS: Dr. Martin Grabmann (N, 1928), 15-16.

ARAM: Anonymous, *Trial and Life of Eugene Aram* (Richmond, 1832), 62.

ARATUS: Plutarch, *Lives* (Modern Library edition, 1250).

ARCHIMEDES: Sir Thomas Heath (L, 1920), 4.

ARETINO: Thomas C. Chubb (N, 1940), 450.

ARGYLL, Marquess of: John Willcock (Edinburgh, 1903), 330

ARGYLL, Archibald: John Willcock (Edinburgh, 1907), 421.

ARMISTEAD: Karl Baedeker, *The United States* (Leipzig, 1909), 194.

ARMSTRONG: John Laurence, *A History of Capital Punishment* (L, n.d.), 131.

ARNAULD: Frances Martin (L, 1873), 324.

ARNOLD, B.: Edward Dean Sullivan (N, 1932), 300.

ARNOLD, T.: A. P. Stanley (L, 1901), 660.

ARRIA: *Oxford Classical Dictionary* (Oxford, 1949), 101.

ARTAGERSES: Plutarch, *Lives* (Modern Library, 1256).

ARUNDEL: Duke of Norfolk, E. M., ed. (L, 1857), 120.

ARVERS: *Poésies*, ed. Abel d'Avrecourt (P, 1900), xvi.

ASCHAM: Disertissimi viri Rogeri Aschami ... familiarum epistolarum (L, 1576), Aa10.

ASTE: Lodovico Maria Pandolfini, *Ristretto della Vita di* (Rome, 1711), 170.

ASTROS: R. P. Caussette, *Vie du Cardinal d'Astros* (P, 1853), 637.

ATCHESON: Berkeley (California) *Daily Gazette*, Aug. 18, 1947, 1.

ATTICUS: Louis L. Snyder, ed., *A Treasury of Intimate Biographies* (N, 1951), 14.

AUBIGNÉ: S. Rocheblave, *Agrippa d'Aubigné* (P, 1910), 47.

AURELIUS, M.: F. H. Hayward (L, 1935), 257.

AURELIUS, Q.: Plutarch, *Lives* (Modern Library, 570).

AURUNGZEBE: Stanley Lane-Poole (Oxford, 1893), 204.

AUSTEN: Elizabeth Jenkins (N, 1949), 395.

AUSTIN: Eugene C. Barker (Nashville, 1925), 520.

BABAR: Sir George Dunbar, *A History of India* (L, 1936), 168. ("Last" words too famous to omit, but Babar lived for three months afterward.)

BABINGTON: *Dictionary of National Biography*, II, 310.

BACHAUMONT: *Mémoires Secrets* (L, 1784), V, 259; cf. edition ed. by P. L. Jacob (pseud. of Paul Lacroix) (P, 1859), 467, note.

BACHMAN: Anonymous, *J o h n Bachman* (Charleston, 1888), 427.

BACON: James Spedding (B, 1878),

II, 620.

BAEDEKER: Robert S. Latimer (L, 1907) , 211.

BAGEHOT: Mrs. Russell Barrington (L, 1915), 453-54.

BAILLY: Fernand-Laurent, *Jean-Sylvain Bailly* (P, 1927) , 455.

BAINHAM: Fox's *Book of Martyrs*, ed. Cumming (L, 1851) , II, 333-34.

BALBOA: Paul Gaffarel ,*Nuñez de Balboa* (P, 1882), 149.

BALDWIN: C. B. Glasscock (Indianapolis, 1933) , 302.

BALZAC: Katherine P. Wormeley (B, 1892) , 344.

BANCROFT: George F. Hoar, *Autobiography of Seventy Years* (N, 1905), II, 206.

BANNISTER: John Adolphus (L, 1838) , II, 339.

BARBUSSE: Jacques Duclos and Jean Fréville, *Henri Barbusse* (P, 1946) , 22.

• BARHAM: *The Ingoldsby Legends* (L, 1889), 331.

BARING: Laura Lovat (L, 1947) , 32.

BARNATO: Richard Lewinsohn (N, 1938) , 265.

BARNAVE: Thomas Carlyle, *The French Revolution*, Book VII, ch. ii.

BARNEVELD: John L. Motley (N, 1904), II, 387.

BARRE: Michaud's *Biographie Universelle*, III, 150.

BARRIE: Dennis Mackail (N, 1941), 717.

BARRON: Arthur Pound and Samuel T. Moore, ed., *They Told Barron* (N, 1930) , xxxii.

BARROW: John Aubrey, *Brief Lives*, ed. Oliver L. Dick (L, 1950), 20.

BARRYMORE: Gene Fowler, *Good*

Night, Sweet Prince (N, 1944) , 468.

BARTON: Blanche Colton Williams (Philadelphia, 1941), 435.

BASEDOW: Richard Diestelmann, *Johann Bernhard Basedow* (Leipzig, 1897) , 89.

BASHKIRTSEFF: Dormer Creston, *Fountains of Youth* (N, 1937), 304.

BASS: Wayne Gard (B, 1936) , 221.

BASTIAT: Georges de Nouvion, *Fréderic Bastiat* (P, 1905), 347.

BAXTER: Frederick J. Powicke (L, 1927) , 165.

BAYARD: Samuel J. Bayard (N, 1874), 274.

BAYARD: Michaud's *Biographie Universelle*, III, 336.

BEARD: *Dictionary of American Biography*, II, 93.

BEATON: James Anthony Froude, *History of England* (L, 1898) , IV, 183.

BEATRIX: Wilhelm Treichlinger, *Abschiedsbriefe* (Berlin, 1934) , 24.

BEAUMONT: Joseph Beaumont (Son) (L, 1856) , 395.

BECKET: James A. Froude, *Short Studies of Great Subjects*, 4th Series (N, 1901) , 113.

BECKFORD: Lewis Melville (L, 1910), 349.

BEDDOES: H. W. Donner, ed., *Works* (L, 1935) , 683.

BEDE: *Dictionary of National Biography*, IV, 101.

BEDELL: [Gilbert Burnet] (L, 1685) , 216.

BEECHER, C.: Lyman Beecher Stowe (Indianapolis, 1934) , 136.

BEECHER, H. W.: Thomas W. Knox (Hartford, 1887), 529.

BEECHER, L.: Lyman Beecher Stowe (Indianapolis, 1934) , 72.

BEETHOVEN: Louis Nohl (Chicago, 1881), 199.

BÉHAINE: J. Jardinier Vervins, *Notice sur* (P, 1866) , 15.

BELL, A.: Henry and Dana Lee Thomas, *Life Stories of the Great Inventors* (N, 1948), 166.

BELL, C.: Amédée Pichot, *Sir Charles Bell, Histoire de sa Vie et de ses Travaux* (P, 1858) , 216.

BELLARMINE: James Brodrick (L, 1928), II, 452.

BENEDEK: Heinrich Friedjung, ed., *Benedeks Nachgelassene Papiere* (Dresden, 1904) , 425.

BENEDICT: Anonymous, *A Memorial of* (Albany, 1866), 85.

BENEZET: Roberts Vaux (Philadelphia, 1817) , 148.

BENJAMIN: Pierce Butler (Philadelphia, 1907), 417.

BENNETT: Reginald Pound (N, 1953) , 367.

BENSON: C. C. Martindale, S. J. (L, 1916), II, 433.

BENTHAM: Charles M. Atkinson (L, 1905) , 207-08.

BENTON: William M. Meigs (Ph, 1904), 517.

BÉRANGER: J. Lucas-Dubreton, *Béranger* (P, 1934) , 272.

BERENGER: Dr. Joseph Schnitzer, *Berengar von Tours* (Stuttgart, 1892), 122, n. 3.

BERLIOZ: Jacques Barzun (B, 1950) , II, 296.

BERNADETTE: Margaret Gray Blanton (N, 1939), 238.

BERNADOTTE: Ralph Hewins (Minneapolis, 1950) , 224.

BERNARD, St.: M. L'Abbé Ratisbonne (N, n.d.), 474.

BERNARD, C.: J. M. D. Olmsted (N, 1938) , 133.

BERRY: [F. A. R.] de Chateubriand, *Mémoires . . . touchant la Vie* (P, 1820), 262.

BÉRULLE: L'Abbé M. Houssaye, *Le Cardinal de Bérulle* (P, 1875) , 494.

BESSARION: Henri Vast, *Le Cardinal Bassarion* (P, 1878) , 430.

BESTOUJEFF: W. J. Linton, *European Republicans* (L, 1892) , 239.

BEZA: Henry M. Baird (N, 1899), 350.

BICKERSTETH: Rev. T. R. Birks (L, 1851) , II, 470.

BILLINGS: Cyril Clemens (Webster Groves, Missouri, 1932), 158.

BILLY THE KID: Walter Noble Burns (N, 1926) , 284.

BIRON: Gaston Maugras, *Le Duc de Lauzon* (P, 1895), 527-28.

BISMARCK: C. Grant Robertson (N, 1919) , 512.

BLACKIE: Anna M. Stoddart (E, 1895) , II, 346.

BLAKE: Mona Wilson (N, 1949) , 317.

BLANDY: August Mencken, *By the Neck* (N, 1942), 253.

BLAURER: Theodor Pressel, *Ambrosius Blaurer's des Schwäbischen Reformators Leben und Schriften* (Stuttgart, 1861) , 512.

BLOMFIELD: Alfred Blomfield (L, 1863), II, 270.

BLÜCHER: Friedrich Foerster, *Der Feldmarshall Fürst Bluecher* (Leipzig, 1821) , 308-09.

BLUM: Wilhelm Liebknecht, *Robert Blum und Seine Zeit* (Nürnberg, 1896), 463.

BLUNTSCHLI: Alphonse Rivier, *Notice sur M. Bluntschli* (Bruelles, 1882) , 5.

BOAS: Paul Rivet in *Renaissance*, I (1943), 313.

BODWELL: Anonymous, *In Memoriam Hon. Joseph R. Bodwell* (Augusta, Maine, 1888) , 16.

BOEHME: Howard H. Brinton,

The Mystic Will (N, 1930), 56.

BOGUE: James Bennett (L, 1827), 365.

BOILEAU: Michaud's *Biographie Universelle*, V, 13.

BOLEYN: Miss [Elizabeth Ogilvy] Benger (Ph, 1822), 372.

BOLINGBROKE: Walter Sichel (N, 1902), II, 399.

BOLIVAR: Thomas Rourke (N, 1939), 357.

BONAPARTE, Mme. Jerome: Eugene L. Didier (N, 1879), 266.

BONAPARTE, P. B.: Joseph Turquan, *Les Soeurs de Napoléon* (P, n.d.), 321.

BONIFACE: Jacobus a Voragine, *Golden Legend*.

BONNET: Le duc de Caraman, *Charles Bonnet, Philosophe et Naturaliste* (P, 1859), 349.

BOOTH, E.: Eleanor Ruggles (N, 1953), 374.

BOOTH, J. W.: Carl Sandburg, *Abraham Lincoln, The War Years* (N, 1939), IV, 402.

BOOTH, J. B.: Mrs. Asia (Booth) Clarke (N, 1870), 153.

BOOTH, W.: St. John Ervine (N, 1935), II, 810.

BORGIA: Ferdinand Gregorovius (N, 1903), 356-57.

BÖRNE: Michael Holzmann, *Ludwig Börne, Sein Leben und sein Wirken* (Berlin, 1888), 360.

BORODIN: M. D. Calvocoressi and Gerald Abraham, *Masters of Russian Music* (N, 1936), 174.

BORROMEO: Margaret Yeo (Milwaukee, 1938), 298.

BOSCO: A. Auffray (L, 1930), 382.

BOSSUET: [Henrietta Farrer] (L, 1874), 582.

BOUFFLERS: Nesta H. Webster (N, 1924), 416.

BOUHOURS: Michaud's *Biographie Universelle*, V, ?11.

BOURBON: Ed. Garnier, *Louis de Bourbon, Evêque-Prince de Liège* (P, 1860), 169.

BOURG: P. Griffet, "Dissertation sur le Procès d'Anne du Bourg," in *Collections des Meilleurs Dissertations . . . relatifs à L'Histoire de France* (P, 1838), XVIII, 16.

BOUVIER: J. Emile Roberty, *Auguste Bouvier, Théologien Protestant* (P, n.d.), 336.

BOWDITCH, H.: Vincent Y. Bowditch (B, 1902), II, 369.

BOWDITCH, N.: Anonymous, *Memoir* (B, 1841), 157.

BOWLES: George S. Merriam (N, 1885), II, 438.

BRACE: *Life . . . told in his own letters*, ed. by his daughter (N, 1894), 479.

BRADFORD: Fox's Book of Martyrs, ed. Cumming (L, 1851), III, 232.

BRAHE: J. T. B. Helfrecht, *Tycho Brahe geschildert nach seinen Leben* (Hof, 1798), 162.

BRAHMS: Richard Specht (L, 1930), 357.

BRAINERD: Jonathan Edwards (New Haven, 1822), 431.

BRANDT: *Time*, June 14, 1948, 22.

BRASIDAS: Thucydides, V, 10.

BREITINGER: J. G. Mörikofer, *Breitinger und Zürich* (Leipsig, 1874), 294.

BREMER: Charlotte Bremer (N, 1880), 98.

BRERETON: Philip W. Sergeant, *Life of Anne Boleyn* (N, 1924), 293.

BRIGGS: William C. Richards (B, 1867), 411.

BRINDLEY: Samuel Smiles, *Lives of the Engineers* (L, 1904), I, 352.

BRISBANE, Albert: Redelia Brisbane (B, 1893), 43.

BRISBANE, Arthur: Oliver Carlson (N, 1937), 346.

BRODERICK: Jeremiah Lynch, *A Senator of the Fifties* (San Francisco, 1910), 224.

BRONTE, A.: Margaret Lane, *The Brontë Story* (N, 1953), 290.

BRONTE, B.: Clement Shorter, *The Brontës* (N, 1900), I, 465.

BRONTE, C.: E, G Gaskoll, Everyman's Library, 400.

BRONTE, E.: *Ibid.*, 258.

BROOK, G.: W. L. Lawrence (Belfast, 1892), 273.

BROOKE, J.: Gertrude L. Jacob, *The Raja of Sarawak* (L, 1876), II, 367.

BROOKE, R.: Arthur Stringer, *Red Wine of Youth* (Indianapolis, 1948), 261.

BROOKE, S.: Lawrence P. Jacks (L, 1917), II, 675.

BROOKINGS: Hermann Hagedorn (N, 1936), 315.

BROOKS, E. G.: E. Streeter Brooks (B, 1881), 240.

BROOKS, P.: Alexander V. G. Allen (N, 1900), II, 940.

BROWN, A.: C. S. Brown (Worcester, 1849), 219.

BROWN, Rev. J.: Anonymous, *Life and Remains* (Aberdeen, 1845), 187.

BROWN, J.: August Mencken, *By the Neck* (N, 1942), 185.

BROWNING, E. B.: David Loth, *The Brownings* (N, 1929), 219.

BROWNING, R.: *Ibid.*, 284.

BRUCE: Jean Froissart, *Chroniques*, I, xx.

BRUNO: V. Spampanato, *Vita di Giordano Bruno* (Messina, 1921), 585.

BRUTUS: Dio, *Roman History*, end of Book XLVII.

BRYAN: Paxton Hibben (N, 1929), 405.

BRYANT: Parke Godwin (N, 1883), II, 405.

BUCER: Alfred Erichson, *Martin Butzer, der Elsässische Reformator* (Strassburg, 1891), 69.

BUCHANAN, G.: D. Macmillan (Edinburgh, 1906), 275.

BUCHANAN, J · George Ticknor Curtis (N, 1883), II, 686.

BUCHANAN, R.: Harriett Jay (L, 1903), 312.

BUCHER: Car. Franc. Christ. Wagner, *Memoriam Viri Perillustris Ioannis Petri Bucheri* (Marburg, 1820), 19.

BÜCHNER: *London Times Literary Supplement*, Dec. 21, 1951, p. 820.

BUCKINGHAM I: Sir Dudley Carleton to Queen Henrietta Maria in *The Five Hundred Best English Letters*, ed. 1st Earl of Birkenhead (L, 1931), 78.

BUCKINGHAM II, Winifred, Lady Burghclere (N, 1903), 398-99.

BUCKLAND: George C. Bompas (L, 1885), 423.

BUCKLE: Alfred Henry Huth (N, 1880), 456.

BUDDHA: *Encyclopaedia Britannica*, 9th ed., IV, 432.

BUDGELL: *Dictionary of National Biography*, VII, 225.

BUDGETT: William Arthur, *The Successful Merchant* (N, n.d.), 410.

BUGEAUD: Count H.d'Ideville (L, 1884), II, 360.

BULL, G.: Robert Nelson (Oxford, 1840), 323.

BULL, W.: Rev. Josiah Bull (L, 1865), 356.

BULLER: Colonel C. H. Melville (L, 1923), II, 288.

BÜLOW: Marie von Bülow, *Leben* (Leipzig, 1921), 573.

BUMBY: Rev. Alfred Barrett (L, 1852), 283.

BUNSEN, Baron: Frances Baroness Bunsen (L, 1868), II, 577.

BUNSEN, Baroness: Augustus J. C. Hare (N, 1879), 475.

BUNYAN: William Hamilton Nelson (Chicago, 1928), 143.

BURGESS: Rev. Alexander Burgess (Ph, 1869), 383.

BURGHLEY: Rev. Edward Nares (L, 1831), III, 483.

BURKE: Ernest Favenc, *The History of Australian Exploration* (Sydney, 1888), 217.

BURN: Anonymous, *Memoirs of the Life of the Late Major-General Andrew Burn* (L, 1815), II, 207.

BURNETT: Vivian Burnett, *The Romantick Lady* (N, 1927), 410.

BURNEY: Percy A. Scholes (L. 1948), II, 259.

BURNS, G.: Edwin Hodder (L, 1890), 501.

BURNS, R.: Preface by Alexander Smith to the *Complete Works* (L, 1868), liii.

BURR: Samuel H. Wardell and Meade Minnigerode (N, 1925), II, 334.

BURROUGHS: Clara Barrus (B, 1925), II, 416.

BURTON, I.: W. H. Wilkins (N, 1908), 770.

BURTON, R.: Seton Dearden (N, 1937), 328.

BUSHNELL: Theodore T. Munger (B, 1899), 351.

BUSONI: Edward J. Dent (L, 1933), 289.

BUTLER, A.: Sir Arthur Quiller-Couch (L, 1917), 223.

BUTLER, B.: *Proceedings and Addresses on the Occasion of the Death of Benjamin F. Butler of New York* (N, 1859), 75.

BUTLER, J.: Thomas Bartlett (L, 1839), 221

BUTLER, S.: Henry Festing Jones (L, 1919), II, 399.

BYRNE: Thurston Macauley (N, 1929), 194.

BYRON: Harold Nicolson (L, 1924), 267.

CABRINI: Theodore Maynard (Milwaukee, 1945), 325.

CADOUDAL: George de Cadoudal, *George Cadoudal et la Chouannerie* (P, 1887), 341.

CAESAR, A.: Suetonius, *Lives of the Twelve Caesars* (Modern Library, 115).

CAESAR, J.: Max Radin, *Marcus Brutus* (N, 1939), 42.

CALHOUN: Dr. H. von Holst (B, 1882), 350.

CALLICRATES: Herodotus, IX, 72.

CALVIN: Philip Schaff, *History of the Christian Church* (N, 1910), VII, 823.

CAMBRONNE: Leon Brunschvigg, *Cambronne, Sa Vie . . .* (Nantes, 1894), 306.

CAMBYSES, Herodotus, III, 65.

CAMBYSES' SISTER: Herodotus, III, 32.

CAMOENS: Wilhelm Storck, *Luis de Camoens Leben* (Paderborn, 1890), 696.

CAMP: Chaplain H. Clay Trumbull, *The Knightly Soldier* (B, 1865), 316.

CAMPAN: Louis B. de Marsangy, *Mme. Campan à Ecouen* (P, 1879), 311.

CAMPBELL: William Beattie (L, 1850), III, 375.

CAMPION: Evelyn Waugh (B,

1946) , 229.

CANIUS: Thomas Lupset, *Life and Works,* ed. John Archer Gee (New Haven, 1928) , 268.

CANNING: Sir Henry Lytton Bulwer, *Historical Characters* (L, 1870), 471.

CANOVA: J. S. Memes (Edinburgh, 1825) , 509.

CAPEL: *The Dying Speeches and Behaviour of the Several State Prisoners that Have Been Executed the Last 300 Years* (L, 1720) , 169.

CARLOS: L. A. Warnkönig, *Don Carlos, Leben* (Stuttgart, 1864) , 159.

CARLYLE, J.: Jane Welsh Carlyle: *A New Selection of Her Letters,* ed. Trudy Bliss (N, 1950), 339.

CARLYLE, T.: David Alec Wilson and David Wilson MacArthur (L, 1934) , 470.

CARNEGIE: Burton J. Hendrick (N, 1932) , II, 384.

CARNOT: A. Lacassagne, *L'Assassinat du Président Carnot* (Lyon, 1894) , 56.

CAROLAN: *Poems* of Carolan, ed. Tomas O Maille (L, 1916) , 41.

CAROLINE: Alice Drayton Greenwood, *Lives of the Hanoverian Queens of England* (L, 1909), I, 411.

CARROLL, C.: Ellen Hart Smith (Cambridge, Mass., 1942) , 311.

CARROLL, L.: Florence Becker Lennon, *Victoria through the Looking-Glass* (N, 1945), 326.

CARSTARES: Robert Herbert Story (L, 1874) , 365.

CARTER: Thomas B. Macaulay, *History of England,* Everyman's Library, III, 97.

CARTERET: W. Baring Pemberton, *The Brilliant Failure of the Eighteenth Century* (L, 1936), 330.

CARUSO: Dorothy Caruso (N, 1945) , 272.

CARY, A.: Mary Clemmer, *A Memorial of Alice and Phoebe Cary* (B, 1885) , 145.

CARY, P.: *Ibid.,* 225.

CASANOVA: Bonamy Dobrée (N, 1933) , 162.

CASAUBON: *Dictionary of National Biography,* IX, 260.

CASSIUS: Plutarch, *Lives* (Modern Library, 1213).

CASTLEREAGH: Ione Leigh (L, 1951), 362.

CATHERINE of Alexandria: Jacobus a Voragine, *Golden Legend.*

CATHERINE of Siena: S. Baring-Gould, *Lives of the Saints* (E, 1914) , IV, 381.

CATHERINE de Medicis: Eugene Defrance, *Catherine de Medicis, Ses Astrologues* (P, 1911) , 295.

CATHERINE of Aragon: Francesca Claremont (L, 1939) , 249.

CATHERINE Howard: Michael Glenne (L, n.d.) , 171.

CATO the Elder: Plutarch, *Lives* (Modern Library, 431).

CATO the Younger: *Ibid.,* 958.

CAUCHY: C. A. Valson, *La Vie et Les Travaux du Baron Cauchy* (P, 1868) , 266.

CAVELL: Helen Judson (N, 1941) , 281.

CAVOUR: Maurice Paléologue (L, 1927) , 294.

CAXTON: Henry R. Plomer (L, 1925), 163.

CAZOTTE: Michaud's *Biographie Universelle,* VII, 290.

CECILIA: Jacobus a Voragine, *Golden Legend.*

CENCI: Carlo Tito Dalbono, *Storia di Beatrice Cenci* (Naples, 1864) ,

405.

CONSTANT: Elizabeth W. Scher-
merhorn (L, 1924), 394.

CONTI: Édouard de Barthelémy,
*La Princesse de Conti d'après sa
Correspondance Inédite* (P, 1875),
177.

COOK: Walter Besant (L, 1890),
144.

COOKE, J.: Ellis Paxson Ober-
holtzer (Ph, 1907), II, 547.

COOKE, W.: Col. W. A. Graham,
The Story of the Little Big Horn
(Harrisburg, 1945), 54.

COOKMAN: Henry B. Ridgaway
N, 1873), 452.

COOPER: Bransby Blake Cooper
(L, 1843), II, 455.

COPLESTON: William James Copleston (L, 1851), 214.

COPLEY: Martha Babcock Amory
(B, 1882), 438.

CORBET: John Aubrey, *Brief Lives*
(ed. Dick, L, 1950, 74).

CORBULO: William Smith, *A New
Classical Dictionary of Greek and
Roman Biography, Mythology,
and Geography,* ed. Charles
Anthon (N, 1851), s.v.

CORDAY: Jules Michelet, *Les
Femmes de la Revolution* in
Barrett H. Clark, ed., *Great Short
Biographies of the World* (N,
1937), 1011.

COROT: Henry and Dana Lee
Thomas, *Living Biographies of
Great Painters* (N, 1940), 216.

CORYAT: *Coryat's Crudities* (L,
1776), III, p. preceding Ff.

COSIN: Percy H. Osmond (L,
1913), 301.

COURTRIGHT: Eugene Cunningham, *Triggernometry* (Caldwell,
Id., 1941), 216.

COWPER: David Cecil, *The
Stricken Deer* (Indianapolis, 1930),
326.

COX: F. Gordon Roe (N, 1924), 34.

CRABBE: George Crabbe (son)
(Oxford World's Classics), 302.

CRAIGIE: *Life of John Oliver
Hobbes told in her Correspondence* (L, 1911), 37.

CRANE, H.: Furnished the compiler by Mr. Samuel Loveman,
who heard it from a passenger
on the "Orizaba."

CRANE, S.: John Berryman (N,
1950), 259-60.

CRANMER: Arthur Styron, *The
Three Pelicans* (N, 1932), 401.

CRANTOR: Diogenes Laertius, IV,
5 (25).

CRATES: *Ibid.*, VI, 5 (92).

CRAWFORD: Maud Howe Elliott
(N, 1934), 308.

CREAM: John Laurence, *A History
of Capital Punishment* (L, n.d.),
125.

CREIGHTON: Mrs. Creighton (L,
1904), II, 464.

CRITTENDEN: Mrs. Chapman
Coleman (Ph, 1873), II, 368.

CROKER: Louis J. Jennings, ed.
(N, 1884), II, 558.

CROLL: James Campbell Irons (L,
1896), 488.

CROME: *Dictionary of National
Biography,* XIII, 142.

CROMWELL, O.: Thomas Carlyle,
ed. S. C. Lomas (L, 1904), III,
218.

CROMWELL, T.: John Stow,
Annals (L, 1615), 580.

CROSBY: Mary Crosby (N, 1892),
66.

CROWFOOT: John Peter Turner,
*The North-West Mounted Police,
1873-1893* (Ottawa, 1950), II, 484.

CUMMINGS: W. N. P. Barbellion,
A Last Diary (N, 1920), xxxiv.

CUMMINS: [Mrs. Alexandrine
Cummins] (N, 1878), 522.

DENNIS: Anonymous, *Life of Mr. John Dennis, the Renowned Critick* (L, 1834) , 57.

DENTON: J. Quinn Thornton, *The California Tragedy* (Oakland, Calif., 1945), 77.

DE QUINCEY: Horace Ainsworth Eaton (N, 1936), 506.

DESCARTES: Elizabeth S. Haldane (L, 1905) , 357.

DESMOULINS, C: Jules Claretie (L, 1876) , 350.

DESMOULINS, L.: *Ibid.*, 364.

DE VEGA: George Henry Lewes, *The Spanish Drama* (in Barrett H. Clark, ed., *Great Short Biographies of the World,* N, 1937, 600-01) .

DEWEY: Laurin Hall Healy and Luis Kutner, *The Admiral* (Chicago, 1944) , 310.

DIAGHILEFF: Arnold L. Haskell and Walter Nouvel (N, 1935), 329.

DICKENS: John Forster (N, n.d.) , 522.

DICKINSON: Martha Dickinson Bianchi (B, 1924) , 100.

DIDEROT: John Morley (L, 1914) , II, 259.

DIENECES: Herodotus, VII, 226.

DIESEL: Henry and Dana Lee Thomas, *Life Stories of the Great Inventors* (N, 1948) , 229.

DIGBY: John Aubrey, *Brief Lives* (ed. Dick, L, 1950, 96) .

DIOGENES: Diogenes Laertius, VI, 2 (32) .

DISRAELI: William F. Monypenny and George E. Buckle (L, 1929) , II, 1488.

DIXON: J. B. Booth (L, 1936) , 278.

DODD: Percy Fitzgerald (L, 1865) , 192.

DODE: Gen. Moreau, *Notice sur le Vicomte* (P, 1852) , 161.

DODGE: Abbie Graham (N, 1926) , 328.

DOLET: Richard Copley Christie (L, 1899) , 475.

DOLLFUSS: J. D. Gregory (L, 1935) , 293.

DOMINIC: Jacobus a Voragine, *Golden Legend.*

DONDEAUVILLE: Anonymous ("trans. from the French"), B, 1878) , 330.

DONNE: Izaak Walton, *Lives* (Oxford World's Classics, 81) .

DOSTIE: Emily Hazen Reed (N, 1868) , 318.

DOUGLAS, H.: S. W. Fullom (L, 1863) , 423.

DOUGLAS, S.: Clark E. Carr (Chicago, 1909) , 143.

DOUGLASS: Booker T. Washington (Ph, 1906) , 341.

DOUMERGUE: *Hommage à Paul Doumergue* (P, n.d.), 115.

DOWSON: Mark Longaker (Ph, 1944) , 268.

DOYLE: Rev. John Lamond (L, 1931) , 260.

DRAPER: Rev. John C. Symons (L, 1870) , 322.

DRAYTON: *Works,* ed. J. W. Hebel (Oxford, 1931) , I, 507.

DREUX: A. Meynier, Jr. (New Orleans, 1883) , 15.

DREW: Jacob H. Drew (N, 1835) , 224.

DREXEL: *San Francisco Chronicle,* "This World," Jan. 25, 1948, p.9.

DRUSUS: *Encyclopaedia Britannica,* 9th ed., s.v.

DU BARRY: Karl von Schumacher (N, 1932) , 302.

DUBOS: Michaud's *Biographie Universelle,* XII, 87-88.

DUCOS: J. B. Weiss, *Geschichte der Französischen Revolution* (Vien-

Élisabeth, Soeur de Louis XVI (P, 1886), 505.

ELIZABETH, St.: Jacobus a Voragine, *Golden Legend.*

ELIZABETH, Queen: Frederick Chamberlin (L, 1923), 312.

ELIZABETH, Empress: Count Egon Corti (New Haven, 1936), 478.

ELLIOTT, E.: John Watkins (L, 1850), 264.

ELLIOTT, H.: Josiah Bateman (L, 1870), 371.

ELLIOTT, J.: *The Faith of John Lovejoy Elliott* (N, 1948), 36.

ELLIS: Françoise Delisle (L, 1946), 488.

ÉLOI: Saint Ouen (de Paris), *Vie de* (P, 1847), 253.

EMERSON: Van Wyck Brooks (N, 1932), 315.

EMMET: Raymond W. Postgate (L, 1931), 314.

ENGHIEN: J. Crétineau-Joly, *Histoire des Trois Derniers Princes de la Maison de Condé* (P, 1867), I, 298.

EPAMINONDAS: Pauly-Wissowa, *Real-Encyclopädie der Classischen Altertumswissenschaft*, V, 2701.

EPICURUS: Diogenes Laertius, X, 16.

ERASMUS: Stefan Zweig (N, 1934), 239.

ERICSSON: William Conant Church (L, 1892), II, 323.

ERRERA: Léon Fredericq and Jean Massart, *Notice sur* (Brussels, 1908), 116.

ERSKINE, R.: A. R. MacEwen (E, 1900), 143.

ERSKINE, T.: William Hanna, ed. *Letters* (E, 1878), 507.

ESSEX: John Stow, *Annals* (L, 1615), 794.

EUGENE: F. von Kausler, *Das Leben des Prinzen Eugen von Sa-* voyen (Freiburg, 1839), II, 771.

EVANS: David Phillips (N, 1843), 167.

EVARTS: E. C. Tracy (B, 1845), 417.

EVERETT: Paul Revere Frothingham (B, 1925), 470.

FAIRBANKS: Ralph Hancock and Letitia Fairbanks (N, 1953), 275.

FALLETTI: Silvio Pellico (L, 1886), 230.

FAWCETT, H.: Winifred Holt, *A Beacon for the Blind* (L, 1915), 311.

FAWCETT, J.: Anonymous, *An Account of the Life, Ministry, and Writings* (L, 1818), 373.

FÉNELON: *Life* by Lamartine in Fenelon's *Adventures of Telemachus*, ed. O. W. Wight (B, 1882), 113.

FERGUSSON: *Poetical Works*, ed. Robert Ford (Paisley, 1905), xlvii.

FERRER: Joseph McCabe (L, 1909), 92.

FESSENDEN: Helen M. Fessenden (N, 1940), 343.

FICHTE: Immanuel H. Fichte, *Leben und Literarischer Briefwechsel* (Leipzig, 1862), I, 457.

FIELD, E.: Slason Thompson (N, 1927), 365.

FIELD, K.: Lilian Whiting (B, 1899), 552.

FIELD, M.: John Tebbel (N, 1947), 109.

FILLMORE: William E. Griffis (Ithaca, 1915), 143.

FINUCANE: James Reynolds (N, 1942), 74.

FISCHER: August Mencken, *By the Neck* (N, 1942), 76-77.

FISK: George Prentice (B, 1890), 275.

FLAVUS: Tacitus, *Annals,* XV, 67.

FLECKER: Geraldine Hodgson (Oxford, 1925) , 229.

FLEMING: *The Complete Marjory Fleming,* ed. Frank Sidgwick (N, 1935) , 182.

FLETCHER: G. W. T. Omond (N, 1897), 148.

FOCH: Sir George Aston (N, 1929) , 449.

FONTAINE MARTEL: Gustave Desnoiresterres, *Voltaire et la Société au XVIII° Siècle* (P, 1871) , I, 471, n. 2.

FONTENELLE: Louis Maignon, *Fontenelle, L'Homme, L'Oeuvre, L'Influence* (P, 1906) , 89.

FONTON: *Genuine and Impartial Memoirs of Francis Fonton, Late of the Bank of England,* by a Student of the Law in the Inner Temple (L, 1790) , 48.

FOOT: *Proceedings on the Death of Hon. Solomon Foot* (Washington, 1866) , 22.

FOOTE: James Mason Hoppin (N, 1874) , 378.

FORREST: James Rees (Ph, 1874) , 488.

FORRESTAL: *Bergen* (Hackensack, N. J.) *Evening Record,* May 23, 1949, 1: Mark Van Doren, ed., *An Anthology of World Poetry* (N, 1939) , 278.

FORSTER: Jac. Moleschott, *Georg Forster, der Naturforscher des Volkes* (Hamm, 1862) , 217.

FOSTER, J.: J. E. Ryland (L, 1852) , II, 183.

FOSTER, S.: Stanley J. Kunitz and Howard Haycraft, ed., *American Authors 1600-1900* (N, 1938) , 285.

FOTHERGILL: George Crosfield (N, 1844) , 542.

FOX, C.: John Drinkwater (N, 1928), 370.

FOX, G.: *An Autobiography,* ed. Rufus M. Jones (Ph, 1919), 578.

FOX, H.: Thad W. Riker (Oxford, 1911) , II, 312.

FOX, H. W.: Rev. George Townshend Fox (L, 1853), 363.

FOX, M.: *Life, Compiled from her own Narrative and Other Sources* (Ph, n.d.) , 71.

FRANCE: Jacques Suffel, *Anatole France* (P, 1946), 373.

FRANCIS: Jacobus a Voragine, *Golden Legend.*

FRANCKE: Hellmuth Heyden, *August Herman Francke, der Mann und sein Werk* (Stettin, 1927) , 40.

FRANKLIN: Carl Van Doren (N, 1938), 779.

FRANZ Joseph: Bertita Harding, *Golden Fleece* (Indianapolis, 1937), 348.

FRASER: *Dictionary of National Biography,* XX, 221.

FREDERICK: T h o m a s Carlyle, *Works* (N, n.d.) , VII, 507.

FREEMAN· W. R. W Stephens (L, 1895), II, 460.

FRELINGHUYSEN: T a l b o t W. Chambers (N, 1863) , 263.

FRENCH: Margaret (French) Cresson, *Journey into Fame* (Cambridge, Mass., 1947) , 303.

FRERE: John Martineau (L, 1895), II, 450-51.

FRICK: George Harvey (N, 1928) , 375.

FRIEDRICH: T. Carlyle, *History of Friedrich II of Prussia* (L, 1905) , III, 273.

FROEBEL: Lina Morgenstern, *Friedrich Froebel, Festschrift* (Berlin, n.d.) , 27.

FROHMAN: Isaac F. Marcosson and Daniel Frohman (N, 1916), 386-87.

FROUDE: Herbert Paul (N, 1906) ,

415.

FRY: Mrs. Francis Cresswell (L, 1856), 580.

FULLER, Andrew: J. V. Morris (L, 1816), 462.

FULLER, Arthur: Richard F. Fuller (B, 1864), 303.

FULLER, M.: Katharine Anthony (N, 1920), 207.

FULLER, M.: William L. King (N, 1950), 329.

FURNIVALL: *A Volume of Personal Record* (L, 1911), lxxxi.

FUSELI: John Knowles (L, 1831), I, 340.

GADSDEN: Rev. James H. Elliott (Charleston, 1872), 23.

GAINSBOROUGH: Sir Walter Armstrong (N, 1906), 218.

GALBA: Plutarch, *Life of Galba.*

GALLAUDET: Rev. Heman Humphrey (N, 1857), 388.

GAMBETTA: P. B. Gheusi (L, 1910), 351.

GANDHI: Louis Fischer (N, 1950), 505.

GARCIA: Walter Noble Burns, *The Robin Hood of El Dorado* (N, 1932), 272.

GARDINER, A.: John W. Marsh and W. H. Stirling (L, 1887), 81.

GARDINER, J.: Sir Walter Scott, *Waverley*, II, note V; "Death of Colonel Gardiner."

GARDINER, S.: *Dictionary of National Biography*, XX, 424.

GARFIELD: William Ralston Balch (Ph, 1881), 706.

GARIBALDI: David Larg (L, 1934), 319.

GARNETT: Anonymous, *The Dying Speeches and Behaviour of the Several State Prisoners that Have Been Executed the Last 300 Years* (L, 1720), 80.

GARRICK: Mrs. Clement Parsons (N, 1906), 367.

GARRICK, Mrs. D.: Percy Fitzgerald, *Life of David Garrick* (L, 1899), 468.

GASPARIN: Theodore Borel (L, 1879), 153.

GASSENDI: Louis Andrieux, *Pierre Gassendi* (P, 1927), 106.

GATES: John Stow, *Annals* (L, 1615), 616.

GAUGUIN: Beril Becker (N, 1931), 329.

GAVESTON: Walter Phelps Dodge (L, 1899), 177.

GEER: Pierre de Witt, *Louis de Geer, Un Patricien au XVII Siècle* (P, 1885), 169.

GELLERT: Mrs. Douglas of Ednam House (Kelso, 1805), I, 158.

GEORGE IV: Percy Fitzgerald (N, 1881), 909, note.

GEORGE V: Harold Nicolson (N, 1953), 530-31.

GEORGE: Henry George, Jr. (N, 1924), 607.

GERSON: A. C. Masson, *Jean Gerson* (Lyon, 1894), 391.

GIANGER: John Fox, *Book of Martyrs*, ed. Cumming, I, 1116.

GIBBON: *Autobiography*, Everyman's Library, 193.

GIBBONS: Allen Sinclair Will (N, 1922), II, 1046.

GIDE: Albert J. Guerard in *The Nation*, April 21, 1951, 371.

GILBERT, A.: Josiah Gilbert, ed., *Autobiography* (L, 1874), 318.

GILBERT, H.: Donald Barr Chidsey (N, 1932), 195.

GILBERT, W.: Sidney Dark and Rowland Grey (L, n.d.), 222.

GILDER: Rosamond Gilder, ed., *Letters* (B, 1916), 498.

GILFILLAN: Robert A. and Elizabeth S. Watson (L, 1892), 447-48.

Haven, 1934), 241.

GUITEAU: August Mencken, *By the Neck* (N, 1942), 89.

GUIZOT: Madame de Witt (B, 1882), 356.

GUNTHER: John Gunther, *Death be Not Proud* (Modern Library), 185.

GURNEY: Joseph B. Braithwaite (Ph, 1855), II, 525.

GUSTAVUS: C. R. L. Fletcher (N, 1890), 284.

GUTHRIE: Anonymous, *Lives of Alexander Henderson and James Guthrie* (Edinburgh, 1846), 173.

HACKMAN: Gilbert Burgess, ed. (L, 1895), 181.

HADRIAN: Spartianus, *Vita Hadriani*, 25.

HAIG: Duff Cooper (L, 1936), II, 433.

HALDANE, J.: "J. B.," *Memoir of Robert Haldane and James Alexander Haldane* (N, 1858), 273.

HALDANE, R.: *Ibid.*, 257.

HALE, E.: Edward E. Hale, Jr. (B, 1917), II, 410.

HALE, N.: Henry Phelps Johnston (N, 1901), 126.

HALL: *Hope for the Hopeless, An Autobiography,* ed. Rev. Newman Hall (N, 1865), 242.

HALLECK: Nelson F. Adkins (New Haven, 1930), 365.

HALLER: Eduard Bodemann, ed., *Von und über Albrecht von Haller* (Hannover, 1885), 182.

HALYBURTON: *Memoirs* (Edinburgh [1847]), 299.

HAMERTON: *Autobiography, with Memoir by his Wife* (B, 1898), 575-76.

HAMILTON, P.: Rev. Peter Lorimer (E, 1857), 154.

HAMILTON, Duke of: Gilbert Bur-

net (L, 1677), 432.

HAMLIN: Margarette W. Lawrence (B, 1854), 281.

HAMMOND: John Fell (Oxford, 1856), 218.

HAMPDEN: *Dictionary of National Biography,* XXIV, 261.

HANCOCK: W. H. Venable (Cincinnati, 1892), 78.

HANNA: Herbert Croly (N, 1912), 455.

HANNIBAL: Plutarch, *Lives* (Modern Library, 464).

HANWAY: R. Everett Jayne (L, 1929), 136.

HARDEN: *Life, Confession, and Letters of* (Hackettstown, N. J., 1860), 46.

HARDEN-HICKEY: Richard Harding Davis, *Real Soldiers of Fortune* (N, 1906), 70-71.

HARDING: Samuel Hopkins Adams, *Incredible Era* (B, 1939), 377.

HARE: John Middleton Hare (L, 1874), 434.

HAROUN: E. H. Palmer (N, n.d.), 125.

HARRINGTON: Mrs. Eliza C. Harrington (Middleton, 1887), 174.

HARRIS: Julia Collier Harris (B, 1918), 588.

HARRISON, B.: *The* (N.Y.) *World,* March 14, 1901, 1.

HARRISON, T.: David Masson, *Life of John Milton* (N, 1946), VI, 96.

HARRISON, W.: Freeman Cleaves, *Old Tippecanoe* (N, 1939), 342.

HARVEY: Anonymous, *Memoir of* (L, 1869), 370.

HASSLER: Floriam C a j o r i (B, 1929), 235.

HASTINGS: Rev. G. R. Gleig (L, 1841), III, 525.

HAUFF: Hans Hofmann, *Eine Dar-*

stellung (Frankfurt, 1902), 111.

HAUSER: Duchess of Cleveland (L, 1893), 56.

HAVELOCK: Rev. William Brock (N, 1860), 288.

HAVERGAL: M. V. G. Havergal (L, 1882), 245.

HAWKER: C. E. Byles (L, 1905), 637.

HAWTHORNE: Julian Hawthorne, Nathaniel Hawthorne and His Wife (B, 1892), II, 369.

HAYDN: Rosemary H u g h e s (L, 1950), 108.

HAYDON: Autobiography and Memoirs, ed. Tom Taylor (L, 1926), II, 818.

HAYES: Charles Richard Williams (B, 1914), II, 398.

HAYNES: Timothy M. Cooley (N, 1837), 309.

HAZLITT: P. P. Howe (L, 1922), 426.

HEARN: V e r a McWilliams (D, 1946), 440.

HEBER: Mrs. Heber (N, 1830), II, 412.

HECKER: Katherine Burton, Celestial Homespun (L, 1943), 381.

HECKEWELDER: Rev. E d w a r d Rondthaler (Ph, 1847), 148.

HEINE: Lewis Browne (N, 1927), 404.

HEMANS: Henry F. Chorley (L, 1837), II, 326.

HENDERSON, A.: Anonymous, Lives of Alexander Henderson and James Guthrie (E, 1846), 58.

HENDERSON, E.: Thulia S. Henderson (L, 1860), 466.

HENLEY, J.: Rev. John G. Avery (Barnstaple, 1844), 419.

HENLEY, W.: John Connell (L, 1949), 377.

HENRIETTA: Julia Cartwright (Mrs. Henry Ady) (N, 1907),

354.

HENRY II: John Richard Green, A Short History of the English People, Everyman's Library, I, 104.

HENRY IV: Raphael Holinshed, Chronicles of England, Scotland, and Ireland (L, 1808), III, 58.

HENRY IV of France: John Bloundelle-Burton (L, n d), 415.

HENRY IV of Germany: Dr. Cosmar Grünhagen, Adalbert, Erzbischof von Hamburg (Leipzig, 1854), 225.

HENRY V: A. J. Church (L, 1889), 147.

HENRY VIII: A. F. Pollard (L, 1905), 424.

HENRY, Prince: Thomas Birch (L, 1790), 354.

HENRY the Lion: Hans Prutz, Heinrich der Löwe (Leipsig, 1865), 435.

HENRY, M.: W. Tong (L, 1716), 387.

HENRY, Patrick: Henry and Dana Lee Thomas, Living Biographies of Famous Americans (N, 1946), 18.

HENRY, Philip: [Rev. Matthew Henry] (L, 1848), 288.

HERBERT of Cherbury: John Aubrey, Brief Lives, ed. A n d r e w Clark (Oxford, 1898), I, 307.

HERBERT, G.: Izaak W a l t o n , Lives (Oxford World's Classics), 318.

HERBERT, S.: Lord Stanmore (L, 1906), II, 441.

HERDER: E u g e n Kühnemann, Herders Leben (Munich, 1895), 375.

HERRICK: Col. T. Bentley Mott (N, 1929), 370.

HERVEY: Méditations d'Hervey, traduites de l'Anglois par M. Le

Tourneur (P, 1771) , 58-59.

HERZL: Josef Patai, *Star Over Jordan* (N, 1946) , 351.

HESSUS: Ioachimi Camerarii *Narratio de Helio Eobano Hesso,* ed. J. T. Kreyssig (Misenae, 1843) , 40.

HEWITT: Allan Nevins (L, 1935), 600.

HEY: Theodor Hansen, *Wilhelm Hey nach seinem eigenen Briefen* (Gotha, 1886) , 398.

HEYLIN: John Barnard, *Theologo-Historicus* (L, 1683) , 291.

HICKOK: Frank J. Wilstach (N, 1937) , 282.

HILARY: John Donne, *Death's Duel* (in *Complete Poetry and Selected Prose,* ed. John Hayward, L, 1936, 751).

HILL, B.: Benjamin H. Hill, Jr. (Atlanta, 1893) , 106.

HILL, U.; *Life,* Dec. 24, 1951, 57.

HILLARY: Lovat Dickson (L, 1950), 195.

HILLMAN: Matthew Josephson (N, 1952) , 670.

HILTON: Edna Nixon (L, 1946), 339.

HILTZHEIMER: *Extracts from Diary,* ed. Jacob Cox Parsons (Ph, 1893) , 260.

HIMMLER: *Time,* June 4, 1945, 27.

HINDENBURG: John W. Wheeler Bennett, *Wooden Titan* (N, 1936), 470.

HINGORO: *New York Times,* April 30, 1954, 4.

HITLER, *Ibid.,* Dec. 31, 1945, 6.

HOBBES: Alexander Chalmers, *General Biographical Dictionary* (L, 1814) , XVIII, 13.

HOCHE: A. Rousselin, *Vie de Lazare Hoche* (P, n.d.) , I, 423.

HODGE: A. A. Hodge (N, 1880) , 582.

HODGSON: Rev. James T. Hodgson (L, 1878), II, 325.

HOEFFLE: *Berkeley* (Calif.) *Gazette,* Dec. 9, 1947, 10.

HOFER: Anonymous, *Memoirs of the Life of Andrew Hofer* (L, 1820) , 196.

HOFFMAN: Theodore Myers Riley (N, 1904), II, 696.

HOFMANNSTHAL: Carl J. Burckhardt, *Erinnerungen an Hofmannsthal und Briefe des Dichters* (Basel, 1944) , 85-86.

HOGG: Henry T. Stephenson, *The Ettrick Shepherd* (Bloomington, 1922) , 106.

HOKUSAI: C. J. Holmes (N, 1901) , 12.

HOLCRAFT: *Memoirs,* ed. W. Hazlitt (Oxford World's Classics), 317.

HOLLAND: Stephen Paget (L, 1921) , 328.

HOLMES: Catherine Drinker Bowen, *Yankee from Olympus* (B, 1944) , 416.

HOLST: Imogen Holst (L, 1938), 168.

HOLTBY: Vera Brittain, *Testament of Friendship* (N, 1940) , 407.

HÖLTY: Hermann Ruete, *Sein Leben und Dichten* (Euben, 1883) , 28.

HOOD, E.: George H. Giddens (L, 1886) , 191.

HOOD, T.: Walter Jerrold (N, 1919) , 395.

HOOK: W. R. W. Stephens (L, 1879) , II, 501.

HOOKER, R.: Izaak Walton, *Lives* (Oxford World's Classics) , 225.

HOOKER, T.: George Leon Walker (N, 1891) , 150.

HOPE: Mrs. Hope, ed. Klein Grant (L, 1844) , 299.

HOPKINS, G.: Eleanor Ruggles (N, 1944), 289.

HOPKINS, H.: Robert E. Sherwood (N, 1948), 931.

HOPKINS, J.: [John Henry Hopkins, Jr.] (N, 1873), 438.

HOPKINS, S.: Williston Walker, *Ten New England Leaders* (B, 1901), 357.

HOUDETOT: Michaud's *Biographie Universelle*, XX, 48.

HOUGHTON: Alfred Marks, *Tyburn Tree* (L, n.d.), 136.

HOUSMAN, A.: Laurence Housman (N, 1938), 121.

HOUSMAN, R.: Robert Fletcher Housman (N, 1846), 371.

HOUSTON: Marquis James, *The Raven* (Indianapolis, 1929), 433.

HOWARD: Hepworth Dixon (L, 1850), 390.

HOWE: Laura E. Richards and Maud Howe Elliott (B, 1916), II, 413.

HOWELLS: Mildred Howells, ed. (N, 1928), II, 399.

HUBBARD: Felix Shay (N, 1926), 551.

HUDSON: Morley Roberts (N, 1924), 304.

HÜGEL: *Selected Letters*, ed. Bernard Holland (L, 1927), 52.

HUGH: *Magna Vita S. Hugonis Episcopi Lincolniensis*, ed. James F. Dimrock (L, 1864), 345.

HUGO: A. F. Davidson (Ph, 1912), 342.

HULL: Bruce Grant, *Captain of Old Ironsides* (Chicago, 1947), 346.

HUMBERT: Ugo d'Andrea, *La Fine del Regno* (Turin, 1951), 55.

HUMBERT, J.: H. Le Vosgien, *Le Général Humbert* (Mirecourt, 1866), 132-33.

HUMBOLDT: [R. H. Stoddard] (N, 1859), 479.

HUME: Henry Calderwood (N, 1904), 157-58.

HUNT, L.: Robert Chambers, ed., *Cyclopaedia of English Literature* (Ph, ca. 1860), II, 802.

HUNT, V.: Edmund Blunden (N, 1930), 311.

HUNTER: *Dictionary of National Biography*, XXVIII, 303.

HUNTINGDON: Anonymous, *Life and Times of* (L, 1844), II, 502.

HUS: Count Lützow (L, 1909), 285.

HUTCHINSON, J.: Lucy Hutchinson (L, 1906), 479.

HUTCHINSON, T.: James K. Hosmer (B, 1896), 348.

HUTTON: Llewellynn Jewitt (L, 1872), 329.

HUXLEY: Houston Peterson (L, 1932), 304-05.

HYDE: *Dictionary of National Biography*, XXVIII, 368.

IBANEZ. Ramon Martinez de la Riva, *Blasco Ibañez, Su Vida* (Madrid, n.d.), 193.

IBSEN: A. E. Zucker (N, 1929), 282.

IGNATIUS: John Fox, *Book of Martyrs*, ed. Cumming, I, 36.

IMPEY: Elijah Barwell Impey (L, 1847), 413.

INGERSOLL: Cameron Rogers (N, 1927), 290.

IRVING, E.: Mrs. Oliphant (L, 1862), II, 404.

IRVING, W.: Pierre M. Irving (N, 1869), III, 419.

ISABELLA: W. H. Prescott, *History of the Reign of Ferdinand and Isabella* (B, 1838), III, 181.

ITO: Kengi Hamada (Tokyo, 1936), 232.

ITURBIDE: *New York Times*, Oct.

9, 1927, Sect. 2, 8.

JACKSON, A.: Marquis James (Indianapolis, 1938), 785.

JACKSON, H.: Ruth Odell (N, 1939), 219.

JACKSON, T.: John Esten Cooke (N, 1897), 444.

JACOB: Genesis, xlix, 29-32.

JACOBI: [Joseph Albrecht von Ittner], *Leben Joh. Georg Jacobi's* (Zurich, 1822), 166.

JACOBS: E. F. Wuestemann, *Friderici Jacobsii Laudatio* (Gotha, 1848), 66.

JAMES the Apostle: John Fox, *Book of Martyrs,* ed. Cumming, I, 22.

JAMES the brother of Jesus: *Ibid.,* I, 25.

JAMES the Dismembered: Jacobus a Voragine, *Golden Legend.*

JAMES I: Clara and Hardy Steeholm (N, 1938), 473.

JAMES II: *A Collection of Scarce and Valuable Tracts* [Somers Tracts], ed. Walter Scott (L, 1814), XI, 343.

JAMES V: *Dictionary of National Biography,* XXIX, 160.

JAMES, H. Sr.: Austin Warren (N, 1934), 188.

JAMES, H.: F. W. Dupee (N, 1951), 288-89.

JAMES, J.: John Campbell (L, 1860), 19.

JAMES, W.: *Letters,* ed. Henry James (B, 1920), II, 350.

JANEWAY: Thomas L. Janeway (Ph, 1861), 260.

JAY, J.: Frank Monaghan (Indianapolis, 1935), 436.

JAY, W.: Syrus Jay (L, 1859), 321.

JEFFERIES: Walter Besant (L, 1893), 364.

JEFFERSON: James Truslow Adams

(N, 1936), 358.

JEFFREY: Lord Cockburn (E, 1852), I, 408.

JEHORAM: 2 Kings, ix, 23.

JEROME: John Fox, *Book of Martyrs,* ed. Cumming, I, 912.

JERROLD: Walter Jerrold (L, n.d.), II, 655.

JESUS CHRIST: Matthew, xxvii, 46—Mark, xv, 34; Luke, xxiii, 46; John, xix, 30.

JEWEL: *Works,* ed. Ayre (Cambridge, 1850), IV, xxii.

JEZEBEL: 2 Kings, ix, 31.

JOAN: V. Sackville West (N, 1936), 341.

JOFFRE: Lt. Col. Charles Bugnet, *Le Maréchal Joffre* (Tours [1932]), 306.

JOHN the Evangelist: Jacobus a Voragine, *Golden Legend.*

JOHN the Almoner: *Ibid.*

JOHN of the Cross: Robert Sencourt, *Carmelite and Poet* (N, 1944), 210.

JOHN the Abbot: Jacobus a Voragine, *Golden Legend.*

JOHN, King: John Stow, *Annals* L, 1615), 174.

JOHN, Don: Padre Luis Coloma (L, 1912), 427.

JOHNSON, J.: Barnie F. Winkelman (Ph, 1942), 278.

JOHNSON, S.: James Boswell (Modern Library, 1191).

JOHNSON, T.: *My Story,* ed. Elizabeth J. Hauser (N, 1911), 312.

JOHNSON, W.: Arthur Pound in collab. with Richard E. Day (N, 1930), 423.

JOHNSTON: Otto Eisenschiml and Ralph Newman, *The American Iliad* (Indianapolis, 1947), 186.

JOKAI: See Budapest Daily *Szabad Ifjusag,* May 4, 1954 (on the authority of Mr. Istvan Csicsery-

Ronay) .

JOLSON: *New York Post,* Oct. 24, 1950, 3.

JONES, H. A.: Doris Arthur Jones (L, 1930) , 400.

JONES, H.: H. J. W. Hetherington (L, 1924) , 154.

JONES, J.: [Robert C. Sands, ed.] *Life and Correspondence* (N, 1830) , 547.

JORTIN: *Dictionary of National Biography,* XXX, 202.

JOSEPH: Genesis, L, 24-25.

JOSEPH II: Michaud's *Biographie Universelle,* XXI, 169.

JOSEPHINE: Baron De Meneval (Ph, n.d.), 256.

JOYCE: *Chamber Music,* ed. W. Y. Tindall (N, 1954) , 38.

JUDAS: Matthew, xxvii, 4.

JUDD: [Arethusa Hall] (B, 1857) , 520.

JUDSON, Adoniram: Francis Wayland (B, 1853) , II, 352.

JUDSON, Ann: James D. Knowles (B, 1831), 338.

JUCURTHA: Plutarch, *Lives* (Modern Library, 500) .

JULIAN: Theodoret 3, 20; Sozomen 6, 2.

KAFKA: Max Brod, *Franz Kafka* (Prague, 1937) , 258.

KALAKAUA: Eugene Burns, *The Last King of Paradise* (N, 1952) , 344.

KANT: Thomas De Quincy, *Collected Writings,* ed. Masson (E, 1890), IV, 376.

KARGE: William A. Packard, (N, 1893) , 30. (One remark not directly quoted intervened.)

KATTE: Thomas Carlyle, *History of Friedrich II of Prussia* (L, n.d.) , II, 341.

KAUFFMANN: Frances A. Gerard

(L, 1893) , 326.

KEAN: F. W. Hawkins (L, 1869) , II, 391.

KEATS: Amy Lowell (B, 1925) , II, 528.

KEMBLE: James Boaden (Ph, 1825) , 581.

KEMP: *An Autobiography,* ed. Helen L. Fairchild (N, 1903) , 198.

KEN: E. H. Plumptre (L, 1890) , II, 202.

KENT: William Kent (B, 1898) , 277.

KEPLER: M. W. Burke-Gaffney (Milwaukee, 1944) , 130.

KERR: *Memorial Address on the Life and Character of* (Washington, 1877) , 31.

KEYSERLING: *New York Times,* Oct. 29, 1951, 17.

KIDD: Sir Cornelius N. Dalton (N, 1911) , 212-13.

KING: Richard Frothingham (B, 1865) , 224.

KINGSLEY: Ed. by Mrs. Kingsley (L, 1878) , II, 460.

KITCHING: *"More than Conqueror"* or *Memorials of* (N, 1873) , 232.

KLÉBER: Count Pajol, *Kléber, Sa Vie* (P, 1877) , 490.

KLEIST: Friedrich Reck-Malleczewen, *Der Letzte Brief* (Frankfurt, 1949) , 71.

KLOPSTOCK: [Miss E. Smith, trans.] *Memoirs of Frederick and Margaret Klopstock* (L, 1809) , 34.

KLOPSTOCK, Mrs.: *Ibid.,* 170.

KLUGE: Milton Shulman, *Defeat in the West* (L, 1947) , 154.

KNIBB: John Howard Hinton (L, 1847) , 526.

KNILL: Charles M. Birrell (L, 1859) , 242.

KNOX: Henry Cowan (N, 1905) ,

[*249*]

370.

KOERNER: Karl Berger, *Theodor Koerner* (Leipzig, 1912) , 256.

KOSSUTH: Budapest Daily *Pesti Naplo,* March 20, 1914 (on the authority of Mr. Istvan Csicsery-Ronay) .

KRAUS: Johannes Voigt, *Das Leben des Professor* . . . (Königsberg, 1819) , 448.

KRAUSE: Charles S. Stanford (Dublin, 1854) , 86.

KUANG-HSU: Daniele Varè, *The Last Empress* (N, 1937) , 278.

KUSAKABE: Robert Louis Stevenson, *Familiar Studies of Men and Books* (N, 1917) , 162.

LA BÉDOYERE: Michaud's *Biographie Universelle,* III, 491.

LABOUCHERE: Algar Labouchere Thorold (N, 1913) , 538.

LACÉPEDE: Michaud's *Biographie Universelle,* XXII, 344.

LACORDAIRE: H. L. Sidney Lear (L, 1882) , 332.

LAENNEC: Paul Sarradon, *Le Docteur Laënnec* (P [1949]) , 190.

LAFAYETTE, Marquis: Brand Whitlock (N, 1929) , II, 410.

LAFAYETTE, Mme.: M. M. Crawford (N, 1907) , 328.

LA FOLLETTE: Edward N. Doan (N, 1947) , 134.

LAGNY: *Nouvelle Biographie Générale* (P, 1878) , XXVIII, 826.

LAHARPE: Gabriel Peignot, *Recherches Historiques* . . . (Dijon, 1820) , 158.

LAKANAL: Paul Le Gendre, *Lakanal* (P, 1882) , 135.

LALANDE: M. Jarrin, *Lalande et La Bresse au XVIIIIe Siècle* (Bourg, 1869) , 72.

LAMB: *Complete Works and Letters* (Modern Library) , 1025.

LAMBALLE: Paul Fassy, *Princesse de Lamballe et La Prison de la Force* (P, 1868) , 40.

LAMBERT: John Fox, *Book of Martyrs,* ed. Cumming, II, 473.

LAMENNAIS: E. Spuller, *Lamennais, Étude* (P, 1892) , 345-46.

LA MOTHE LE VAYER: Florence L. Wickelgren, *Sa Vie et Son Oeuvre* (P, 1934) , 21.

LANDIS, C.: *Berkeley* (Calif.) *Gazette,* July 6, 1948, 1.

LANDIS, K.: J. G. Taylor Spink (N, 1947) , 291.

LANDRU: J. B. Jean Belin, *Secrets of the Sureté* (N, 1950) , 85.

LANE: Anne Wintermute Lane and Louise Herrick Wall (B, 1922) , 464-65.

LANIER: Aubrey Harrison Starke (Chapel Hill, 1933) , 432.

LAPLACE: H. Andoyer, *L'Oeuvre Scientifique de Laplace* (P, 1922) , 14.

LARCOM: Daniel D. Addison (B, 1897) , 290.

LA SALLE: Armand Ravelet, *Le Bienheureux J. B. De La Salle* (Tours, 1888) , 424.

LATIMER: *Encyclopaedia Britannica,* 9th ed., XIV, 326-27.

LAUD: Robert P. Tristram Coffin (N, 1930) , 318-19.

LAURENCE: John Fox, *Book of Martyrs,* ed. Cumming, I, 93.

LAURIER: Oscar D. Skelton (N, 1922) , II, 554.

LAVAL: *New York Times,* Oct. 16, 1945, 1.

LAWRENCE, D.: Frieda Lawrence, *Not I, but the Wind* (N, 1934) , 295.

LAWRENCE, H.: Sir Herbert B. Edwardes and Herman Merivale (L, 1873) , 612.

LAWRENCE, J.: Albert Gleaves

(N, 1904) , 195.

LAWRENCE, T.: *Letters*, ed. David Garnett (L, 1938) , 872.

LEAR: Angus Davidson (L, 1938) , 268.

LE CLERC: Aldous Huxley, *Grey Eminence* (N, 1941) , 329.

LECOUVREUR: Cécile Sorel, *La Vie Amoureuse d'* (P, 1925) , 148.

LEE, C.: John Richard Alden (Baton Rouge, 1951) , 298.

LEE, J.: *The Mormon Menace, being the Confession of John Doyle Lee Danite* (N, 1905) , 354.

LEE, R.: J. C. Young, *Marse Robert* (N, 1929) , 355.

LEEUWENHOEK: Paul de Kruif, *Microbe Hunters* (N, 1926) , 24.

LEGER: Jacobus a Voragine, *Golden Legend.*

LEHAR: Maria von Peteani, *Franz Lehar, Seine Musik* (Vienna, 1950) , 232.

LEICHHARDT: Ernest Favenc, *History of Australian Exploration* (Sydney, 1888) , 417.

LENCLOS: *Lettres*, ed. A. Bret (P, n.d.) , 98.

LEO: Ludwig Pastor, *History of the Popes from the Close of the Middle Ages* (L, 1908) , VIII, 63.

LEOPARDI: Iris Origo (L, 1935) , 190.

LEOPOLD I: Dr. Egon Caesar Corti (L, 1923) , 299.

LEOPOLD II: Comte Louis de Lichtervelde (N, 1929) , 348.

LEPELLETIER: *Nouvelle Biographie Générale* (P, 1862) , XXX, 834.

LESPINASSE: Camilla Jebb, *A Star of the Salons* (L, 1908) , 333.

LEWIS, E.: Burton A. Konkle (Ph, 1907) , 258.

LEWIS, S.: Reported to the compiler by Mr. Mark Schorer, who

has in preparation the authorised biography.

LEY: *New York Times,* Oct. 27, 1945, 4.

LIEUTAUD: Michaud's *Biographie Universelle,* XXIV, 514.

LIEVEN: Lytton Strachey, *Portraits in Miniature* (N, 1931) , 135.

LIGNE: Ernst Benedikt, *Karl Josef, Fürst von Ligne* (Vienna, 1937) , 295.

LINDSAY: Edgar Lee Masters (N, 1935) , 361.

LINDSEY: Thomas Belsham (L, 1873) , 312.

LINTON: George Somes Layard (L, 1901) , 371.

LISLE: Cecil Deedes, *Royal and Loyal Sufferers* (L, 1903), 120.

LISZT: James Huneker (N, 1911) , 25.

LIVINGSTONE: W. Garden Blaikie (N, 1880) , 464

LODGE: John A. Garraty (N, 1953) , 424.

LODY: John Laurence, *A History of Capital Punishment* (L, n.d.) , 155.

LONDON: Joan London (N, 1939) , 375.

LONG: Carleton Beals (Ph, 1935) , 404.

LONGFELLOW: Samuel Longfellow (B, 1891) , III, 325.

LOPEZ: William E. Barrett, *Woman on Horseback* (N, 1938) , 311.

LOTHAR: Gregory of Tours, *History of the Franks,* IV, 21 (14) , trans. O. M. Dalton (Oxford, 1927) .

LOUIS I: Michaud's *Biographie Universelle,* XXV, 150.

LOUIS I de Bourbon: Duc d'Aumale, *History of the Princes de Condé in the XVIth and XVIIth*

185.

MAINTENON: Mme. Saint-René Taillandier (L, 1922) , 283.

M'KAIL: John Howie, *The Scots Worthies* (Glasgow, 1835), I, 318.

MALHERBE: Michaud's *Biographie Universelle*, XXVI, 244.

MANDRIN: Anonymous, *Histoire de Louis Mandrin* (Montbéliard, n.d.) , 107.

MANN: Louise Hall Tharp, *Until Victory* (B, 1953) , 313.

MANNING: Edmund Sheridan Purcell (L, 1895) , II, 806.

MANSFIELD, K.: *Letters to J. Middleton Murry* (N, 1951) , 701.

MANSFIELD, R.: William Winter (N, 1910) , I, 325.

MARAT: F. Chevremont (P, 1880) , II, 352.

MARC: [Joseph Donzé de Verteuil] *Derniers Sentiments des Plus Illustres Personnages Condamnés à Mort* (P, 1775) , I, 19.

MARCONI: Douglas Coe (N, 1943), 253.

MARGARET of Antioch: Jacobus a Voragine, *Golden Legend.*

MARGARET: *Ibid.*

MARGARET of Angoulême: A. Mary F. Robinson (B, 1886) , 312.

MARGARET of Austria: Eleanor E. Tremayne, *The First Governess of the Netherlands* (N, 1908), 288.

MARGARET of Scotland: *Dictionary of National Biography,* XXXVI, 138.

MARIANNE: L. V. Jacks (N, 1935), 169.

MARK: Jacobus a Voragine, *Golden Legend.*

MARLBOROUGH: Winston S. Churchill (L, 1938) , IV, 649.

MARQUETTE: Agnes Repplier (N, 1929) , 241.

MARRYAT: Florence Marryat (L, 1872) , II, 300.

MARSH: George D. Lyman (N, 1930), 321.

MARTI: Félix Lizaso (Albuquerque, 1953) , 250.

MARTIN: Frederic W. Farrer, *Lives of the Fathers* (L, 1907) , 1, 656.

MARVELL: Augustine Birrell (N, 1905) , 18.

MARY Queen of Scots: Maurice Baring, *In the End is My Beginning* (N, 1932), 309.

MARY I: *Dictionary of National Biography,* XXXVI, 351.

MARY II: Mary F. Sandars, *Princess and Queen of England* (L, 1913) , 365.

MASANIELLO: Michaud's *Biographie Universelle,* XXVII, 173

MATA HARI: Maj. Thomas Coulson (N, 1930) , 309.

MATHER, C.: Rev. Abijah P. Marvin (B, 1892) , 570-71.

MATHER, I.: Kenneth B. Murdock (Cambridge, Mass., 1925) , 388.

MATHEWS: Mrs. Mathews (L, 1839) , IV, 414.

MATURIN: Maisie Ward (L,1920) , 60.

MAURICE: C. F. G. Masterman (L, 1907) , 197.

MAURY: Charles Lee Lewis (Annapolis, 1927) , 239.

MAXIMILIAN: Bertita Harding, *Phantom Crown* (Indianapolis, 1934), 330.

MAZARIN: Comte de Cosnac, *Mazarine et Colbert* (P, 1892) , II, 425.

MAZZINI: Gwilym O. Griffith (L, 1932) , 355.

MEADE: George Meade (N, 1913) , II, 303.

MEDICI: William Roscoe (L, 1895), 330.

(L, 1932), 204. It is also said: "He moved his beard from the block with the remark that 'it had never committed treason.'" *Dictionary of National Biography*, XXVIII, 439.

MOREAU: Ernest Daudet, *L'Exil et la Mort du* (P, 1909), 250.

MOREHEAD: Samuel Trexler (N, 1938), 161.

MORGAN: Lewis Corey (N, 1930), 411.

MORIALE: Henry Smith Williams, *The Historians' History of the World* (L, 1908), IX, 228.

MORRIS: J. W. Mackail (L, 1911), II, 332.

MORSE: Carleton Mabee, *The American Leonardo* (N, 1943), 377.

MORTON: William D. Foulke (Indianapolis, 1899), II, 501.

MOULE: John B. Harford and Frederick C. Macdonald (L, n.d.), 349.

MOZART: Edward Holmes (L, 1878), 233.

MUHLENBERG: Anne Ayres (N, 1880), 503.

MUNRO: *Short Stories of Saki* (N, 1930), 714.

MÜNSTERBERG: Margaret Münsterberg (N, 1922), 302.

MURAT: Marquis de Sassenay, *Les Derniers Mois de Murat* (P, 1896), 199.

MÜRGER: Arthur Moss and Evalyn Marvel, *The Legend of the Latin Quarter* (N, 1946), 188.

MURPHY: John P. Emery (Ph, 1946), 169.

MURRIETA: Walter Noble Burns, *The Robin Hood of El Dorado* (N, 1932), 275.

MUSSET: Arvède Barine (N, 1906), 169.

MUSSOLINI: Paolo Monelli (L, 1953), 290.

MUSSORGSKY: M. D. Calvocoressi (L, 1946), 61.

NAPOLEON: Emil Ludwig (Modern Library), 674.

NAPOLEON II: Octave Aubry (Ph, 1932), 261.

NAPOLEON III: Archibald Forbes (N, 1897), 341.

NARVAEZ: Andrés Révesz (Madrid, 1953), 249.

NEANDER: Philip Schaff (L, 1886), 160.

NELSON: A. T. Mahan (B, 1899), 740.

NERO: Arthur Weigall (N, 1930), 382.

NEVIN: John Tasker Howard (N, 1935), 340.

NEWELL [Rev. Leonard Wood] (Ph, 1831), 249.

NEWTON: R. Cecil (L, 1824), 85.

NEY: A. Hilliard Atteridge, *The Bravest of the Brave* (L, 1912), 349.

NICHOLAS, St.: Jacobus a Voragine, *Golden Legend*.

NICHOLAS II: Jean Jacoby, *Le Tsar Nicolas II* (P, 1931), 341.

NICOLL: T. H. Darlow (L, 1925), 446.

NIEBUHR: Chevalier Bunsen and Profs. Brandis and Lorbell (N, 1852), 489.

NIJINSKY: Romola Nijinsky, *Last Years of* (N, 1952), 251.

NODIER: Mme. Mennessier-Nodier, *Charles Nodier* (P, 1867), 367.

NOTHNAGEL: Friedrich Reck-Malleczewen, *Der Letzte Brief* (Frankfurt, 1949), 132.

OATES: Martin Lindsay, *The Epic of Captain Scott* (L, 1934), 157.

O'BRIEN: Michael MacDonagh (L, 1928), 261.

O'CONNELL: Sean o'Faolain, *King of the Beggars* (N, 1938), 328.

OGILVY: J. M. Barrie (N, 1896), 206.

OLGIATTI: John Addington Symonds, *Renaissance in Italy* (Modern Library), I, 85.

OLIPHANT, L.: Margaret Oliphant (N, 1891), II, 369.

OLIPHANT, M.: *Autobiography*, ed. Mrs. Harry Coghill (N, 1899), 440.

O'NEILL: *New York Times*, Sept. 26, 1950, 26.

OPIE: Jacobine Menzies-Wilson and Helen Lloyd (L, 1937), 291.

O'REILLY: James J. Roche (N, 1891), 355.

ORLEANS, Duchess of: Ernest F. Henderson, *A Lady of the Old Regime* (N, 1909), 235.

ORLEANS, Louis: Evarts S. Scudder, *Prince of the Blood* (L, 1937), 312.

OSLER: Harvey Cushing (Oxford, 1926), II, 685.

OTHO: Plutarch, *Lives* (Modern Library, 1295).

OUGHTRED: John Aubrey, *Brief Lives*, ed. Dick, 225.

OUIDA: Eileen Bigland (N, 1951), 262.

OUTLAW: Eugene Cunningham, *Triggernometry* (Caldwell, Id., 1941), 247.

OWEN, J.: S. Austin Allibone, *A Critical Dictionary of English Literature* (Ph, 1899), II, 1472.

OWEN, R.: Frank Podmore (N, 1907), II, 629.

OWEN, W.: *Poems*, ed. E. Blunden (N, 1931), 38-39.

OZANAM: Kathleen O'Meara (N, n.d.), 345.

PADEREWSKI: Aniela Strakacz (New Brunswick, 1949), 332.

PAGE: Rosewell Page (N, 1923), 207.

PAINE: Hesketh Pearson (N, 1937), 287.

PALM: Friedrich Reck-Malleczewen, *Der Letzte Brief* (Frankfurt, 1949), 62-63.

PALMER, C.: *Courtlandt Palmer: Tributes Offered by Members of the Nineteenth Century Club to its Founder and First President* (N, 1889), 97.

PALMER, W.: *San Francisco Chronicle*, "This Week," March 9, 1947, 10.

PALMERSTON: Herbert C. F. Bell (L, 1936), II, 419.

PANCRATIUS: Jacobus a Voragine, *Golden Legend*.

PARKER: Henry Steele Commager (B, 1936), 309.

PARNELL: Katharine O'Shea (N, 1914), II, 258.

PARRY: Rev. Edward Parry (L, 1857), 385.

PASCAL: Morris Bishop (N, 1936), 343.

PASCIN: Wilhelm Treichlinger, *Abschiedsbriefe* (Berlin, 1934), 231.

PASTEUR: René Vallery-Radot (N, 1937), 464.

PATMORE: Derek Patmore, *Portrait of my Family* (L, 1935), 237.

PATON: [John Howie] *Biographia Scoticana* (Dundee, 1809), 294.

PATTISON, D.: Margaret Lonsdale, *Sister Dora* (B, 1880), 271.

PATTISON, W.: Chard Powers Smith, *Annals of the Poets* (N, 1935), 268.

PAUL: II Timothy iv, 21-22.

PAULINUS: Henry Vaughan,

Works, ed. L. C. Martin (Oxford, 1914), I, 381.

PAVLOVA: V. Dandré (L, 1932), 360.

PAYNE: Thomas Wright (L, 1919), 266.

PAYSON: Asa Cummings (B, 1830), 370.

PEACE: Charles Whibley, A Book of Scoundrels (N, 1897), 258.

PEACOCK: Works, with a Biographical Notice by Edith Nicolls (L, 1875), I, li.

PEARSON: William Stebbing, ed. (L, 1900), 309.

PEEL: Priate Letters of, ed. George Peele (L, 1920), 288.

PEERSON: John Fox, Book of Martyrs, ed. Cumming, II, 622.

PÉGUY: René Johannet, Vie et Mort de (P, 1950), 441.

PELAGIA: Jacobus a Voragine, Golden Legend.

PELLICO: Ilario Rinieri, Della Vita e delle Opere di (Turin, 1899), II, 334.

PENN, G.: L. V. Hodgkin (L, 1947), 197.

PENN, S.: Ibid., 200

PENROSE: Walter Davenport, Power and Glory (N, 1931), 238-39.

PENRUDDOCK: Anonymous, The Dying Speeches and Behaviour of the Several State Prisoners that Have Been Executed the Last 300 Years (L, 1720), 206.

PEPONILA: Dio's Roman History, Epitome of Book LXV, 16.

PERCEVAL: Spencer Walpole (L, 1874), II, 296.

PERICLES: Plutarch, Lives (Modern Library, 211).

PETACCI: Paolo Monelli, Mussolini (L, 1953), 290.

PÉTAIN: Marquis de Belleval, Le Cri de la France (P, 1951), 297.

PETER, St.: Eusebius, Church History (in a Select Library of Nicene and Post-Nicene Fathers of the Christian Church, ed. Schaff and Wace, 2nd Series N, 1890, I, 162).

PETER Martyr: Jacobus a Voragine, Golden Legend.

PETER I: Stephen Graham (N, 1929), 329.

PETER III: R. Nisbet Bain (Westminster, 1902), 186.

PETER, Prince: J. P. Oliveira Martins, The Golden Age of Prince Henry the Navigator (N, 1914), 302.

PETERS: Dictionary of National Biography, XLV, 75.

PHILIP II: Martin A. S. Hume (L, 1897), 260.

PHILLIPS: Isaac F. Marcosson (N, 1932), 303.

PHILOPOEMEN: Plutarch, Lives (Modern Library, 448).

PHOCION: Cornelius Nepos, Life of.

PIKE: Fred W. Allsopp (Little Rock, 1928), 310.

PILKINGTON: Charles F. Harford-Battersby (N, 1899), 337.

PIRANDELLO: Stanley J. Kunitz and Howard Haycraft, Twentieth Century Authors (N, 1942), 1109.

PITMAN: Alfred Baker (L, 1913), 326.

PITT the Elder: Basil Williams (L, 1913), II, 331.

PITT the Younger: J. Holland Rose (L, 1911), 558.

PIUS IX: Giuseppe Sebastiano Pelczai, Pio IX (Turin, 1911), III, 394.

PIZARRO: Frederick A. Ober (N, 1906), 289.

PLATT: Louis A. Coolidge (N, 1910), 585.

PLOTINUS: Michaud's *Biographie Universelle,* XXXIII, 528.

PLOWMAN: *Bridge Into the Future,* Letters of, ed. D. L. P. (L, 1944) , 771.

PLUMB: William E. Connelley (Chicago, 1913) , 430.

POE: Hervey Allen, *Israfel* (N, 1934) , 675.

POLK: Martha McBride Morrel, *"Young Hickory"* (N, 1949) , 365.

POLYCARP: John Fox, *Book of Martyrs,* ed. Cumming, I, 41.

POMPADOUR: Edmond et Jules de Goncourt, *Madame de Pompadour* (P, 1906) , 406.

POOLE: *The New Yorker,* March 20, 1954, 42.

POPE: Samuel Johnson, *Lives of the English Poets, Works* (Oxford, 1825) , VIII, 305.

PORCARI: Lloyd W. Eshleman, *Molders of Destiny* (N, 1938) , 40.

PORTER, N.: George S. Merriam, ed. (N, 1893), 195.

PORTER, W.: William W. Williams, *The Quiet Lodger of Iring Place* (N, 1936) , 251.

PORTEUS: *Works,* with Life by Rev. Robert Hodgson (L, 1823) , I, 253.

POTTER: Margaret Lane (L, 1946) , 173-74.

PRESCOTT: George Ticknor (B, 1864) , 443.

PRESTON: Thomas Ball (L, 1885), 174.

PRIESTLEY: *Dictionary of National Biography,* XLVI, 365.

PROTASIUS: Jacobus a Voragine, *Golden Legend.*

PROUST: André Maurois (N, 1950) , 313.

PUCCINI: Dante del Fiorentino, *Immortal Bohemian* (N, 1952) ,
219.

PULITZER: Don C. Seitz (N, 1924) , 415.

PURCELL: J. A. Westrup (L, 1937), 85.

PUSEY: Henry Parry Liddon (L, 1897) , IV, 385.

PUSHKIN: Ernest J. Simmons (Cambridge, Mass., 1937) , 423.

QUARLES: *Complete Works,* ed. A. B. Grosart ([E], 1880) , I, xxiii.

QUEZON: Sol H. Gwekoh (Manila, 1948), 246.

QUIJANO: *New York Herald-Tribune,* Oct. 7, 1927, 1.

QUIN: Anonymous, *Life of Mr. James Quin* (L, 1887) , 62.

RABELAIS: Burton Rascoe, *Titans of Literature* (N, 1932) , 176.

RADCLIFFE, A.: Aline Grant (Denver, 1951), 147.

RADCLIFFE, James: William Sidney Gibson, *Dilston Hall,* (L, 1850) , 153.

RADCLIFFE, John: Earl of Birkenhead, *The Five Hundred Best English Letters* (L, 1931) , 211-12.

RALEIGH: Milton Wadman (N, 1928) , 237.

RALSTON: George D. Lyman N, 1937), 312.

RANDOLPH: William Cabell Bruce (N, 1922) , II, 46.

RAVAILLAC: Michaud's *Biographie Universelle,* XXXV, 241.

RAVEL: Madeleine Gros (N, 1940) , 257.

RAY: Charles E. Raven (Cambridge, 1942) , 306.

READE: Malcolm Elwin (L, 1931), 359.

RÉCAMIER: H. Noel Williams (N, 1907) , 326.

REED: Howard A. Kelley (N, 1906), 248.

REMINGTON: Harold McCracken (Ph, 1947), 121.

RENAN: Henriette Psichari, *Renan d'Après Lui-Meme* (P, 1937), 289.

RENOIR: Georges Rivière, *Renoir et Ses Amis* (P, 1921), 265.

REYNOLDS, J: James Northcote (L, 1813), 370.

REYNOLDS, S.: *Letters of,* ed. Harold Wright (Richmond, Eng., 1923), 346.

RHODES: Sarah Gertrude Millin (N, 1933), 403.

RIBBENTROP: *New York Times,* Oct. 16, 1946, 1.

RICE: *N.Y. Sunday Mirror,* July 18, 1954, 51.

RICHARD III: James Gairdner (Cambridge, 1898), 241.

RICHELIEU: Hilaire Belloc (Ph, 1929), 383.

RICHELIEU, Duc de: Thomas Carlyle, *The French Revolution,* I, Book iii, end.

RICHMOND: Rev. T. S. Grimshawe (N, 1857), 416.

RICHTER: Walther Harich, *Jean Paul* (Leipzig, 1925), 856.

RIDLEY: *Fathers of the English Church* (L, 1809), IV, 24.

RILKE: Nora Wydenbruck (L, 1949), 363.

RIZAL: Charles Edward Russell and E. B. Rodriguez, *The Hero of the Filipinos* (N, 1923), 308.

ROBERTSON, F.: Stopford A. Brooke (B, 1865), II, 237.

ROBERTSON, G.: *Letters from,* ed. Kerrison Preston (L, 1953), 527.

ROBERTSON, J: Charles W. Gordon (Ralph Connor), (N, 1908), 393.

ROBERTSON, T.: Maynard Savin (Providence, 1950), 44.

ROBESPIERRE: Hilaire Belloc (N, 1908), 364.

ROBINSON, E.: Hermann Hagedorn (N, 1938), 381.

ROBINSON, H.: *Diary, Reminiscences and Correspondence,* ed. T. Sadler (B, 1869), II, 509.

ROB ROY: Sir Walter Scott (B, n.d.), Introduction, xliv.

ROCHESTER: Gilbert Burnet (L, 1680), 157.

RODGERS: Charles Oscar Paullin (Cleveland, 1910), 396.

RODIN: Judith Cladel (N, 1937), 328.

RODIN, Mrs.: Anna Leslie, *Immortal Peasant* (N, 1937), 354.

RODNEY: David Hannay (L, 1891), 218.

ROHAN-CHABOT: Ch. Baille in *Académie des Sciences, Belles-Lettres et Arts* (Année 1896), 220.

ROLAND, Madame: *Private Memoirs of,* ed. Edward Gilpin Johnson (Chicago, 1900), 33.

ROLAND de la Platière: Thomas Carlyle, *French Revolution,* II, vii, ch. ii.

ROMAINE: *Works,* ed. William B. Cadogan (L, 1813), I, ci.

ROMMEL: Desmond Young (N, 1950), 210.

ROOSEVELT, F.: *1946 Britannica Book of the Year,* 648.

ROOSEVELT, T.: Joseph B. Bishop (N, 1920), II, 474.

ROSA: Lady [Sydney] Morgan (L, 1855), 246.

ROSCOMMON: S. Johnson, *Lives of the Poets, Works* (Oxford, 1825), VII, 168.

ROSSETTI, C.: Marya Zaturenska (N, 1949), 292.

ROSSETTI, D.: Evelyn Waugh (L, 1928), 220.

ROSSETTI, Mrs.: Violet Hunt (N, 1932), 305.

ROSSINI: Francis Toye (L, 1934), 237.

ROTHSCHILD: John Reeves (Chicago, 1887), 51.

ROTHSTEIN: Damon Runyon, *Trials and Other Tribulations* (Ph, 1947), 222.

ROUSSEAU: Henri Beaudouin, *La Vie et Les Oeuvres de* (P, 1891), II, 559-60.

ROYER-COLLARD: E. Spuller (P, 1895), 213.

RUBINSTEIN, A.: Catherine Drinker Bowen, *"Free Artist"* (N, 1939), 367.

RUBINSTEIN, N.: *Ibid.*, 274

RUDOLF: H. R. H. Princess Stephanie of Belgium, *I Was to be Empress* (L, 1937), 248.

RUNYON: Edward Weiner (N, 1948), 255.

RUSH: Nathan G. Goodman (Ph, 1934), 346.

RUSSELL, C.: R. Barry O'Brien (N, 1901), 382.

RUSSELL, J.: Bertrand and Patricia Russell, *The Amberley Papers* (N, 1937), II, 576.

RUTHERFORD: *Letters,* ed. Rev. Andrew A. Bonar (E, n.d.), 22.

RUTHVEN: Charles Williams, *James I* (L, 1934), 158.

RYLAND: *Hymns and Verses on Sacred Subjects* (L, 1862), ix.

SACCO: Leo W. Sheridan, *I Killed for the Law* (N, 1938), 31-32.

SAINT-EDME: Firmin Maillard, *Le Requiem des Gens de Lettres* (P, 1901), 137.

SAINT-GAUDENS: *Reminiscences,* ed. Homer Saint-Gaudens (N, 1913), II, 359.

SAINT-PIERRE: Joseph Drouet, *L'Abbé de Saint-Pierre* (P, 1912), 103.

SAINT-SIMON: Friedrich Muckle, *Henri de Saint-Simon, Die Persönlichkeit* (Jena, 1908), 116.

SALADIN: Stanley Lane-Poole (N, 1898), 366.

SAMSON: Judges, xvi, 30.

SAND: Frances Winwar, *The Life of the Heart* (N, 1945), 296.

SANDERSON, F.: H. G. Wells, *The Story of a Great Schoolmaster* (N, 1924), 170.

SANDERSON, R.: Izaak Walton, *Lives* (Oxford World's Classics), 414.

SANDOZ: Marie Sandoz, *Old Jules* (B, 1935)), 424.

SAN MARTIN: Margaret H. Harrison, *Captain of the Andes* (N, 1943), 196.

SANTO-IRONIMO: A. Lacassagne, *L'Assassinat du Président Carnot* (Lyon, 1894).

SAPPHO: *Songs,* trans. David Moore Robinson (N, 1925), 201.

SARPI: Samuel Johnson, *Works* (Oxford, 1825), VI, 269.

SARSFIELD: John Todhunter (L, 1895), 202.

SAUCKEL: *New York Times,* Oct. 16, 1946, 19.

SAUL: II Samuel, i, 9.

SAUNDERS: John Fox, *Book of Martyrs,* ed. Cumming, III, 30.

SAVAGE: Samuel Johnson, *Lives of the Poets, Works,* (Oxford, 1825), VIII, 187.

SAVINA: Jacobus a Voragine, *Golden Legend.*

SAVINIANUS: *Ibid.*

SAVONAROLA: Pasquale Villari (N, 1896), 757.

SAXE: Saint - René Taillandier, *Maurice de Saxe* (P, 1865), 396.

SCARRON: Jacques Jéramec, *La*

SMITH, E.: Filson Young, *Titanic* (L, 1912), 164.

SMITH, J.: Fawn M. Brodie, *No Man Knows My History* (N, 1945), 394.

SMITH, S.: Hesketh Pearson (L, 1934), 324.

SNYDER: Leo W. Sheridan, *I Killed for the Law* (N, 1938), 41.

SOCRATES: Plato, *Phaedo,* 118.

SOLEYMAN: Count Pajol, *Kléber, Sa Vie* (P, 1877), 494.

SOMERSET: James A. Froude, *History of England* (L, 1898), V, 51.

SOPHIA: Jacobus a Voragine, *Golden Legend.*

SOPHONISBA: Livy, XXX, 15.

SPENCER: David Duncan (N, 1908), II, 227.

SPENGLER: John Fox, *Book of Martyrs,* ed. Cumming, II, 113.

SPIES: August Mencken, *By the Neck* (N, 1942), 77.

SPIESSHEIMER: Wilhelm Treichlinger, *Abschiedsbriefe* (Berlin, 1934), 26-27.

STAEL: R. McNair Wilson (N, 1931), 347.

STAFFORD: Anonymous, *The Dying Speeches and Behaviour of the Several State Prisoners that Have been Executed the Last 300 Years* (L, 1720), 362.

STANFORD: Bertha Berner (Stanford, [1935]), 207.

STANISLAS: Pierre Boyé, "Les Derniers Moments du Roi Stanislas," *Mémoires de la Société d'Archéologie Lorraine* (Nancy, 1898), 286.

STANISLAVSKY: David Magarshack (L, 1950), 404.

STANLEY: Jacob Wassermann, *Bula Matari* (N, 1933), 337.

STANTON, C.: George R. Stewart, *Ordeal by Hunger* (N, 1936), 125.

STANTON, E.: Constance Buel Burnett, *Five for Freedom* (N, 1953), 128.

STEDMAN: Laura Stedman and George M. Gould (N, 1910), II, 489.

STEIN: Furnished the compiler by Mr. Addison M. Metcalf, quoting from a letter from Miss Alice B. Toklas to Mr. Carl Van Vechten. The version in Donald Sutherland's biography (New Haven, 1951) is (203): "What *is* the answer? . . .In that case, what is the question?"

STEINMETZ: Jonathan Norton Leonard, *Loki* (N, 1929), 290.

STEPHEN: Acts, vii, 60.

STEPHENS: Rudolph von Abele (N, 1946), 315.

STERNE: Wilbur L. Cross (New Haven, 1925), II, 165.

STEVENSON: John A. Steuart (B, 1924), II, 296.

STEWART: *Letters of the Right Hon. Lady Jane Douglas* (L, 1767), 155-56.

STOLBERG: Theodor Menge, *Der Graf Friedrich Leopold Stolberg und seine Zeitgenossen* (Gotha, 1862), II, 523.

STONE: Alice Stone Blackwell (B, 1930), 282.

STOWE: Forrest Wilson, *Crusader in Crinoline* (Ph, 1941), 639.

STRAFFORD: C. V. Wedgwood (L, 1935), 341.

STRATHCONA: Beckles Willson (B, 1915), II, 452.

STRAUS: Filson Young, *Titanic* (L, 1912), 126.

STRAUSS: H. E. Jacob (N, 1940), 342.

STRAW: John Stow, *Annals* (L, 1615), 292.

STREICHER: *New York Times,*

Oct. 16, 1946, 19.

STRINDBERG: Elizabeth Sprigge (N, 1949), 224.

STROZZI: Michaud's *Biographie Universelle*, XL, 327.

STUART: Otto Eisenschiml and Ralph Newman, *The Amercan Iliad* (Indianapolis, 1947), 577.

SUDBURY: John Stow, *Annals* (L, 1615), 287.

SULLIVAN: Herbert Sullivan and Newman Flower (L, 1927), 263.

SUMNER: George H. Haynes (Ph, 1909), 433.

SUN YAT-SEN: Stephen Chen and Robert Payne (N, 1946), 220.

SURRATT: August Mencken, *By the Neck* (N, 1942), 137.

SUTTER: Julian Dana (N, 1934), 395.

SWEDENBORG: Benjamin Worcester (B, 1883), 403.

SWETCHINE: Count de Falloux (B, 1867), 369.

SWIFT: E. S. Fay (L, 1939), 279.

SYDNEY: Alexander Charles Ewald (L, 1873), II, 318.

SYNGE: M a u r i c e Bourgeois (L, 1913), 235.

TABOR: Caroline Bancroft, *Photo Story of the Matchless Mine* (Denver, 1953), [4].

TAFT: Jhan and June Robbins, *Eight Weeks to Live* (N, 1954), 22. The second remark, being an idiom, is transferred from indirect discourse. Presumably Taft said more, unrecorded.

TAIT: Randall T. Davidson and William Benham (L, 1891), II, 596.

TALLEYRAND: Bernard de Lacombe (L, 1910), 324.

TALMA: Regnault-Warin, *Mémoires sur Talma* (P, 1904), 263.

TAMERLANE: Harold Lamb (N, 1928), 251.

TANEY: Carl B. Swisher (N, 1935), 577.

TASSO: Rev. R. Milman (L, 1850), II, 287.

TAYLOR, B.: Marie Hansen-Taylor and Horace E. Scudder (B, 1884), II, 765.

TAYLOR, J.: Edmund Gosse (N, 1904), 207.

TAYLOR, Z.: Silas Bent McKinley and Silas Bent, *Old Rough and Ready* (N, 1946), 287.

TEKAKWITHA: Daniel Sargent (N, 1936), 242.

TENNYSON: *Works*, ed. Hallam, Lord Tennyson (L, 1921), lvii.

TERESA of Avila: Helen H. Colvill (N, 1909), 319.

TERRY: Edward G. C r a i g (N, 1932), 196.

THACKERAY: Lewis Melville (L, 1910), II, 60.

THAYER: Mrs. Edith Reid (N, 1936), 232.

THEODORA: Jacobus a Voragine, *Golden Legend*.

THEODORE: *Ibid.*

THEODORIC: T h o m a s Hodgkin (N, 1891), 423.

THEOPHRASTUS: Diogenes Laertius, V, 2 (41).

THERAMENES: William Smith, *A New Classical Dictionary*, ed. Charles Anthon (N, 1851), s.v.

THERESA: Constance Lily Morris (N, 1937), 332.

THOMAS, St.: Jacobus a Voragine, *Golden Legend*.

THOMAS: Rose Fay Thomas (N, 1911), 543.

THOMPSON: Lloyd Wendt and Herman K o g a n (Indianapolis, 1953), 356.

THOREAU: Léon Bazalgette (N,

VIGNY: Arnold Whitridge (L, 1933), 211.

VILLARS: Michaud's *Biographie Universelle*, XLIII, 431.

VINCENT: Theodore M a y n a r d, *Apostle of Charity* (N, 1939), 311.

VITELLIUS: Tacitus, *History*, III, 85.

VOLTAIRE: James Parton (B, 1881), II, 610.

WAGNER: Henry T. F i n c k (N, 1893), II, 449.

WAIBLINGER: Karl Frey, *Wilhelm Waiblinger, Sein Leben* (Aarau, 1904), 240.

WALKER: Gene F o w l e r, *Beau James* (N, 1949), 377.

WALLACE: Isabel Wallace (Chicago, 1909), 199.

WARD: Maude Howe Elliott (N, 1938), 683.

WARWICK: Charlotte F. Smith (L, 1901), 344.

WASHINGTON, B.: Basil Mathews (Cambridge, Mass., 1948), 301.

WASHINGTON, G.: Washington Irving (N, 1869), V, 336.

WASSERMANN: Marta Karlweis, *Jakob Wassermann, Bild, Kampf und Werk* (Amsterdam, 1935), 471.

WATERFORD: Augustus J. C. Hare, *The Story of Two Noble Lives* (L, 1893), III, 476.

WATSON: William E. Brewton (Atlanta, 1926), 398.

WATT: Samuel Smiles (Ph, 1865), 506-07.

WATTS: [E. Paxton Hood?] (L, n.d.), 264.

WAYNE: John Hyde Preston, *A Gentleman Rebel* (N, 1930), 343.

WEBB: Thomas Moult (L, 1932), 287.

WEBER: Lucy Poate Stebbins and Richard Poate Stebbins, *Enchanted Wanderer* (N, 1940), 273.

WEBSTER, D.: Claude M. Fuess (B, 1930), II, 354.

WEBSTER, N.: Harry R. Warfel (N, 1936), 436.

WEED: Thurlow W. Barnes (B, 1884), II, 576.

WELLINGTON: G. R. Gleig (L, 1865), 456.

WELLS: Vincent Brome (L, 1951), 226.

WESLEY: C. E. Vulliamy (N, 1932), 349.

WHATELY: E. Jane Whately (L, 1866), II, 418.

WHITE, J.: John Hamilton Thom, ed. (L, 1845), III, 310.

WHITE, K.: *Poems, Letters*, ed. John Drinkwater (Muses' Library), 240-41.

WHITEFIELD: J a m e s Paterson Gladstone (N, 1901), 340.

WHITGIFT: W. F. Hook, *Lives of the Archbishops of Canterbury* (L, 1875), V, 184 N.S.

WHITMAN: Edgar Lee Masters (N, 1937), 289.

WHITNEY: Mark D. Hirsch (N, 1948), 595.

WHITTIER: Whitman B e n n e t t (Chapel Hill, 1941), 325.

WICKSTEED: C. H. Herford (L, 1931), 179.

WIELAND: J. G. Gruber, *Wieland* (Leipzig, 1816), II, 550.

WILBERFORCE: R. Coupland (Oxford, 1923), 517.

WILD: Frederick J. Lyons (L, 1936), 218-19.

WILDE: T. G. Wilson, *Victorian Doctor* (N, 1946), 311.

WILHELM I: Ernst Berner, *Kaiser Wilhelms des Grossen Briefe, Reden und Schriften* (Berlin, 1906), II, 429.

WILHELM II: *Time,* J u n e 16, 1941, 34.

WILLARD: L y d i a Jones Trowbridge (Chicago, 1938) , 192.

WILLIAM the Conqueror: Phillips Russell (N, 1933), 299.

WILLIAM II: A. Thierry, *History of the Conquest of England by the Normans* (Everyman's Library) , I, 335.

WILLIAM III: Thomas B. Maculay, *History of England* (Everyman's Library) , III, 747.

WILLIAM the Silent: Nina B. Baker (N, 1947), 256.

WILLIAMS, A.: Leonard C l a r k (Bristol, 1945) , 187.

WILLIAMS, H.: Robert W a t s o n Winston (Chapel Hill, 1942), 309.

WILLIAMS, J.: George C. Osborn (Baton Rouge, 1943) , 476.

WILLKIE: Joseph Barnes (N, 1952) , 385-86.

WILSON, E.: George Seaver (N, 1937), 294.

WILSON, W.: Harold Garnet Black (N, 1946) , 248.

WINDOM: *Memorial Tributes to* (Cambridge, Mass., 1891) , 160.

WIRZ: August Mencken, *By the Neck* (N, 1942) , 118.

WISHART: *Dictionary of National Biography,* LXII, 251.

WITT, C.: Antonin Lefèvre Pontalis, *John de Witt* (L, 1885), II, 492.

WITT, J.: *Ibid.*

WOLCOT: Theodore Reitterer, *Leben und Werke Peter Pindars* (Vienna, 1900) , 40.

WOLFE, C.: *Remains,* ed. John A. Russell (L, 1832), 210.

WOLFE, J.: Beckles Willson (N, 1909) , 494.

WOLLSTONECRAFT: Ralph M.

Wardle (Lawrence, Kansas, 1951), 306.

WOLSEY: Mandell Creighton (L, 1888) , 206.

WOOD: Darrell Garwood, *Artist in Iowa* (N, 1944), 249.

WOOLF: *New York Times,* Apr. 20, 1941, 6.

WOOLLCOTT: Samuel Hopkins Adams (N, 1945) , 369.

WOOLMAN: Janet Whitney (B, 1942), 429.

WOOLSTON: Anonymous, *T h e Life of Mr. Woolston* (L, 1733) , 29.

WOOLTON: *The Christian Manual,* ed. for the Parker Society (Cambridge, 1851), iv.

WORDSWORTH: George McLean Harper (N, 1916) , II, 436.

WRIGHT: Elizabeth Mary Wright (L, 1932), II, 682.

WYATT: John Stow, *Annals* (L, 1615) , 624.

WYCHERLEY: Ed. W. C. Ward (L, 1948), xlii.

WYLIE: Nancy Hoyt (Indianapolis, 1935) , 187.

XAVIER: S. Baring-Gould, *Lives of the Saints* (E, 1914), XIV, 673.

XIMENES: Walter Starkie, *Grand Inquisitor* (L, 1940), 447.

YANCEY, R.: Rebecca Yancey Williams, *The Vanishing Virginian* (N, 1940) , 277.

YANCEY, W.: John W. Du Bose (N, 1942), II, 735.

YEATS, J.: Van Wyck B r o o k s, *Scenes and Portraits* (N, 1954) , 188.

YEATS, W.: Richard Ellmann (N, 1948) , 285.

YOUNG: M. R. Werner (N, 1925) , 459.